FOUR MASTERWORKS OF AMERICAN INDIAN LITERATURE

Four Masterworks of American Indian Literature

QUETZALCOATL / THE RITUAL OF CONDOLENCE
CUCEB / THE NIGHT CHANT

Edited, and with commentaries and new translations, by John Bierhorst

THE UNIVERSITY OF ARIZONA PRESS / TUCSON

THE UNIVERSITY OF ARIZONA PRESS
First printing 1984
Manufactured in the U.S.A.

The preparation of this book was assisted by a grant
from the Center for Inter-American Relations.

Library of Congress Cataloging in Publication Data

Main entry under title:

Four masterworks of American literature.

    Reprint. Originally published: New York : Farrar,
Straus, and Giroux, 1974.
    Includes bibliographies and index.
    Contents: Quetzalcoatl – The ritual of condolence –
Cuceb – The night chant.
    1. Indian literature – Translations into English.
2. American literature – Translations for Indian languages.
3. Indians – Religion and mythology. I. Bierhorst, John.
PM197.E1F68   1984   897   84-8462
ISBN 0-8165-0886-0

CONTENTS

The Ritual of Condolence

AN IROQUOIS CEREMONIAL

Cuceb

A MAYA PROPHECY

The Night Chant

A NAVAJO CEREMONIAL

NOTE

In the translations that follow, italics are used to indicate words added to clarify the text or complete its meaning. A somewhat fuller statement about the use of italics will be found in the closing paragraphs of each of the four introductions, where the reader will also find a brief guide to pronunciation.

Citations given in the notes by author only, or by author and date, can be traced in the bibliography at the close of the section. The bibliographies are not alphabetical, however, as they are intended to serve not only as a catalogue of references but as a guide to the library resources in each field. Only the most significant works have been included, and these have been listed in order of importance.

The four maps—of Mexico, Iroquoia, Yucatan, and the Navajo country—give preference to aboriginal place names, with modern or acculturated usages set off by parentheses.

FOREWORD

This volume is intended as a first step toward establishing a body of standard works, a canon, of native American literature. That there exists a sizable legacy of verbal art surviving more or less intact from preconquest times (and recorded either by Euro-American linguists or by Indian scribes using the Latin alphabet) is a fact reasonably well known. But what are the major works of Indian literature? And where can they be read?

For one reason or another some of the most important texts have been at least partially hidden from readers of English. Either they have not been translated or they have been inadequately translated. Or, if adequately translated, they have remained, so to speak, dismembered, for the simple reason that they were recorded in pieces over a period of years and never assembled.

Such has been the case with the four works offered here—each of which, reconstituted or retranslated, is presented as an outstanding´ example, perhaps the leading example, of the bardic, oratorical, prophetic, and incantatory styles characteristic of the cultures that produced them: the Aztec, the Iroquois, the Maya, and the Navajo, respectively. (Whether or not these ethnic groups deserve precedence over their neighbors, it may be pointed out that these four, together with the Inca, are the most heavily documented and for this reason, if for no other, the most difficult to ignore. Unfortunately, while much has been written on the subject of Inca civilization, very little authentic Inca literature remains. Most of the latter-day Quechua material sometimes passed off as "Inca" is substantially acculturated. An extended list of areas worthy of attention would include, in addition to the Inca, or Quechua, the Zuni, the Kwakiutl, the Quiché, the Uitoto, and the Winnebago, not to mention at least a dozen others where gifted ethnographers have been matched with gifted informants.)

So poorly known are these works that with the exception of the much-abused Quetzalcoatl no previous attempt has been made to interpret them from a literary point of view. Nor is there a critical tradition upon which to build. The school of literary anthropology D. G. Brinton might have founded in the 1880's failed to materialize in the tide of reaction that swept American Indian studies into the twentieth century (leaving the cult of myth and even the comparative method, the lifeblood of literary anthropology, far behind). In recent years the pursuit of myth, including New World myth, has been enlivened by the followers of Claude Lévi-Strauss and, to a lesser extent, by the Jungians. Yet in both cases the mythic works themselves have been subordinated to the exposition of theory. The structuralists have made it a matter of principle that myth requires no special handling as art. And yet it can still be demonstrated, one hopes, that the singling out of superior materials at the expense of lesser works that may indeed deserve burial, coupled with a close attention to both form and content, will yield results of genuine literary interest.

The genius of mythic literature lies in its ability to express ideas and relationships without the use of abstractions. Its peculiar idiom moves unobtrusively from one particularity to the next, covering much the same ground as its modern counterpart, yet without ostentation and sometimes with enviable efficiency. It must not be supposed that Indian languages are devoid of abstractions, even if they prefer to operate with concrete symbols. Yet it is nothing less than this "preference" that gives the ancient mode its twentieth-century appeal:

> It is said that he completely burned his house of gold, his house of redshell. And the other Toltec treasures, the splendid things, the precious things: all were buried, all were concealed in inaccessible places, in the interior of a mountain or in chasms. (Quetzalcoatl, Fragment D, twelfth "chapter")

The same passage, fully paraphrased, might read something like this: "Even as the sun departs from its western home in a blaze of red and gold, hiding its light beneath this mountain Earth or in her deepest crevices, so does the light of civilization fade from the world. Alas, the sun has set on the Toltec empire."

But in most cases it must be conceded that the mythic mode, whether employed in myth per se or in what we call ritual, assumes the more leisurely, the more deliberate pace. It takes the entirety of the Quetzalcoatl story, for example, to cover the same ground that the poet Shelley covers in a few phrases about leaves from an enchanter fleeing, or Verlaine with his long-sobbing violins of autumn. Compared to the deft calculus of the Western idiom, the ancient usage seems more like a species of geometry, putting the graspable parts of an idea together by a process of careful summation, or moving from one idea to the next through a series of incremental changes. The relative merits depend upon one's point of view. The Wordsworthian "Sunshine is a glorious birth" may strike some ears as painfully direct. And yet this kind of metaphysical shorthand does get to the point quickly. On the other hand, let us see how precisely the same idea is expressed, through summation, in the text of a Navajo song:

> Ína hwié! my grandchild, I have eaten.
> Ína hwié! my grandchild, I have eaten.
> Ína hwié! my grandchild, I have eaten.
>> Hastshéhogan. His food I have eaten.
>> The pollen of evening. His food I have eaten.
>> Much soft goods. His food I have eaten.
>> Abundant hard goods. His food I have eaten.
>> Beauty lying behind him. His food I have
>>> eaten.
>> Beauty lying before him. His food I have
>>> eaten.
>> Beauty lying above him. His food I have
>>> eaten.
>> Beauty lying below him. His food I have
>>> eaten.
>> Beauty lying all around him. His food I have
>>> eaten.

> In old age wandering. I have eaten.
> On the trail of beauty. I have eaten.
> Ína hwié! my grandchild. I have eaten. Kolagane.

Lengthy as it is, this is only one half—the second half—of the complete idea. Whether it is performed or not, the singer and the hearer will understand that there must be another fifteen-line verse virtually the same as the one just given, except that "Hastshéyalti" will be substituted for "Hastshéhogan," "I am about to eat" will be substituted for "I have eaten," and "evening" will be made "morning." Hastshéhogan, though a male deity, represents the female sun as it sinks in the west; Hastshéyalti, the male sun as it rises in the east. Added together, they make for a whole sun. Their proffered "food" is sunlight, symbolized by vegetable pollen, which the singer actually ingests as he recites these lines. The glorious presence of the deity is imagined both materially (soft goods plus hard goods) and spiritually (the aureole of "beauty," or ideality). Identifying himself with this imagined presence, the singer embarks upon the circular "trail of beauty"—the conventional transformation mystery of Navajo religion—which turns him from old age to youth.

Again the same idea is expressed in these measured words from the Iroquois Condolence:

> Now, we attach the Sun again in its place for thee;
> that then shall come to pass, when the time shall
> come for the dawning of a new day, that verily thou
> shalt see the Sun when it shall come up out of the
> horizon, when, indeed, our Elder Brother, *the Sun*,
> who lights up the earth shall come over it. Thus,
> then, my offspring, thy eyes shall rest on it as it
> draws ever closer to thee. That, therefore, when the

> Sun shall reach, or place itself in mid-heaven then
> around thy person rays or haloes of light will
> abundantly appear. Then, indeed, shall thy mind
> resume its wonted moods.

The speaker addresses himself to ailing society, which he intends to renew through the agency of sunlight. But notice that here the idea is expressed in terms of a gradual movement from darkness to light. The sun is not merely placed in the sky but hauled up from the horizon by degrees ("it draws ever closer to thee") until it reaches the desired zenith. Here, then, is a typical example of Iroquois progressionism. But we will find it also in the Aztec, Maya, and Navajo texts. The incremental itineraries of the hero Quetzalcoatl, the meting out of the Maya katun by tuns and years, and even the "I am about to eat, I have eaten" in the Night Chant song quoted above are all examples of Indian progressionism.

From the foregoing samples two conclusions may be drawn: (1) that Indian literature, if symbolic, is far from chaotic—each verbal element has a contributory meaning and each element has its proper place—and (2) that this literature, owing to its "geometrical" bias, cannot be read for style in the usual sense of the term; the ideas and images are there, but generally unwrapped (and spread out) rather than neatly packaged. Hence the paradox that Indian languages, while often synthetic *as languages*, are typically analytic in their *modus operandi*.

Though an artist may still be regarded as a "high priest" and his works occasionally cited for "cathartic" or "therapeutic" value, art in the West is no longer regarded as a department of religion, nor is it intimately associated with medicine. The traditional art of the New World, by contrast, has remained a *whole art,* capable of combining the aesthetic, the sacred, and the medicinal in varying proportions and without discrimination.

The method of whole art is to create a model, a replica, such that the original may be forcibly perfected or, variously, manipulated for the benefit of the communicant. The original upon which the model is based may be anything in the environment that is thought to be worth controlling; it may be represented in effigy form, or re-created in a verbal formula, with the idea of coercing it, beseeching it, propitiating it, or disarming it through adoration. Or the original may be the environment itself, in which case the artist's work becomes a replica of the natural world as a whole, to be manipulated, or transfigured, with the intention of influencing communal (and personal) destiny.

The classic example of the world replica is the man-made temple: a vaulted space scrupulously arranged with reference to the four world-quarters, east, south, west, and north, and generally facing into or away from the rising sun. This is the plan of the Greek temple, the Christian cathedral, the Navajo hogan (whose floor plan is a quartered circle), the Iroquois longhouse, and the pyramid temples of Quetzalcoatl. In the case of the pyramid temple the model includes not only the four-chambered world-vault but also the "mountain"—the earth—that supports it.

If the temple provides a static model of the natural realm, there may also be room for a dynamic model, re-creating the great system in its time-changing aspect. Of this the conspicuous example is the mass, or restoration ritual, in which the universal cycle of analysis, synthesis, and reanalysis is carefully iterated through symbol in such a way that the transition from analysis to synthesis, or, as we may as well say, from death to birth, is made to appear as though there need be no loss of former identity. And so the natural process, manipulated, becomes resurrection.

Both the Iroquois Condolence and the Navajo Night Chant are rituals of restoration. So are—or were?—the myth of Quetzalcoatl and the Cuceb before their assimilation to the narrative and prophetic modes. The question of which came first, the myth or the ritual, the gospel or the mass, or even whether the two forms are in fact lineally related, need not concern us here. The point is that all four works serve to idealize the common flux of decay and reintegration, summoning to mind the "circle" of death and life familiar in popular writing and in fact often specified in ancient lore.

The revivalist narrative (or ritual) may be viewed as a focused progression away from the old and into the new, building to a climax in which the awaited transition is at last made possible through the mechanism of a sacred "mystery." The mystery may be thought of as a kind of trick. But no impertinence is intended. Ambiguity and titillation are part of the process. Verbalized, the mystery may even take the form of a pun. At exactly this point the terror of death gives way to the joy of birth; and in ritual the denouement may include comedy and irreverence and, in some cases, sexual license.

In the variant of the myth recorded by Sahagún the transformation of Quetzalcoatl is accomplished by means of the cross that symbolizes both Quetzalcoatl himself and the quadripartition of the cosmos. By traveling the circuit of the cross—that is, by passing from the eastern point to the southern to the western to the northern and back again to the eastern—the hero identifies himself with the inevitable cycle of nature and, like the world as it moves through the seasons, he is made new.

The return to the eastern point is the resolving fifth term that "completes" the number 4. So the number 5, a special case of 4, is also sacred.

In Navajo ritual the same clockwise circuit is called the path of ideality, or "trail of beauty" in the phrase made famous by Washington Matthews. The Night Chant text contains numerous references to this "trail," and one is obliged to make clockwise, or sunwise, circuits throughout the ceremony. The moment for the mystery to take effect—that is, the moment in which the communicant's old life is decisively made new—is determined by numerical calculation. In the Night Chant there is no death qua death but rather a series of evacuations in which the participant is drained of evil, interconnected with a series of rechargings in which he is instilled with new power. As with the approach of an electrical storm, both the voiding, or negative, procedures and the attractive, or positive, ones are accumulated until, at the prescribed moment, the tension is concentrated in a towering prayer to the spirit of thunder:

> With the far darkness made of the dark cloud on
>   the ends of your wings, come to us soaring . . .
> With the near darkness made of the dark cloud, of
>   the he-rain, of the dark mist, and of the
>   she-rain, come to us . . .

The prayer is answered:

> Above it thunders,
> His thoughts are directed to you . . .

And the tension is broken. In the ensuing flood of recapitulative song (accompanied by dance) the rain spirit takes the role of an irreverent clown, mocking the dancers and provoking general laughter.

In the lesser-known versions of Quetzalcoatl the transformation of the old into the new is achieved through the hero's cremation (in Fragment C and in the second ending of Fragment B) or by dint of an implied ritual murder (in the main portion of Fragment B).

Resurrection in the Cuceb also hinges on a fantasized murder. Here the imagined victim is a surrogate for the time god called Katun, whose old self is dispatched (the victim's soul floats up to paradise), making way for a new incarnation. With the arrival of the incoming katun the world is made over, rain requickens the dead earth, the tree of life grows green, and we note the appearance of a sacred clown.

Similarly the Ritual of Condolence depends upon the (circumstantial) death of a chief—who may or may not have been murdered. The chief, therefore, is dead before the ritual begins, but he has not been *eliminated*. The ceremonial high point comes with the singing of the Hymn that bids farewell to the dead chief's soul. Only then can the new chief be raised up in his place. But as in the case of the Maya Katun the transition from old to new is ambiguous. Of necessity the old lord suffers replacement; ideally he lives again through the continuance of his name, transferred to his chosen successor. It is said, therefore, that the chief has been resurrected. On another level society itself, which had been laid low with mourning, is also resurrected. As the ritual draws to a close, a speaker rises and invites the assembly to dance, making a common sexual innuendo that invariably provokes laughter.

In conjunction with the sacred mystery—the cross, the trail of beauty, the ritual murder, or whatever it may be—there is a medicinal element that should not be overlooked. The mystery answers the implicit cry, "Make me new"; the medicine, or tonic, responds to the same inner voice, calling, "Make me whole" (or "Make my people whole"). It may even be said that the progress from debility to restored health is a necessary condition for the journey from death to birth (or from old age to youth). The typical operant is the elixir. In the Night Chant the patient literally absorbs the infusion of herbs known as night medicine; in the Ritual of Condolence the patient receives the rhetorical Water-of-pity, which figuratively restores his body to normalcy. In the Aztec myth (Fragment D) it is Quetzalcoatl himself who is the patient. As his life ebbs, he finds that his flesh is "sapped, as though it had been cut to pieces." The remedy is the agave wine, the pulque, that gives him the required strength to make his journey through death to new life. And it is probable that the mysterious wine of the katun, mentioned in the Cuceb, serves a similar purpose. (In certain instances the progress from debility to health may acquire a moral interpretation, where debility is equated with moral weakness, or guilt, and restoration becomes contingent upon punishment. In Fragment D of the Quetzalcoatl myth the "laxity" of the Toltecs and the intemperance of the hero—he drinks *too much* agave wine—are punished by the fall of Tollan. Explicit sexual transgressions play a comparable role in Fragments C and D of Quetzalcoatl and in the Cuceb.)

It will be noticed that the transition from old life to new is worked out in the literature through an interplay of simple and complex metaphors. In the Cuceb, to take one of the easiest examples, we have the recurring symbolism of drought, relieved by rain. In the Iroquois Condolence the sun is "lost," but the ritual restores it to its former position. Again, in the Quetzalcoatl cyclus, the passage from death to birth is elevated to a metaphorical plane by the figure of the sun, overcome by night but reemerging at dawn. Of comparable value is the *light* of the sun, exalted in Navajo ritual as the instigator of vegetable life. Rain plays a similar role. Or the metaphorical burden may be shifted to the earth as it turns from winter to spring. These, then, are the familiar nature images fondly catalogued by old-fashioned mythographers, yet nonetheless operative for their having been overvalued and, worse, incorrectly described. The problem is that they must sometimes be pieced together out of far-flung clues demanding a thorough knowledge of the related ethnography (of which we have more now, naturally, than we did formerly). But once this is done the nature metaphor is easy enough to grasp, appealing as it does directly to the conscious mind. It requires no acquaintance with deep structures to see the link between resurrection and sunrise.

Not so with a second, and perhaps more interesting, class of metaphor that may be said to depend upon a hidden lens within the brain—through which the *thing* or *condition* is perceived as halved (or doubled) and the *happening* as a reunifying merger. The formal recognition of this quirk, this "dualism," is as old as Hegel and as new as French structuralism. In modern literature it generally passes unrecognized; in myth it comes to the fore. Notice that Quetzalcoatl is perceived as half female and half male ("I *am* the one in quechol plumes, I *am* the lord who pierces"—both are solar images: see Fragment E and note 105). But in the course of his journey he will become a child (in Fragment D, "chapter" 4). Likewise the Night Chant's promised rain is divided into "he-rain" and "she-rain." But at the ceremonial climax the goal is achieved through the aid of a thunder spirit identified with "child-rain."

To take another example: in the Aztec myth the concept of fate is analyzed into light and dark components, metaphorically represented in Fragment B as day and night (or sun and stars) and in Fragment C as Quetzalcoatl and Tezcatlipoca, the alternating tutelaries of human destiny. But at the close of Fragment C the "day" and the "night" are merged in the bright spot of dawn (Quetzalcoatl himself), the hopeful synthesis that gives the myth its forward momentum. (This identification of Quetzalcoatl with the morning star is echoed in the Night Chant and in the Cuceb, where the hero Nayénezgani and the Lord of the Katun are similarly apotheosized.) But according to the doctrine, the morning star is the "child" of the sun. Thus we have an interlocking of the two metaphorical systems, male-female-child and light-dark-dawn. And these, moreover, are merely two of the links in a luxuriantly proliferating chain of dyadic or, if we count the merging member as an independent third term, triadic metaphor. The reader is invited to continue the game.

In offering these few general remarks, I do not wish to imply that the following works were chosen to illustrate a thesis. On the contrary, they were selected exclusively for their appeal to literary interest.

And yet the four have much in common, especially as they reveal the impress of the revivalist ritual. If there is any conclusion to be drawn it is perhaps that this ritual pattern is indeed for modern literature the prototype par excellence (as literary anthropologists working with Old World materials have shown again and again).

I hope I have made clear at least a few of the essential differences between mythic and modern literatures. I hope it is also clear that the term "literature"—as it attracts to itself the connotation of Art—is applicable to the former as well as the latter.

It may be true that myths, like dreams, are mere products of nature. Yet it is equally true that the most compelling dreams, ancient or modern, have been mysteriously vouchsafed to artists. Let this book be dedicated to them: to Ah Kauil Ch'el, Hatali Natloi, Chief John Arthur Gibson, and the anonymous informants of Sahagún.

J.B.

New York
February 8, 1973

FOUR MASTERWORKS OF
AMERICAN INDIAN LITERATURE

Quetzalcoatl

AN AZTEC HERO MYTH

"And when you return, you shall
have again been made a child."

INTRODUCTION

American Indian religion in one of its many phases has tended to conceptualize the universe in terms of its halves—the familiar Mother Earth and Father Sky, or Mother Earth and Father Sun—whose mystical product is the hero-child known to the Navajo as Nayénezgani or to the ancient Mexicans as Quetzalcoatl. (To the earth-sky pair belongs the power of being, to the offspring is given the power of doing. The former, in other words, enjoys eternal or at least prior existence, serving as a reservoir of procreative and salutary energy upon which the hero draws in order to finish the work of the world.) What is noteworthy, though hardly unique, about the deity Quetzalcoatl is that he represents not only the heroic "product," but the generative "halves" as well. He is synonymous with the omnipotent Spirit of Duality, the sophisticated Mexican concept incorporating earth and sky. His generative power, specifically, is felt to be present in the wind, regarded as the breath of life, which he sometimes personifies. As the sacred child, Quetzalcoatl, like his counterparts in other mythologies, is sometimes the culture hero, sometimes the religious reformer. (As such, he becomes the natural patron of art, technology, religious science, and wizardry.) To him fall the tasks of improving, redressing, or rescuing the world. In ancient Mexico he was sometimes, but by no means always, identified with solar light (not necessarily the same as the sun itself) or with the closely related morning star, which appears to rekindle the solar disc or to revive it, so to speak, by chasing away the gloom of night.

The name Quetzalcoatl means literally "plumed serpent," from *quetzalli,* feather of the precious green quetzal, and *coatl,* a snake. From one point of view the ubiquitous bird-snake of Mexican art, architecture, and pictography would appear to be an ideogram for sky and earth, the above and the below. From another point of view it may be seen as a precious, or idealized, form of the archetypal serpent who imparts cultural knowledge (see p. 190). By manipulation it can be made to stand for specific attributes. In the minds of some informants, for example, the snake apparently symbolized the writhing wind, while its plumes were the softer, more "feathery" breezes. Other evidence would certainly show that the plumed serpent represented the earth itself clothed in fresh vegetation. A particularly ingenious reinterpretation, involving a double pun, transforms "bird-snake" into "precious twin," an epithet of the morning star, considered the twin of the evening star (*quetzal* = "quetzal" or "precious"; *coatl* = "snake" or "twin").

The myth of Quetzalcoatl is always a myth of regeneration, of death and revival, illustrating the perennial power of nature to make things new. It may take the form of a contest between night and day, with night as the temporary victor and day the inevitable revenant. It may foreshadow, or hark back to, the cataclysmic destruction of the universe and its subsequent re-creation. It may be an allegory based on the alternation of winter and spring, or on the disappearance and return of the planet Venus.

Or the god may be historicized and his promised return postponed—turning the revivalist myth into its familiar messianic variant. According to fifteenth-century Aztec belief, Quetzalcoatl had come to earth during the semilegendary Toltec period (A.D. 600–1100) as a flesh-and-blood culture bringer, religious reformer, and princely ruler. Driven away by adversaries, so it was imagined, he would someday come back to right old wrongs and reestablish his earthly kingdom. In this phase of his cult the hero-god is sometimes known as Topiltzin Quetzalcoatl or simply Topiltzin ("Our Dear Prince"). The city with which he is associated is Tollan, the ancient Toltec capital, whose ruins have been located by archaeologists near the present-day town of Tula, fifty miles north of Mexico City. But the "Tollan" of the culture hero, as Brinton once attempted to show, is basically the mythic garden of the western sun, the analogue of the Navajo "garden of Hastshéhogan," transposed to an earthly site. As for the hero himself, the ancient chroniclers have done their work well. It would not be an easy task at present to disestablish the historicity of Topiltzin Quetzalcoatl. The early missionaries accepted it without question—and so have a number of modern investigators.

The most readily believable accounts, in order of importance, are Ixtlilxochitl's *Relaciones,* Torquemada's *Monarquía indiana* (Bk. I, ch. 14), *Annals of Cuauhtitlan,* and Chimalpahin's *Memorial breve.* The first two, which evidently derive from a single source, do not include a Quetzalcoatl among the eight or nine kings of Tollan, nor are any of these kings identified with either the familiar culture bringer or the religious reformer. (It may, of course, be argued that the Quetzalcoatl we are looking for served not as king but as high priest and so would not necessarily be included in a list of rulers. It may also be argued that *every* Toltec king bore the title Quetzalcoatl in honor of the god whom he represented, so that any of the Toltec rulers might have been the nucleus that attracted the myth.) Now the third and fourth accounts do give space to a Quetzalcoatl. Yet in both cases he is worked into the list as a patently fabulous inclusion. *Annals of Cuauhtitlan* places him among the earliest rulers; Chimalpahin puts him toward the very end. All four accounts, however, give notice of a final or near-final ruler whose historicity is more than probable and whose story is of considerable interest.

The king in question is known in *Annals of Cuauhtitlan* as Huemac, in Chimalpahin's account as either Huemac or Tepiltzin ("One's Dear Prince"), and in Ixtlilxochitl's *Relaciones* as either Topiltzin ("Our Dear Prince") or Meconetzin ("Dear Child of the Maguey"). For convenience I will refer to this person as Huemac, or as Topiltzin Huemac, in order to distinguish him from Topiltzin Quetzalcoatl, whom I will consider for the moment to be entirely mythical.

It would appear that Huemac had been elected to the throne of Tollan in a manner less than satisfactory to certain rival interests. Hostile feelings were immediately aroused, and eventually an unmistakable and perhaps long-latent factionalism. As a result the Toltecs were plunged into civil strife and the kingdom was destroyed—enabling outside groups to gain control by default. Huemac himself, though he ultimately disappeared or was executed, left behind him an infant son named Pochotl, from whom later dynasties were to claim descent.

Further details, if indeed these few, can hardly be imparted with any assurance of mundane truth. Even in the relatively sober account written by Ixtlilxochitl, the biography of Hue-mac (whom he calls Topiltzin) rapidly grades into saga. In *Annals of Cuauhtitlan*, in Torquemada, in *Legend of the Suns*, in *Historia Tolteca-Chichimeca*, and in Sahagún (Fragment D), it reaches its full development.

Huemac becomes the now tragic, now evil king who inevitably brings his people to ruin. Ghastly omens foretell the end, and variation after variation is played on the same recurring motifs: a monstrous corpse that cannot be removed, an odor of death that kills on contact, feverish dances in which the participants are slain, an outrageous sexual transgression, celestial omens, etc. At last the people are decimated. The few that remain are dispersed, and Huemac repairs to the cave called Cincalco, where he presumably enters the underworld, remains in exile, or is apprehended and hanged.

The Huemac material gives rise to some of the most colorful passages in Mexican literature, inviting a detailed analysis that unfortunately cannot be included here. It may be noted in passing, however, that the concept of sin and retribution is among the driving forces behind this lore. The fall of Tula is felt to have been brought about by the sins of Huemac, the sins of the people, the evils of Huemac visited upon the people in payment for their sins, or some similar variation of the same idea. Much like the polluted and overripe figure of the aging Quetzalcoatl, Huemac becomes the symbol of an accumulated guilt that can finally be tolerated no longer. Each in his own way serves to implement the theory of renewal: Quetzalcoatl, being a god, will be born again, but Huemac, a mortal, can only be replaced. The dualistic tension between the two figures is operative at several different levels. As a crude generalization it would be possible to say that together they represent the spiritual and earthly aspects of a single personality. Yet for the most part the myth and the saga are kept separate by the ancient narrators, and accordingly there will be no attempt here to include the saga except (as in Fragment D) where it forcibly works its way into the myth.

The corpus of Quetzalcoatl encompasses a dozen or more variants, preserved in Spanish, French, Italian, or Nahuatl. Of these only five have survived in the Nahuatl (or "Aztec") language. They are as follows:

Fragment A / The Restoration of Life. In the opening episode Quetzalcoatl descends to the underworld, seeking the bones left over from previous creations. He obtains them, brings them to paradise, and, placing them in the "precious" womb of the earth mother, which he inseminates with his own blood, gives birth to a new race of humans. But death has won a partial victory. In his frailty Quetzalcoatl had permitted the underworld spirits to nibble the bones, compromising them in such a way that humans would forever be denied immortality. In a second episode the hero discovers maize, which he likewise brings to paradise: "and the gods then chewed it. Then they laid it upon our lips so that we were made strong." But Quetzalcoatl himself does not have the strength to procure the entire treasure of maize for future generations. In the third and final episode the god Nanahuatl, personifying lightning, splits open the fabulous cache (i.e., the "mountain" of food that is the earth) in order to make its contents available to man. But no sooner has he done so than the rain gods appear; they steal not only the maize but all the foods contained in the "mountain." Though the subject of the myth is the creation of life, its thrice-iterated theme is life's uncertainty. And its ultimate effect is to establish the symbolic connection between rain and birth, or, alternately, drought and death. A structuralist summary of the myth's three parts would yield the equation: birth is to death (i.e., human mortality) as feast

is to famine as rain is to drought. In the triumphant conclusion
to Fragment D, below, the spirit of rain will point the way to
rebirth.

Fragment B / The Ceremonial Fire. The young planet Venus
finds that his father, the sun, has been murdered by the stars
and covered up in the sands of the western sea (a conventional
allegory of the setting sun). Retrieving the corpse, the hero
inters it within a sacred "earth mountain" (in allusion to the
belief that the sun between dusk and dawn passes through the
heart of the earth, that is, through the underworld realm of
the dead). Ultimately the hero succeeds in lighting a fire at
the top of the "mountain," outwitting, then slaying, the stars
who attempt to thwart him. (The exploit accords with the
perceived function of the planet as morning star, rising just
before dawn to rekindle the solar fire. It also recalls the Aztec
new-fire ceremony—performed at the close of each fifty-two-
year "calendar round" to give the world a new lease on life,
prompting the sun, specifically, to renew its struggle against
the forces of night.) Having renewed the sun, the hero proceeds to renew himself, restating, as it were, the basic theme:
traveling eastward across the earth (in allusion to the nocturnal
west-east progress of the sun's lost light), the hero reaches the
shore, dies, and is transformed by fire (into the newborn
morning star). In this particular story the protagonist is
known only by the epithet Ce Acatl, an alternate name for the
planet Venus.

Fragment C / A Cycle of Transformation. Fragment C is an
interweaving of at least four separate traditions, bound together by the commonality of the savior doctrine and the
pervasive symbolism of light. The hero, to begin with, is cast
in the role of a culture bringer, a discoverer of plants, gems,

metals, etc., and the originator of fine arts. Accordingly he is associated with the precious "treasure" of the sun (i.e., its light), which he buries, or "hides," beneath the earth as his death (i.e., night) approaches. A second tradition contributes the theme of the religious reformer, the model of chastity and penance, the abjurer of human sacrifice, who preaches the cult of a supreme Spirit of Duality. But the jealous god Tezcatlipoca (the tutelary of night and the diviner of secret thoughts) contrives to make the hero both drunk and incestuous, effectively stripping him of his priesthood and forcing him to flee. A third tradition supplies the essential framework of the myth —the story of the personified planet Venus, who, as in Fragment B, inters the corpse of his murdered sun-father, proceeds eastward across the earth, dies, and is transformed into the morning star (thus delivering the world from darkness). Fourthly and lastly, the hero is identified with a particular aspect of Venus known as Tlahuizcalpanteuctli, "Lord of the House of Dawn," the warlike vindicator whose "arrows" strike humankind (i.e., human guilt?) generally, allowing the myth as a whole to be read as a vengeful triumph of light over dark. (For the doctrine of guilt and punishment, with reference to Quetzalcoatl, see especially Codex Vaticanus 3738.)

Fragment D / The Fall of Tollan. This important fragment, part myth, part saga, casts Quetzalcoatl in the double role of prototypal priest and culture bringer, emphasizing his virtues as a patron of crops. As the myth develops, the hero acquires the traits of a vegetation god; and his story, on one level, becomes an allegory of winter and spring. The text falls readily into three divisions. Part I describes a mythical Tollan patterned after the garden of the western sun. As it slips into decline, its abstemious ruler, Quetzalcoatl, succumbs to the wiles of a perennially jealous Tezcatlipoca (here referred to as

Titlacahuan, "He to Whom We Are Slaves"). In an episode reminiscent of Fragment C, Titlacahuan makes Quetzalcoatl drunk and sends him away. Part II transports us to a semi-historical Tollan where, leaving myth behind, we enter the realm of geste. The narrative becomes noticeably more stylish, with identifiable "literary" flourishes. What we have, in fact, is a version of the Huemac saga, illustrating the fall of the Toltec empire in a series of allegorical legends—and culminating in a symbolic drought with (unsuccessful) sacrifices to the gods of rain. Part III returns to the interrupted story of Quetzalcoatl. Now, in a mythopoeic tour de force, both the hero and, symbolically, the topography are led through a five-stage "initiation" into the mysteries of death. As a consequence the hero's entourage of hunchbacks (the diminutive spirits of rain) freeze in a snowy pass. But gazing eastward, the "dead" king sees the mountain home of pent-up rain and, moving toward it, is turned clockwise in a five-stage cycle of rebirth in which he and, again symbolically, the topography are both revived. Continuing eastward, he merges with the rising sun. (Note the relationship between the "real-life" ordeal of Huemac and the mythic triumph of Quetzalcoatl. The saga leaves the question of death unresolved; the myth supplies the answer—rebirth.)

Fragment E / A Song of Survival. In a three-act masque with parts for several singers, a poet whose name, ironically, does not survive develops the theme of immortality-through-art. The program is an outgrowth of ritual, based on the death of a god (Topiltzin Quetzalcoatl), followed by the birth of a related god (Cinteotl, the spirit of maize); the material itself, however, has been redigested and philosophized. Act I laments the departure of Topiltzin, suggesting from the very first line that his name will live on in perdurable works of wood and stone. The egregiously clever verses of Act II describe the birth of an ear of maize as though it were a poem created by the Author of Life. As art, the "poem" will continue to live in the minds and hearts of men. In Act III the poet steps forward and speaks with his own voice, introducing himself in an opening stanza as a humble singer in the service of others. In a second stanza he asserts that his songs will endure like the timeless wood and stone monuments left behind by Topiltzin. The third stanza, recalling the imagery of Act II, has him "transplanting" his song as a sprig of divine inspiration, so that "taking root" on earth it will live forever. Finally he relies on the metaphor of the flower, the conventional symbol of song, imagining that his own "flower" has become one with the quintessential Peyote, Cacao, and Prince flowers. The key sentiment is expressed in the phrase "a remembrance of me, that my name might endure."

Though adapted to serve a quite different purpose, the Quetzalcoatl material in Fragment E, historicized as it is, clearly belongs to the messianic tradition. The same could be said of Fragment D and, to a lesser extent, Fragments C and even B. Commentaries obtained from native informants and preserved in various sixteenth-century documents indicate that by late Aztec times the myth of Topiltzin, or Ce Acatl, Quetzalcoatl had come to be generally regarded as messianic. The received idea was that Quetzalcoatl would return in the flesh during a year beginning with the day Ce Acatl, or "1 Reed," the traditional date for the reappearance of Venus after inferior conjunction with the sun. Coincidentally a year 1 Reed was just coming around as Cortés, in 1519, began his march inland from the Veracruz coast, displaying, inevitably, the cross (of the four world-quarters) and accompanied by light-haired "children of the sun." Mexicans immediately made the connection, and the manner in which the Spaniards were greeted—with mingled reverence and hostility on the part of the Aztec leadership, with a sense of relief on the part of rivals who had chafed under the Aztec yoke—contributes an element of curious fatalism to the story recorded in Book XII of Sahagún's great *Historia,* in Bernal Díaz's *True History of the Conquest of New Spain,* and of course in Prescott's well-known *Conquest of Mexico.*

As early as the mid-1520's Nahuatl texts composed prior to the Conquest were being rescued by missionary-ethnographers and by native savants who had learned to write their own language in the new Latin script. Presumably the old pictographic books had memorialized certain songs, myths, and sagas. But these could have served only as mnemonic aids for poets and priests who had been trained orally.

A number of the texts pertaining to Quetzalcoatl were committed directly to Spanish or were promptly translated from Nahuatl originals now lost. In this category belong the important historical works of Ixtlilxochitl, the works of Mendieta, "Historia de los mexicanos por sus pinturas," "Histoyre du Mechique" (known only in the French version), and Codex Vaticanus 3738 (known only in the Italian). In none of these works, valuable as they undoubtedly are, does the flavor of Nahuatl utterance survive.

The known Nahuatl sources, all dating from either the second or third quarter of the sixteenth century, are *Historia general de las cosas de Nueva España,* compiled by Fray Bernardino de Sahagún and preserved both in Spanish and Nahuatl, viz., in codices now in Madrid and in Florence (Fragment D is from the Florentine Codex); the codex *Can-*

tares mexicanos (source of Fragment E); *Annals of Cuauhti-tlan* (source of Fragment C); and *Legend of the Suns* (source of Fragments A and B). *Annals of Cuauhtitlan* and *Legend of the Suns* are preserved, together with other matter, in a dossier known variously as "The History of the Kingdoms of Colhuacan and Mexico," Codex Chimalpopocatl, or, confusingly enough, "Annals of Cuauhtitlan." In Sahagún's compilation there is yet another account of Quetzalcoatl, aside from Fragment D; but this, though composed in Nahuatl, is more in the spirit of reportage than of myth, and it has consequently been omitted.

With the exception of the interesting pastiche brought out by Garibay in his little volume *Épica náhuatl,* no previous attempt has been made to collate these materials or to present them in a unified modern-language translation. The present work, while new, has been facilitated by the published versions of particular codices, or excerpts from codices, by Lehmann, Garibay, Anderson and Dibble, Seler, Velázquez, and Schultze-Jena. All of these versions are useful (and without them the work at hand would have been quite impossible), yet none can be certified as error-free. Accordingly the translations offered below attempt to correct minor faults—without straying from the mainstream of twentieth-century Nahuatl scholarship.

The translations are cautiously literal, with glosses and added connectives supplied in italic, including Sahagún's "chapter" headings in Fragment D. (In these italicized headings the general rule has been inverted, so that gloss words appear in roman.) Wherever possible an effort has been made to preserve the Nahuatl cadence:

> uel itech peuhtica,
> uel itech quiztica,

in Quetzalcoatl
in ixquich in toltecayotl, in nemachtli

The lexical reading yields "truly of-him it-began, truly of-him it-flowed-out, Quetzalcoatl all art, knowledge." The final reading:

Truly with him it began,
truly from him it flowed out,
from Quetzalcoatl
all art *and* knowledge.

Note that the expletive "truly" has not been discarded. For honesty's sake, most expletives have been similarly retained, whether or not in violation of current taste. On the other hand, pronouns belonging to the second person have (usually) been given simply as "you," "your," or "yours," avoiding the more correct "ye" and "thou" forms preferred by many linguists. Verb tenses are also handled with a certain degree of freedom, there being no attempt here, for instance, to duplicate the Nahuatl "historical present."

A number of words and phrases have been retained in the original language. In keeping to the traditional orthography it has been necessary to sacrifice refinements like the glottal stop and the lengthened vowel. As a rough guide to pronunciation the following rules may be observed: vowels are sounded as in Spanish (ah, eh, ee, oh, oo), consonants as in English, with these exceptions: *x* has the value of English *sh;* *qu* has the value of *k; tl,* whether at the beginning or end of a syllable, is pronounced virtually the same as the *tl* in the English word *atlas* (hence ket-sal-CO-atl, not ket-sal-CO-waddle —though in conversation most English speakers will avoid the former pronunciation as too pretentious); *u* before a vowel has the value of English *w*; *z* has the value of *s* as in *sun*; *ll* is sounded as in English, not as in Spanish. Note the following examples.

> Coatlicue (ko-ah-TLEE-kway)
> Toueyo (toh-WAY-yo)
> Huemac (WAY-mock)
> Xiuhtlacuilolxochitzin (shoo-tla-KWEE-lol-sho-
>   CHEET-seen)
> Cuauhtitlan (kwow-TEE-tlan)
> Mimixcoa (mee-meesh-KO-ah)
> Tlahuizcalpanteuctli (tla-wees-kahl-pahn-
>   TAYook-tlee)

Nahuatl words are generally stressed on the penult. Readers acquainted with modern Mexican usage may wish to break this rule in the case of familiar names like Chapultepec (cha-PULL-te-pek), Cuauhtitlan (kwow-tee-TLAN), Quetzal-coatl (ket-SAL-co-ATL), and of course the name Mexico itself. Yet the only genuine exception occurs in a word like *Toltecaye* ("O Toltecs!") where the final syllable, being an interjection of sorts, must receive the main stress (tol-tek-ah-YAY).

QUETZALCOATL

Translated from the Nahuatl by John Bierhorst

Fragment A / The Restoration of Life

And the gods assembled then, *and* they said, "Who
shall live? The skies have dried, the Earth Lord
has dried. *But* who, O gods, shall live?" They
were therefore troubled:[1]

Skirt-of-Stars Light-of-Day, Lord-*Drawn*-to-the-
Water *Lord*-Issuing-Forth, Who-Firms-the-Earth
Who-Tills-*the-Earth*, Quetzalcoatl Titlacahuan
were their names.[2]

But Quetzalcoatl went to the Dead Land then, *and*
came to the Dead Land Lord, to the Dead Land
Lady, saying, "These, the precious bones in your
keeping, for these I have come, *and* these I would
take." And he was answered at once: "To make
what, Quetzalcoatl?" And therefore he spoke
again: "The gods are troubled, *asking*, 'Who shall
live on earth?' "

And so too the lord of the Dead Land spoke again:
"Very well. Blow my trumpet shell and circle
four times round my emerald realm."[3] But his
trumpet shell was not hollow.

Then *Quetzalcoatl* summoned worms, who
hollowed it out, *and* at once bees and hornets
went in. Then he blew. *And* the lord of the Dead
Land heard.[4]

And so too the lord of the Dead Land spoke once
more: "Very well. Take them." But then to his
subjects, the Micteca, the lord of the Dead Land
said, "*My* holy ones, tell him he must but
relinquish them!"

And at once Quetzalcoatl said, "But no! I have
them already *and* forever." But his nahual said to
him, "Merely answer: 'I do but relinquish
them.' "[5] *Quetzalcoatl* spoke at once, he cried out,
"I do but relinquish them!" Yet in fact he
ascended *with them.*

Then truly he took up the precious bones, the
bones of man *where* they lay to one side, *and* so
too the bones of woman *where* they lay to one
side. Quetzalcoatl took them at once, then he
wrapped them up, then he carried them off.

But the lord of the Dead Land now spoke again
to his subjects: "Holy ones, Quetzalcoatl is truly
removing the precious bones. Holy ones, make
him a crypt!" Then they made it for him. He was

startled by quail moreover, and so he fell into the crypt, he stumbled, he fell unconscious.[6]

And the precious bones were therefore immediately scattered. Then the quail bit into them *and* nibbled them. And when Quetzalcoatl regained his senses, he wept. Then he said to his nahual, "My nahual! How will it be?" And at once he was answered, "How will it be? It *will* be undone. *But* let it be as it will."[7]

And then he gathered *and* reassembled *the bones and* bundled them up. Then he brought them to Tamoanchan.

And when he arrived there, then she *who is* called Quilaztli, she, Cihuacoatl, reduced them to powder, which she even placed in a jadestone bowl. And thereupon Quetzalcoatl bled his member.[8]

Then all the gods did penance, *and* they will be named herewith: Lord-*Drawn*-to-the-Water, Who-Tills-*the-Earth*, *Lord*-Issuing-Forth, Who-Firms-the-Earth, He-Who-Falls-Headlong— *and* the sixth *who* is Quetzalcoatl.[9]

And then they spoke: "Born are the servants of the gods." For indeed they did penance for us.

Again they spoke: "*But* what will they eat, O gods? Let food be discovered." And then the ant brought maize kernels out of the heart of Food Mountain.

And at once Quetzalcoatl confronted the ant, asking, "Where did you find it? Tell me." But she would not tell him. Over and over he asked her *and* at last she said to him, "There!" Then she showed him the way and at once Quetzalcoatl changed himself into a black ant.

Then she showed him how to enter inside. Then together they dragged it out. The red ant, it seems, showed Quetzalcoatl the way.[10] At the exit he laid down the kerneled maize. Then he took it to Tamoanchan. And the gods then chewed it. Then they laid it upon our lips so that we were made strong.

And they spoke then: "What shall we do with Food Mountain?" And at once Quetzalcoatl set out again, *and* he trussed it with cords *and* attempted to carry it *with him*. But he could not lift it.

And then Oxomoco divined with the kernels. And so too did Oxomoco's wife, Cipactonal, divine thereupon. Indeed the woman *is* Cipactonal.[11]

And then Oxomoco *and* Cipactonal announced, "It is Nanahuatl who must break open Food Mountain. Indeed it has been determined."

But suddenly rain gods came forth: blue rain gods, white rain gods, yellow rain gods, red rain gods. Then Nanahuatl broke open *the mountain*, and then the rain gods stole the food:

white, black, yellow, *and* red maize; beans,
amaranth, sage, *and* argemone. All the foods were
stolen.[12]

Fragment B / The Ceremonial Fire

And in coming forth he greatly afflicted his
mother for the duration of four days.[13] Thereupon
by that time *and* in this manner Ce Acatl was
born.[14] But as he was born, then already his
mother was dead.

And Ce Acatl was reared by Quilaztli, the
Serpent Woman.

But when he had grown, then he went *and* made
war with his father. And as a warrior he proved
himself in a place called Xihuacan such that he
took captives there.

But there in that place *were* Ce Acatl's uncles, the
four hundred Mimixcoa. Now they hated *and*
therefore killed his father. And when they had
killed him, they covered him up in the sand.[15]

And Ce Acatl looked for his father then. *And*
therefore he asked, "Where is my father?" And at
once a vulture said to him, "Aye, they have
killed your father. Yonder he lies. Aye, they have
buried him."[16]

And then he retrieved *the corpse and* placed it
within its temple, *called* Cloud Serpent
Mountain.[17]

And the uncles who killed his father were named
Apanecatl and Zolton and Cuilton.[18] Now he
asked them, "What shall I sacrifice to the temple?
Perhaps a rabbit, perhaps a snake!"

And immediately they said to him, "We would be
vexed indeed. Better a jaguar, an eagle, a wolf!"[19]

Ce Acatl answered, he said to them, "Very well.
It shall be." Then he called to the jaguar, the eagle,
the wolf, saying, "Come, my uncles! They say I
must sacrifice you to my temple, *but* in truth
you shall not die. In truth it is they whom you
shall devour, when indeed I sacrifice them to my
temple—*them*, my father's brothers!" And merely
for appearance' sake did he tie them by the neck.

And Ce Acatl called then to moles, telling them,
"Come, my uncles, we must dig a passage in our
temple." And at once the moles dug through *and*
burrowed out a passage. *And* Ce Acatl entered in,
emerging at the summit of his temple.

Now his father's brothers *had* said, "It is we who
shall light the fire at the summit." *But* they were
much diverted, watching the jaguar, the eagle,
and the wolf *make* a show of anguish. And when
they'd recovered some presence of mind, Ce Acatl
already was lighting the fire.

And the uncles were very angry then, *and* they started at once. Apanecatl led the way, hurriedly scaling *the temple*.

But immediately Ce Acatl rose up, *and* striking him full in the face sent him tumbling down, *and* he fell to the base *of the mountain*.

Next he seized Zolton *and* Cuilton; *and as* the animals blew *on the fire*, then he put them to death: he spread them with chili *and* slashed their flesh; and when he had tortured them, then he cut open their breasts.[20]

And then once again Ce Acatl *set out to* make conquests, toward the place called Ayotlan. And when he had conquered, he went on to Chalco *and* Xicco. *There* too he made conquests.

And when he had conquered *there*, he went on to Cuixcoc and made conquests.

And then to Zacanco he went and made conquests. Then he went on to Tzonmolco, making conquests, then to Mazatzonco, whereupon he made conquests, then to Tzapotlan. And there *too* he made conquests.

And then he proceeded to Acallan, where he crossed the water. And also there he made conquests.

Until he reached Tlapallan.[21] But then in that

place he fell sick. Five days he was sick.²² And
by then he was dead. And when he was dead, then
they set him on fire. *And* he was consumed in
flames.²³

Fragment C / A Cycle of Transformation

In the year 1 Reed it is told, they say—in its time
in that *year*—Quetzalcoatl was born, called
Topiltzin Priest 1-Reed Quetzalcoatl, and his
mother they say was named Chimalma, and they
say that *this was* the manner in which
Quetzalcoatl was placed in his mother's belly: she
swallowed an emerald.²⁴ *Came the years* 2 Flint, 3
House, 4 Rabbit; 5 Reed, 6 Flint, 7 House, 8
Rabbit; 9 Reed.²⁵

Then in the time of 9 Reed, when he'd reached
some awareness, when he'd reached his ninth year,
he asked for his father, saying, "What does my
father resemble? May I see him, may I see his face?"²⁶

Thereupon he was told: "He is dead, he is buried
yonder. Go see!" Quetzalcoatl went there at once,
and he opened the earth. He searched for the
corpse, and he gathered the bones. In a place
called the shrine of Quilaztli he buried them.
Came the years 10 Flint, 11 House, 12 Rabbit; 13
Reed, 1 Flint, 2 House, 3 Rabbit; 4 Reed, 5 Flint,
6 House, 7 Rabbit; 8 Reed, 9 Flint.

10 House: this *was* the year of the death of
Cuauhtitlan's king who was Huactli; for sixty-two
years he had ruled. This was the king who did not
know how to plant edible corn.[27] Nor could his
subjects weave robes. As yet they dressed only in
hides. As yet their food was but birds, snakes,
rabbits, *and* deer. As yet they were homeless.
Rather they wandered from place to place.

In the year 11 Rabbit, lady Xiuhtlacuilolxochitzin
ascended the throne. Her house of thatch stood
beside the square, where today it is *paved with
stones.* And they say that this lady was given the
city because she was Huactli's wife; moreover
she ably invoked the "devil" Itzpapalotl.[28] 12
Reed, 13 Flint, 1 House.

2 Rabbit *it was,* when Quetzalcoatl came to
Tollantzinco. There he remained four years and
built his house of penance, his turquoise house of
beams. From there he passed on to Cuextlan, so
crossing the river; *and* in that particular place he
erected a bridge that still stands, they say.[29]
3 Reed, 4 Flint.

In the year 5 House the Toltecs came for
Quetzalcoatl to install him as king in Tollan, and
he was their priest. The story thereof has been
written elsewhere.[30] 6 Rabbit. 7 Reed *was* the
time of lady Xiuhtlacuilolxochitzin's death.
Twelve years had she ruled in Cuauhtitlan. In the
year 8 Flint, at the place called Palace in the

Woods, Ayauhcoyotzin ascended the throne as
Cuauhtitlan's king.

9 House, 10 Rabbit; 11 Reed, 12 Flint, 13 House,
1 Rabbit. 2 Reed: according to the tradition of
Texcoco, this *was the year of* the death of
Quetzalcoatl, prince of Tollan Colhuacan.[31] *But*
in 2 Reed *it was* that he built his house of penance,
his place of worship, his place of prayer. He the
prince, 1-Reed Quetzalcoatl, built his house as
four: house of turquoise, house of redshell,
house of whiteshell, house of precious feathers.[32]
There he worshipped, did his penance, and also
fasted.

And even at midnight he went down to the
stream, to the place called Edge of the Water,
where the water moss was.

And he set thorns *into his flesh* on the summit of
Xicocotl, also on Huitzco, also on Tzincoc, also
on Mount Nonohualca. And he made his thorns of
jadestone.

His fir boughs *were* quetzal plumes.[33] And his
thorns of turquoise, of jadestone, of redshell were
fumed with incense. And the offerings that he
sacrificed were snakes, birds, *and* butterflies.

And it is related, they say, that he sent up his
prayers, his supplications, into the heart of the
sky, and he called out to Skirt-of-Stars Light-of-
Day, Lady-of-Sustenance Lord-of-Sustenance,

Wrapped-in-Coal Wrapped-in-Blood,
Tlallamanac Tlallichcatl.[34]

And they knew that he was crying out to the
Place of Duality, which lies above the ninefold
heavens. And thus they knew, they who dwell
there, that he called upon *them* and petitioned
them most humbly and contritely.

And also in his time he discovered great riches:
jadestone, fine turquoise, and gold, silver, redshell,
whiteshell, plumes of quetzal, cotinga, roseate
spoonbill, oropendola, trogon, *and* blue heron.[35]

And also he discovered cacao of various colors
and cotton of various colors.

And truly in his time he was a great artisan in all
his works, in the blue, green, white, yellow, *and*
red painted earthenware from which he drank
and ate, and in many other things besides.

And in the time that he lived Quetzalcoatl
started *and* began his temple and raised *its*
serpent pillars, but he did not finish or complete
it.

And in the time that he lived he did not show
himself in public. Deep within his house he
dwelled, protected. And his pages guarded him
at many points surrounding him. In each
apartment there were pages, and his apartment
was the last.

And in his house were mats of jewels, mats of
precious feathers, mats of gold. And his house of
penance, so they say, was built as four, they say.

And it is told *and* related that many times during
the life of Quetzalcoatl *certain* sorcerers
attempted to shame him into making human
offerings, into sacrificing humans. But he would
not consent. He would not comply, because he
greatly loved his subjects, who were Toltecs.[36]

The offerings he made were always *and* only
snakes, birds, *and* butterflies.

And it is related, they say, that he thereby angered
the sorcerers, so that they took to mocking and
taunting him. *And* the sorcerers asserted *and*
willed that Quetzalcoatl be vexed and put to
flight. *And* so it happened, it came to pass. 3 Flint,
4 House, 5 Rabbit; 6 Reed, 7 Flint, 8 House, 9
Rabbit; 10 Reed, 11 Flint, 12 House, 13 Rabbit.

In the year 1 Reed Quetzalcoatl died. And they
say that he went to Tlillan Tlapallan to die.[37]

Thereupon *his successor*, called Matlacxochitl,
ascended the throne and ruled in Tollan.

Then they tell how Quetzalcoatl departed: it was
when he refused the sorcerers' *decree* that he
make human offerings, that he sacrifice humans.
Thereupon the sorcerers deliberated among
themselves, they whose names were Tezcatlipoca,

Ihuimecatl, and Toltecatl.[38] "He must leave his
city, *for* we shall live here," they said. *And* they
said, "Let us make pulque. We will have him
drink it, to corrupt him, so that he will no longer
perform *his* sacraments."

And then Tezcatlipoca said, "I, I say we must
give him his body to see!"

But who can say how or in what manner they
conspired together to do such things?

Tezcatlipoca went first, carrying a two-sided
mirror the size of an outstretched hand, concealed
in a wrapping.

And when he had come to where Quetzalcoatl
was, he said to the pages who guarded him,
"Announce to the priest: 'Lord, a servant has
come to show you your body that you may see
it!' "

The pages went in *and* informed Quetzalcoatl,
who answered, "What *is* this, grandfather page?
What body of mine does he bring? Examine it!
Only then may he enter."

But Tezcatlipoca would not let them see it. He
said, "I, I myself will show it to the priest. Tell
him!" *And* they told him. "He refuses," *they said.*
"He insists upon showing it to you *himself.*"
Then Quetzalcoatl said, "Let him come,
grandfather."

Tezcatlipoca was summoned; *and* he entered,
greeting him, saying, "My son, Priest 1-Reed
Quetzalcoatl! Lord, I have come to salute you
and show you your body."

Said Quetzalcoatl, "You have taken great pains,
grandfather. From where have you come? *And*
what *is this* body of mine? May I see it!"

He answered, "My son, lord priest, I am your
servant, come from the slopes of Mount
Nonohualca. May it please you to see your body."
Thereupon he presented the mirror, saying,
"Behold *and* envision yourself, my son. It is here
in the mirror you shall appear."

And the moment he saw himself, Quetzalcoatl
was filled with fear. He said, "If my subjects
were to see me, would they not take flight?" For
the eyelids *were* greatly swollen, the eye sockets
deeply sunk, the face much distended all over
and bilious.[39]

Looking into the mirror, he said, "Never shall
my subjects see me. Here alone will I stay."

Then Tezcatlipoca took leave *and* departed and
conferred with Ihuimecatl in order that they
might indeed deride him. Said Ihuimecatl, "He,
the artist, Coyotlinahual, shall be the one to go."
And they informed him that it would be he who
must go. *And* the artist Coyotlinahual said, "Very
well, I shall go. I shall see Quetzalcoatl."

He went at once, *and* to Quetzalcoatl he said,
"My son, I say come out! Let your subjects see
you. I will dress you that you may be seen." "My
grandfather, do it!" he said. *"This* I would like to
see."

And the artist Coyotlinahual proceeded at once.
First he made Quetzalcoatl's plumes. Then he
made him his turquoise mask, taking red to color
the mouth, taking yellow to lattice the forehead,
then gave him his serpent teeth, then made him
his beard of cotinga *and* spoonbill plumes, neatly
swept back.

When he'd arranged Quetzalcoatl's attire in this
manner, then he gave him the mirror. *And* he
looked at himself, greatly admiring himself. Then
at once Quetzalcoatl abandoned his refuge.

Then the artist Coyotlinahual went to tell
Ihuimecatl. "I have brought Quetzalcoatl out.
Now go!" *And Ihuimecatl* answered, "Very
well"; then he fell in with *the sorcerer* called
Toltecatl *and* together they went on their way.

Soon they arrived at the Place Where Onions
Are Washed, where they lodged with the
harvestman Maxtla, *who was* keeper of Toltec
Mountain.[40] Thereupon they stewed potherbs,
tomatoes, hot peppers, young corn, *and* beans.
And this continued for several days.

And *as* magueys were *found* there as well, they

obtained some from Maxtla. *And* in only four
days they prepared, then decanted, the pulque.

It was they who discovered the wild honeycombs,
and so *with honey* they blended the pulque.[41]

They went then to Tollan, to the house of
Quetzalcoatl, bringing all their potherbs, their
peppers, et *cetera*, also the pulque.[42]

They arrived *and* confronted Quetzalcoatl's
guards, who refused them permission to enter.
Twice, thrice they were turned away. *Indeed*
they were not admitted. At last they were asked
where their home *was*.

They replied, saying, "Yonder it lies at Priests'
Mountain, at Toltec Mountain." As Quetzalcoatl
heard this, he said, "They may enter."

They entered and greeted him. Also they gave
him the potherbs et *cetera*. And when he had
eaten, they entreated him further *and* offered the
pulque. But he said to them, "No, I cannot drink
it. No, I abstain. Does it take away the senses? Is
it fatal?" They answered him, "Taste it with the
tip of your finger. It's strong, it's newly made."

Quetzalcoatl tasted it with the tip of his finger
and, finding it good, said, "I would drink *more*,
grandfather. Three more *draughts*!" They
answered him, "Four more shall you drink."

Thus they gave him even his fifth, saying, "This is your sacrament."[43]

When he had drunk, then they served all his pages, *and* each took five *draughts*. They made themselves utterly drunk.

Again the sorcerers addressed Quetzalcoatl: "My son, may it please you to sing. Here is the song you shall give *us*." Then Ihuimecatl recited it for him:

> "House of quetzal, of quetzal,
>   Of zacuan, of redshell,
>   I leave thee! An ya'!"[44]

And Quetzalcoatl said joyously, "Bring *me* my elder sister, Quetzalpetlatl, that we may be drunk together."[45]

His pages repaired to the place where she fasted, to Mount Nonohualca, saying, "Quetzalpetlatl, penitent lady, my daughter! We have come to fetch you. The priest Quetzalcoatl awaits you. Go and be with him." She said, "Very well, grandfather page. Let us go."

And arriving, she seated herself next to Quetzalcoatl, whereupon she was given the pulque, four *draughts* and one more, the fifth, as her portion. Thus Ihuimecatl and Toltecatl made *both of them* drunk. Then to Quetzalcoatl's sister they presented a song, singing:

> "Where *now* is your home,
>   My sister, *my* Quetzalpetlatl?
>   Oh it's here, where you tipple!
>   Ayn ya′, ynya yn′, ye an′!"

Having made themselves drunk, no more did they
say, "We are fasting." And then they went down
to the river no more. No more did they puncture
themselves with thorns. Nothing more did they
do at the break of day. And at dawn they were
filled with remorse, their spirits were heavy.

Thereupon Quetzalcoatl said, "Unfortunate me!"
Then he raised the lament he'd composed for his
going away. And he sang:

> "No more.
>   The days will be counted no more in my house,
>   *and* it shall be empty.
>   For only beyond I awaken.
>   From earth, from the flesh, I depart: quickly
>   from burning *and* pain.
>   Never *more* do I thrive."

Then he sang the words of another song:

> "She will nurse me no more,
>   She, my mother, an ya′!
>   She of the Serpent Skirt,
>   Ah, the holy one![46]
>   I, her child, alas,
>   Am weeping, iya′, ye an′!"

As Quetzalcoatl sang, then all were made sad. And
so his pages wept then, and sang, saying:

> "No more we delight in him,
>   Him our noble one,
>   Him Quetzalcoatl.
> No more thy precious crown!
> The bleeding thorns *are* broken.[47]
> We mourn for him,
> We weep, alas."

And when Quetzalcoatl's pages had sung, then
he spoke to them: "Grandfather page, enough!
I am leaving the city, for *now* I depart. Give the
command that a funeral urn be made." Then
quickly a funeral urn was carved. And when it
was carved *and* finished, they placed Quetzalcoatl
in it.

But he lay only four days in the funeral urn.[48]
And when he felt discomfort, then he said to his
pages, "Enough, grandfather page! We will go!
But everywhere bury, conceal the things we've
created, the beauty, the joy, our wealth, all of it,
our treasure." And his pages did so. They hid it
where Quetzalcoatl's bathing place was, at the
place called Edge of the Water, where the water
moss was.

Then Quetzalcoatl departed. He got up, called
together his pages, *and* wept over them. *And*
then they set out, seeking Tlillan, *the Black Land;*

Tlapallan, *the Red Land;* Tlatlayan, *the Fire
Land.*[37]

And he traveled *and* ventured widely, *though*
no place was pleasing to him. Yet he reached the
place he was seeking. Then again, in that place,
he wept. He was miserable.

And so in the time, in the year 1 Reed, when he'd
reached the sacred shore, the celestial water—so
it is told, they say—then he halted *and* wept *and*
gathered up his attire *and* put on his plumes, his
turquoise mask, et *cetera.*[49] And when he was
dressed, then at once he set fire to himself, he
surrendered himself to the flames.

Thereafter they called it Tlatlayan, where
Quetzalcoatl surrendered to the fire.

And they say as he burned, his ashes arose. And
all the precious birds appeared *and* were seen
rising upward into the sky. Roseate spoonbill,
cotinga, trogon, blue heron, yellow parrot,
scarlet macaw, and white-fronted parrot were
seen—*and* all the other precious birds.[50]

When the ashes were gone, then the heart of the
quetzal rose upward at once.[51]

They saw. And therefore they knew he had gone
to the sky, he had entered the sky. The old people
say he was changed to the star that appears at
dawn. Therefore they say it appeared when

Quetzalcoatl died, and so they called him Lord of
the House of Dawn.

And it is said when he died he disappeared for
four days. Then he dwelled in Mictlan, they say.
And for four days also he made himself arrows.
And so in eight days he appeared, the great star.[52]
And they said *it was* Quetzalcoatl. Then, they
said, he ascended his lordly throne.

And when he appeared they knew also, according
to sign, whom he would shoot with his arrows
and strike *and* wound.[53] If he comes on 1
Crocodile he strikes the old men, the old women,
all *whomsoever*. If *on* 1 Jaguar, if *on* 1 Deer, if
on 1 Flower, he strikes little children. And if *on*
1 Reed, he strikes at kings, all *whomsoever, and
even so* if *he comes on* 1 Death. And if *on* 1 Rain,
he strikes the rain: no rain will fall. And if *on* 1
Movement, he strikes young men, young women.
And if *on* 1 Water, then drought will occur. Et
cetera. Therefore in each of these *signs* did the
elders pay him their homage.

Such was the life, in its entirety, of him who was
called Quetzalcoatl. He was born in 1 Reed. And
also he died in 1 Reed, and so it is reckoned he
lived for fifty-two years. And so it is finished: in
the time, in the year, 1 Reed.

Fragment D / The Fall of Tollan

PART I

*The third "chapter": which tells the history of
the great enchanter Quetzalcoatl, how he was
king, and what he did when he went* away.[54]

Quetzalcoatl was looked upon as a god. He was
worshipped *and* prayed to in former times in
Tollan, and there his temple stood: very high,
very tall. Extremely tall, extremely high. Very
many *were* its steps *and* close together, hardly
wide, but narrow. Upon each *step* indeed one's
foot could not be straightened.

And they say that he was always veiled, always
his face was veiled: and they say that he was
monstrous, his face like a pitifully battered thing,
pitifully covered with lumps—inhuman. Also his
beard *was* very long, exceedingly long *and*
copious.[55]

And his subjects, the Toltecs, were highly skilled.
Nothing *was* difficult for them to do. They cut
jadestone and cast gold, and pursued yet other
crafts. Highly skilled indeed *they were* in feather
work.

Truly with him it began, truly from him it
flowed out, *from* Quetzalcoatl all art *and*
knowledge.

And there his house of jadestone stood, and his
house of gold, and his house of redshell, and his
house of whiteshell; and his house of beams, his
turquoise house, and his house of quetzal plumes.[56]

And *for* his subjects, the Toltecs, *there was* no
place *too* remote to reach. Indeed they quickly
arrived where they were going. And because
they ran exceedingly, one called them "they who
crook the knee all day."[57]

And there was a mountain called Crying Out
Mountain, still so called today. They say that
there a herald stood. *And* whatever was needed,
he stood there crying out. *From* there indeed it
spread over Anahuac, indeed it was clearly heard
in all places, whatever he uttered, whatever law
had been ordered.[58] *And* quickly all hastened
to hear what Quetzalcoatl commanded.

And also they had great abundance. Cheap were
foods *and* all the crops. They say the calabashes
were enormous, some *a fathom* round, the corn
ears very much like mulling stones, extremely
long: they merely rolled them *to pulverize the
grain*. And amaranths *grew as* palms: they truly
climbed them, they truly could be climbed.

And there as well grew tinted cotton: crimson,
yellow, rose, violet, pale green, azure, dark green,
orange, brown, purplish, dark gold, *and* coyote-
colored cotton. All these kinds were immediately
thus. They did not dye them.

And all the precious birds dwelled *there:* cotinga, quetzal, oropendola, roseate spoonbill, also all the different birds that very ably sing, that ably warble, in the mountains.

And also gold *and* jadestone—all of it was scarcely prized, so much did they possess.

And cacao, flower cacao, also grew.[59] Indeed in many places there were cacao trees.

And the Toltecs were very prosperous *and* comfortable. They never wanted. There was nothing lacking in their houses, they were never hungry. And they didn't need the stunted ears of corn except *as fuel* to heat the baths.

And Quetzalcoatl did penance also. He bled *the flesh of* his shinbone, he stained maguey thorns with blood. Also he bathed at midnight. And his pool was where he bathed himself—the place called Turquoises Are Washed Here.

He was imitated by the incense keepers and the priests. The life of Quetzalcoatl became a pattern for the life of *every* priest: so it was established— the regimen of Tollan--so it was adopted here in Mexico.

The fourth "chapter": which tells how the glory of Quetzalcoatl was ended and how three enchanters came to him and what they did.

But it so happened that Quetzalcoatl and all the
Toltecs grew lax. And then at once there came
three sorcerers, contriving evil: Huitzilopochtli,
Titlacahuan, *and* Tlacahuepan.[38] All three
contrived by evil to destroy Tollan.

It was Titlacahuan who began to work the evil.
They say he changed himself, impersonated *and*
dissembled a little old man, very stooped, very
white—indeed a little *old* white-headed man.[60]
Thereupon he went to the house of Quetzalcoatl.
And as he arrived, then at once he announced:
"I wish to see the lord Quetzalcoatl." Whereupon
he was answered: "Be gone, old man! The lord
is ill *and* you will disturb him."

Then the little old man replied, "But no! I must
truly see him, I truly must come to his side."
And they said, "Very well. *But* first you wait.
First we must advise the lord."

And with that they informed Quetzalcoatl at
once. They advised him, "My prince, a little old
man has arrived who would see you. *He seems*
like a net for you, like a snare for you. We turned
him away, but he would not go. He merely
answers, 'I must see the lord.' "

Then Quetzalcoatl said, "Let him come, let him
enter. It is he whom I have awaited *for many
days*, even for five, even for ten."

Then to Quetzalcoatl at once they conducted the little old man, who greeted him then, saying, "Lord my grandchild, what of your health? Here is the potion I bring to you. You will drink it!"

And then Quetzalcoatl spoke: "Come close, old one. You are tired, you have toiled *to reach me*. Already for five, for ten, *for many days*, I have awaited you."[61]

And the old man said to him then, "My prince, what indeed of your health?" Whereupon Quetzalcoatl answered, "Truly, much do I ail in all parts. Nowhere *am I* well. My hands, my feet —my flesh indeed is sapped, as though it had been cut to pieces."

And then the old man said, "Indeed, here is the potion, delicious *and* smooth—and it works within one. If you drink it, it will work in you. Also it will soothe your body. Also you will weep. Your heart will feel deserted, you will think upon your death. And you will think also upon the place where you are to go."

Then Quetzalcoatl said, "Where am I to go, old one?" Then the little old man answered him, "Indeed, only there—toward Tollan Tlapallan— shall you go.[37] A man *stands* guard there, one already aged.[62] You *and he* shall take counsel together. And when you return, you shall have again been made a child."[63] Quetzalcoatl was overwhelmed.

But the little old man spoke again: "Come, you must drink the potion!" Quetzalcoatl answered, "Old one, truly I shall not drink it." Then the old man said to him, "Drink it! You will find it tempting. Or set it down in front of you at least. Your fate will tempt you. Merely taste a little!"

And Quetzalcoatl then tasted a little, and then drank deeply.

And then Quetzalcoatl spoke: "What is it? *It is* delicious. Already the illness is cured. Where has the pain gone? No more am I sick."

The little old man then said to him, "Drink another! The potion is good. Your body will strengthen thereby."

And then he drank once again, then he made himself drunk. Then he wept, he was stricken with sorrow.

Quetzalcoatl was overwhelmed. His heart was broken. He could put it from his mind no longer, but lived in anguish: he lived with his remorse.

Indeed, they say the sorcerer deceived him. And the potion that he gave him—this, they say, *was* white wine. And this, they say, *is* made with the juice of Sacred Maguey.[64]

PART II

*The fifth "chapter": which tells of another evil
wrought by the enchanter Titlacahuan.*

And here is another thing Titlacahuan did—how
he wrought an evil.

He dissembled—he impersonated—a Toueyo *and*
went simply *in the nude, with his penis* dangling,
selling chili peppers, seated in the market square,
in the palace entrance court.[65]

Now the daughter of Huemac was most
appetizing. Indeed, many Toltec men desired her.
And they petitioned her that they might marry
her. But Huemac favored no one. To no one
would he give her.

Now this daughter of Huemac looked out into
the market square and saw the Toueyo *with his
penis* dangling. And seeing it, she immediately
went *back* inside. She was immediately ill,
swollen, *and* inflamed, tantalized by the Toueyo's
tototl.[66]

And when Huemac learned that his daughter was
ill, he said to the women who guarded her, "What
has happened? What is this? How did it come to
be that my little daughter is inflamed?"

Then the women who guarded her answered
him, "A Toueyo selling chili peppers made her
hot *and* indisposed her. So it came to be, so the
illness seized her."

Now King Huemac gave orders at once, saying,
"Toltecs! Let him be looked for! A Toueyo
selling chili peppers! He shall appear!"

Then they looked for him everywhere. And
when no one appeared, then a herald cried out at
Crying Out Mountain, saying, "Toltecs! If
anywhere you see a Toueyo selling chilis,
bring him in! The lord is looking for him."
Whereupon they looked *and* went everywhere,
went picking through Tollan, looking.

And when they'd grown weary, finding him
nowhere, then they went to inform the king that
indeed they had found him nowhere.

And at last he appeared on his own—just so—come
to sit down even there where at first he'd
appeared. And when he'd been seen, they went
rushing at once to report it.

They spoke: "The Toueyo has truly appeared."
Then Huemac replied, "Have him come quickly!"

Then at once the Toltecs went rushing to fetch
the Toueyo. They brought him before the king.
And when they had brought him, the king then
inquired of him, "Where *is* your home?"

Whereupon he was answered: "I *am* indeed a Toueyo, I sell little chilis."

The king then said to him, "Where *indeed* are you going? Put on a loincloth! Cover yourself!" Whereupon he was answered: "But we truly *are* thus."[67]

And the king then replied, "You have indisposed my little daughter. You yourself shall be the remedy."

And he was answered: "My dear stranger, my prince! Truly it would not be proper. Kill me, take my life, let me die! What can you mean? I am nothing but a chili peddler."

And the king replied at once, "Nay, you shall cure her. Have no fear."

And then they trimmed his hair. They immersed him *and* bathed him. Then they rubbed him with tincture. They gave him a loincloth *and* tied it around him.

And when they'd adorned him, the king then said to him, "Look upon my daughter there *where* she is guarded." And when he went there, then he knew her. Then the woman was cured. He did at last become the son-in-law of the king.

The sixth "chapter": which tells how the Toltecs
were impatient with the marriage of Huemac's
daughter. Also: another evil wrought by
Titlacahuan.

And then the Toltecs laughed *and* made fun of it.
They were scornful, saying, "It seems the king has
married his daughter to a Toueyo."

At length the king summoned the Toltecs *and*
spoke to them: "I have indeed heard ridicule
against me, mockery against me, for having taken
a Toueyo as my son-in-law. Now you must betray
him—abandon him—at Zacatepec, at Coatepec."

Thereupon the Toltecs issued a call to arms *and*
set forth in a body. Thereupon they departed,
that they might abandon the son-in-law.

And as they went into battle, then they ditched[68]
the Toueyo, together with all the dwarfs *and*
the cripples.

And when they had ditched them, then the
Toltecs went on to take captives—to capture the
Coatepec foemen.

But to all the dwarfs *and* the cripples the Toueyo
said, "Have no fear. Here we will conquer them,
here will they die by our hands."

And after a while, then the foemen routed the
Toltecs—who believed the Toueyo would surely

be killed there, as they had betrayed and
abandoned him, leaving him behind to die. And
thereafter they came to inform King Huemac,
telling him, "We did indeed abandon the Toueyo,
who had been your cherished son-in-law."

And Huemac rejoiced greatly, believing truly
without a doubt that it was thus achieved. For
he was ashamed that he had taken a Toueyo as his
son-in-law.

But he, the Toueyo, whom they'd gone to
abandon in battle—when the Coatepec, the
Zacatepec foemen came, then he took command
of the dwarfs, the hunchbacks. He said to them,
"Pay good heed *and* fear not! Don't be terrified,
don't despair! I know already that you will
capture them, every one. We will some way kill
them all."

And as the foemen came to attack them, came
running toward them, then in a fury they
counter-attacked, trampling them, killing them,
slaughtering them, annihilating them. Multitudes
without number did they kill of the foemen.

And when the king heard of it, he was most
uneasy and distressed. Then he summoned the
Toltecs *and* said to them, "We must go to greet
this cherished son-in-law of yours."[69]

And then the Toltecs broke apart—they spilled
forth. Then already they were going with the

king. They came scattering toward him, falling
in around him, as he went to make the greeting.

The Toltecs came in their regalia: quetzal
headdress and turquoise shield. *And* when they'd
reached him, then they shared it with him, they
apportioned him a quetzal headdress and a
turquoise shield. In full regalia did they come.

They came dancing in his honor, came as dancing
victors. They came stepping in a lordly manner;
they came vaunting. In a company did they come.

They came singing to him, came adorning *him*
with song. They came honoring with song. They
came blowing *flutes* for him—came with the shell
trumpet roaring, came with the conch horn barking.

And as they neared the palace, then they crowned
him with plumes and yellowed him with yellow
tincture and went and rouged his face. And all
his companions were embellished likewise.

And then Huemac spoke to his son-in-law:
"Indeed, now are the hearts of the Toltecs
satisfied that you *are* my son-in-law. You have
done well. Be received on this soil. Rest your
feet."[70]

The seventh "chapter": wherein is related another
evil wrought by the enchanter, such that Toltecs
perished as they stepped and *danced.*

Yet a second evil: —*Now* this very sorcerer, when as champion he'd been plumed with yellow parrot feathers, thereupon proposed that they make music *and* yield themselves to song.

And so a herald cried out from the summit of Crying Out Mountain. He cried *and* called out to the lands surrounding. Wide indeed could the cry of the herald be heard. And very quickly did they come.

And then *the sorcerer* went to Where the Crags Are. And all the people, the common people, went *with him*. And all the youths *and* young women were assembled, numberless—a throng.

The sorcerer began to sing, to drum, to strike a beat for them upon his drum. At once there was dancing.

And so they went leaping, hand in hand, turning back to back. Great was the rapture as everyone sang, *as* the song came surging and ebbing.

And the song that he sang he invented right there. And as he sang out, they answered right then, taking the song from his lips.

And the singing commenced at dusk, and it ended at flute call.

And as they danced, they came stepping feverishly, entranced. Many fell onto the crags

in the gorge *and* all of them died there. At once
they were turned into stones.

And as for the others, *there* at the craggy gorge
—the sorcerer broke the bridge, and *yet* the bridge
was of stone. All of them fell there at once, into
the water, there at the bridge, *and* all were
turned into stones.

But how it had happened the Toltecs no longer could
tell, *for* they were as drunk.

And many a time was there singing, there Where
the Crags Are. And as many times as there was
song, then as many times was there death. They
were thrown on the crags, they were scattered
below. The Toltecs indeed were destroyed.[71]

*The eighth "chapter": which tells of another
evil wrought by the same enchanter, whereby
many more Toltecs died.*

Behold another! And the sorcerer brought it to pass:

They say that he once took the guise of a warrior
and summoned the herald, the crier, that he might
cry out to the world, that all might come. *And*
the herald gave voice: "The people, the common
people, all shall come! You shall come to a halt
at Xochitlan to work the chinampa, to reap!"

Then all the common people came *and* they

halted *there* at Xochitlan. (And they called it
Xochitlan, *Place of the Flowers*, because, they
say, it was the quetzalcoatl's garden of flowers.)[72]

And when the Toltecs had come together, had
gathered, *and* were crowded, then the warrior
slew them, he smote them, he smote them at the
nape.

Many indeed, without number, died by his hand
as he took their lives. And others, who fled, who
took flight—who were saved from his hand, who
escaped his grasp—toppled down as they ran *and*
were killed at once. And the others were trampled
and crushed. *And* all of them died there.

*The ninth "chapter": which tells of another evil
wrought by this same enchanter, whereby many
more Toltecs perished.*

Behold *yet* another work of the sorcerer:[73]

Now he who was called Tlacahuepan or
Cuexcoch had seated himself at the center of the
market square, where he caused a manikin to
dance (they say that this *was* Huitzilopochtli).
And in his hand he held it as he made it dance.

And when the Toltecs saw him, they came
stampeding toward him, tumbling toward him,
that they might see it. Indeed many people were

trampled there. They died in the crush, they were
crushed to death.

And as it happened that many were killed many
times in this manner—upon seeing the dancing—
the sorcerer himself cried out, saying, "Toltecs!
What evil *is this*? *Is this* not an evil to us, *this*
dancing? And him! Let him be killed! Let him be
stoned!" Whereupon they stoned him. He was
felled by the stones. And after a while he reeked.

Indeed it was frightful the way he reeked. Indeed
it was overpowering. And wherever the wind
bore the stench, the people died.

And when many had died of the stench, then the
sorcerer spoke to the Toltecs *and* said, "Get rid
of this dead one! Cast him out! Truly the stench
is ruinous. Let him be tugged *away*." And the
Toltecs trussed him with ropes and they tugged
him.

And *yet* as they tugged him, he failed to move, so
heavy *he was*. At first they dismissed it, they
thought nothing of it. Then at last they issued a
summons, and the herald gave voice: "Let every
man come! Bear him off, lug him with ropes! Let
the dead one be cast away!"

And as the Toltecs came and assembled, they
trussed the dead one with ropes. Then they struck
up a chanty, they voiced it:

"Toltecaye! Macuele! Ma tlatilinilo! *O Toltecs!*
Onward! Heave!"

And even so, they failed to move him. Nor could
they stir him at all. And whenever one of the
ropes would break, then all would be killed, all
in a line, down along the rope. They fell,
they came tumbling one on another, and so they
were killed.[74]

And as indeed he could not even be stirred, as
indeed he could not be removed, then the
sorcerer said to the Toltecs, "O Toltecs! He must
have a song of his own!" Then the Toltecs
chanted the song, singing:

"Xitlahuilanacan ye tohuepan Tlacahuepan,
tlacatecolotl! *Pull ye now our log Tlacahuepan,*
the sorcerer!"[75]

And as they chanted, then at once the dead one
stirred: they made him move, they brought him
forth. *And* when a rope broke, then the log would
ram them all, would run them over.[76] Also *there*
were many merely trampled: they were crushed
and so they died.

Yet together they removed him, they threw him
away, this dead one, this Tlacahuepan.
Thereupon they returned as if they'd seen
nothing of what had been done to them all. They
no longer perceived it as evil, *for* they were as
drunk.

*The tenth "chapter": which tells of another evil
wrought by the same enchanter, such that he
cursed Tollan.*

Behold also how the sorcerer cursed Tollan:

It is said that a white hawk, pierced through the
head by an arrow, came flying *and* swooping not
far from the Toltecs, nearing the earth as it
swooped. Indeed it was seen overhead coming
down from above, coming near.[77]

Behold, too, another evil—wrought as a curse
upon the Toltecs:

They say a mountain burned, called Grass
Mountain. At night it appeared in the distance,
burning. The distant flames rose upward. When
the Toltecs saw it, they were very troubled *and*
alarmed. They threw their hands up, screaming,
crying out aloud.[78]

No longer were they tranquil. There was no
more peace. And if they saw an evil thing, they
said, "O Toltecs! All things now, *and* even we,
must pass.[79] *For* even now the Toltec way is
passing. We are truly cursed. What now? Where
to? Unhappy we! *Now at last* are ye aroused."

Behold another evil:

Stones, they say, rained down upon the Toltecs.[80]
And when the stones had rained, then a sacrificial

altar descended out of the sky. There it fell—
behind Chapultepec. And afterward an old
woman lived there selling banners, crying, "Have
your banners!" And they who were destined to
die would answer *among themselves*, "You shall
buy them." Then they passed to where the
sacrificial altar was. No one asked, "What *is this*
you do *to me?*" Thus they lost their lives.[81]

*The eleventh "chapter": wherein is related
another evil wrought by the same enchanter,
whereby he teased the people, whereby he undid
Tollan, killing not merely a few of the Toltecs.*

Behold also how the Toltecs were cursed:

It is said that the food turned bitter, utterly bitter
and bitter to the core: it could no longer be
placed on the lips. The Toltecs indeed had been
tricked.[82]

Now an old woman (it seems, so they say, that
this was the sorcerer, dissembling *and* taking the
shape of an old woman) came to sit in Xochitlan
and there she roasted maize. And the maize she
roasted could be scented far and wide. Indeed
it wafted to the people, spreading far and wide.

The odor of roasted maize spread over the land.
And when the Toltecs smelled the roasting maize,
they found it savory, found it fragrant—found it
good.

And when they had smelled it, they came forth
quickly. In but a moment they had arrived, for
they say the Toltecs thought nothing of distance.

They did *indeed* think nothing of distance. Even
though they were far away, they could quickly
get to where they were going *and* just as quickly
to where they had come from.

But when in numbers they had gathered there
together, she killed them all, she took their lives
entirely. Never more were they to make their
journey back, their journey home.

Indeed the Toltecs had been teased—in such a
way that very many were disposed of by the
sorcerer. Indeed, he made sport of the Toltecs.

PART III

*The twelfth "chapter": which tells of the flight—
of the flight and exile—of Quetzalcoatl, how he
went to Tlapallan, and of all that he did on the way.*

And many another evil was done to the Toltecs
that Tollan might be destroyed. And because it
was so, Quetzalcoatl suffered. He grieved. Then
he remembered that he was to go, that he was to
leave his city of Tollan. Then he made his
preparations.

It is said that he completely burned his house of gold, his house of redshell. And the other Toltec treasures, the splendid things, the precious things: all were buried, all were concealed in inaccessible places, in the interior of a mountain or in chasms.[83]

And he also changed the cacao trees to mesquites. And all the precious birds, the quetzal, the cotinga, the roseate spoonbill—he sent them on ahead.[84] They led him onward, they proceeded to Anahuac.[85] So it was. And so he started out, and so he followed on.

And soon he reached the site of Cuauhtitlan— *Beneath the Tree.*[86] The tree rose very broad and very tall. He stopped beside it. Then he asked to have his mirror, then he saw himself: he looked at his reflection, saying, "Truly I *am* old." And there he dubbed it Old-Age Cuauhtitlan—*Beneath the Old-Age Tree.*

Thereupon he stoned the tree. He pelted it. And as he pelted it, the stones grew all encrusted *and* fixed themselves upon the old-age tree.[87] This is how it always looked—it appeared just so— beginning at the root, extending to the crown.

And as Quetzalcoatl followed on, they[88] preceded, blowing *flutes* for him.

Again he rested—at a place where he sat himself upon a rock, leaning *forward* on his hands. Suddenly then in the distance he saw Tollan,

and then he wept. Sighing, he wept. His tears
rained down as hail, *and* his tears slid down his
face. As they dropped, they pierced the very
rock.

The thirteenth "chapter": where it is told of the
mark Quetzalcoatl made in the rock with his
hands where he rested, where he sat.

And as he leaned on the rock with his hands, he
pressed *them* down, just as one would make
impressions with one's palms in clay.[89] His
buttocks likewise were upon the rock and so were
impressed *and* bemired. Indeed the indentations
can be seen. So he gave *this* place the name
Temacpalco—*Where the Handprints Are.*

And then he arose *and* went on to a place called
Tepanohuayan—*At the Stone Bridge—where* a
river lies, a river flowing, spread out wide. He
laid stones to make a bridge, *and* then and there
crossed over. And thereupon he called it
Tepanohuayan.

And again he set forth, and arrived at a place
called Coahapan—*At the Water of the Serpent.*
There *were* sorcerers there who wished to turn
him back, reverse him, *and* they blocked his way
and asked him, "Where are you going? Where
are you bound? Why are you leaving the city?
To whom have you left *it*? Who shall do
penance?"

Then Quetzalcoatl answered the sorcerers, "This cannot be permitted. I must go on."

Then the sorcerers asked Quetzalcoatl, "Where do you go?" And Quetzalcoatl answered, "Tlapallan *is* where I go *and* what I seek."[37]

And they asked him, "What business have you *there*?" Then Quetzalcoatl said, "I have been summoned there—the sun has called me."[90]

Then they answered, "Very well. You must relinquish all the Toltec arts."

And there he did relinquish all the Toltec arts: the art of casting gold, the art of cutting *jewels*, the art of carving wood, the art of working stone, the art of painting *books*, the art of *feather*-working.

They made him yield it all, they took it all by force—they seized it all.

So it was. Then Quetzalcoatl threw his jewels upon the water and they were swallowed up. And so he gave the place a name: Cozcahapan, *At the Water of the Jewels*, now called Coahapan, *At the Water of the Serpent*.

And then he traveled on, reaching the place called Cochtocan—*Where He Lay Sleeping*. And there a sorcerer came to meet him *and* said to him,

"Where are you going?" Then he answered,
"Tlapallan *is* where *I go and* what I seek."

Then the sorcerer said, "Very well. Drink this
wine that I have brought here." Quetzalcoatl
answered, "No, I must not drink, nor even taste
but a little."

Then the sorcerer spoke to him again: "It cannot
be allowed that you fail to drink, that you *even*
fail to taste it. *For* I give leave to no one, I let no
one pass, unless I serve him wine *and* have him
drink—*and* make him drunk. Now do it! Come!
And drink this!"

Then Quetzalcoatl drank the wine *through* a reed.
And when he had drunk, he fell fast asleep in the
road. He thundered as he slept: his snoring could
be heard from afar. And when he woke, then he
glanced from side to side. He looked at himself
and arranged his hair; then he gave the place a
name: Cochtocan, *Where He Lay Sleeping.*

*The fourteenth "chapter": which tells how
Quetzalcoatl's subjects were chilled* and *frozen
to death as they passed between Iztactepetl and
Popocatepetl—and of the other things that
he did.*

Then again he set forth, climbing up between
Iztactepetl and Popocatepetl. *And* all the dwarfs

and the hunchbacks *who were* his servants went
with him. It snowed on them all, they were chilled
there, they died of the cold.[91] And Quetzalcoatl
was shaken by it. He wept. He sang. Weeping
greatly, he sighed.

Then he saw in the distance another white
mountain, called Poyauhtecatl.[92] *And* again he set
forth *and* went everywhere, touching at towns
and villages everywhere. And they say that he
left a great number of traces behind him—his signs
—by which he was signified:[93]

At a certain spot on a mountain, they say, he
would frolic *and* tumble *and* fall to the bottom,
and for his recovery he left in place a towline *of
maguey*.[94]

At another site he laid out a ball court all of stone.
And through the middle, where the center line
lay, it was entrenched. *And* the entrenchment ran
deep.[95]

And in another place he shot a ceiba,[96] shooting it
so that he himself passed through the heart of the
ceiba.[97]

And in another place he built a house
underground. *And* the site is called Mictlan.[98]

And in yet another place he erected a stone, a
great stone phallus. They say that anyone, *even* a
child, might once have pushed it with his finger.

It had indeed been set in motion, rocking back
and forth. Yet, they say, when many pushed it,
then it absolutely would not move. Though many
together might make the effort, desiring to push
it, it could not be moved.

And still many other things did he do in towns
and villages everywhere. And they say that he
named all the mountains. Here *and* throughout he
bestowed all the names.

And at last he arrived at the seashore. Then he
constructed a litter of serpents.[99] *And* when it
was finished, he sat himself on it: it served as his
boat. And so he set off *and* was carried away by
the sea.

No longer does anyone know how he reached
Tlapallan.[90]

Here ends the third book.[100]

Fragment E / A Song of Survival

I / A LAMENT

Singer:[101] In Tollan stood the house of beams,
where still the serpent columns stand deserted.
Gone away is Nacxitl Topiltzin.[102]

Chorus: Departing, he is wept for by our princes. He goes away; goes to where he rests, in Tlapallan.

Singer: Now he leaves them in Cholollan, traveling through the land of Poyauhtecatl, going to Acallan.[103]

Chorus: Departing, he is wept for by our princes. He goes away; goes to where he rests, in Tlapallan.

Topiltzin: I am bound for Nonohualco,[104] I the one in quechol plumes, I the lord who pierces.[105]

Prince Matlacxochitl: I am grieving, my lord attired in plumes has gone away, he abandons me,[106] I, Matlacxochitl.[107]

Topiltzin: As the mountain falls, I weep. Alas, the ocean sands rise up.[108]

Matlacxochitl: I am grieving, my lord attired in plumes has gone away, he abandons me, I, Matlacxochitl.

Singer: In Tlapallan you are awaited. You are bidden there to sleep.

Chorus: You are moving onward now, my lord attired in plumes. You are bidden now to Xicalanco, to Zacanco.

Singer: Ah, but no! Your palace, your temple—these you leave behind you here in Tollan Nonohualco.[109]

Chorus: We weep for the lord, the noble one.

Singer: Your palace, your temple—these you leave behind you here in Tollan Nonohualco. The painted stones, the beams, you left them here behind you, in Tollan where you came to rule.

Chorus: Nacxitl Topiltzin! Never can your name be lost, for your people will be weeping.

Singer: The turquoise house, the serpent house, you built them here in Tollan where you came to rule.

Chorus: Nacxitl Topiltzin! Never can your name be lost, for your people will be weeping.

11 / THE BIRTH OF CINTEOTL

Cinteotl: I, the variegated maize, came forth.[110]

Chorus: The multicolored flower of life expands. It stood up shining, it flourished, in the sacred presence of Our Mother.[111]

Cinteotl: The water splashes, the precious water-leaf puts forth buds. I am a work of the Only God. I am his creation.

Chorus: Your heart is alive in the painted *kernels (or words).*[112] The waterweed *(or book) is your* throne: there you sing, that the princes might dance; there you reign *(or speak)* at the water's edge *(or in flowing words).* He made you: in a garden of flowers *(or poems)* he gave you birth: he paints your name in song. The artists indite it. The book is complete. Your heart is perfected.

Cinteotl: Here, through art, I live.

III / THE POET SPEAKS

Who will have me? Who would be with me?
Here I stand: will you take me? *I am* a singer.
My fragrant songs, my flowers, fall *like strewn
petals* in the presence of others.

Great are the stones as I carve them, massive
the beams as I paint them: they are *my* song: for
it shall be heard when I have departed. I leave my
song-sign behind me on earth: here my soul will
continue to live: a remembrance of me, that my
name might endure.

I weep as I speak, I cry to my soul: would
that I might see the song-root, would that I might
transplant it, would that it might grow on earth
when it comes. Let it come: a remembrance of me,
that my name might endure.

The Prince Flower[113] breathes its aroma. Our
flowers are one. My song is heard, it takes root.
My transplanted word is sprouting. Our flowers
stand up in the rain.

Sweet flower of Cacao bursts open with
perfume. The fragrant flower of Peyote falls in a
raining mist. I the singer, I live. My song is heard,
it takes root. My transplanted word is sprouting.
Our flowers stand up in the rain.

NOTES

Fragment A / The Restoration of Life

1 / The world, or more specifically the sun, had been created and
destroyed four times before the advent of the present, or fifth,
sun. It was during the fourth sun (immediately after the deluge
that destroyed the fourth world, but prior to the creation of the
fifth sun per se) that the god Quetzalcoatl brought forth the human race as we now know it. In the interim the troubled gods
ask, "Who shall live *on earth?*" i.e., Who shall perform the de-
votions that gods require?

2 / The eight names of the supreme Spirit of Duality are arranged
in four complementary pairs, each of which expresses a cosmic
idea. The first pair, Skirt-of-Stars (*Citlallinicue*) and Starlight-of-
Sustenance (*Citlallatonac*), alludes to what might be called the
womb of night, already containing within it the seminal light of
dawn. The idea of starlight as the antecedent of sunlight and thus
the ultimate source of food is a widespread Indian concept. *Citlallatonac* has therefore been freely translated as "Light-of-Day." The
second pair, Lord-Beside-the-Water (*Apanteuctli*) and Who-
Comes-Over-in-Place-of-Others (*Tepanquizqui*), may represent
the sinking sun or evening star (drawn down to the western sea)

and the rising sun or morning star (issuing forth in place of the stars). The interpretation is uncertain and I have translated the epithets freely. The third pair harks back to primeval times when the earth was still soft. One of the tasks of the American Indian demiurge is to make the earth solid, as in the Pima myth recorded by Frank Russell, *Bureau of American Ethnology, Twenty-sixth Annual Report,* 1908, p. 207, or the Mandan myth given by Edward Curtis, *The North American Indian,* Vol. V, 1909, p. 39. Not until it has been firmed can it be tilled. Quetzalcoatl is sometimes shown in the pictographic codices holding a tilling instrument and it is probably he—in his Venusian, demiurgic, and agricultural functions—who is indirectly referred to in the second and third pairs of this list. See note 9. The relationship between Quetzalcoatl and Titlacahuan is discussed in note 38.

3 / The adjective "emerald" is roughly comparable to the English expression "golden," meaning "precious." The setting is Mictlan, the underworld, literally "Dead Land"; its ruler is Mictlanteuctli ("Dead Land Lord")—Mictlancihuatl ("Dead Land Lady"), and his-her subjects are the Micteca ("Dead Ones"), mentioned below.

4 / This portion of the myth would appear to be a parody. Although the original upon which it is based has not survived, it may be reconstructed from the analogous Navajo creation story (see Washington Matthews's *Navaho Legends,* 1897, p. 69) and from the allusion contained in a line found in *Cantares mexicanos* (folio 15), which reads: "For our sake he circled four times round *the perimeter of* Tamoanchan." The primal scene in Tamoanchan, the Aztec paradise, would presumably have had Quetzalcoatl Ehecatl (i.e., Quetzalcoatl "the Wind") circling four times round the inert flesh, while imparting to it the breath of life by means of the wind emblem, or conch horn. (The transformation of the story into an underworld descent suggests the identification of Quetzalcoatl with the planet Venus as it passes beneath the earth between its disappearance as evening star and

its reemergence as morning star. Hence the rather static creation myth becomes an exploit—a hero myth—in its own right.) In a similar Iroquois episode the hero wins the gift of life from his spirit father, Wind, by racing around the perimeter of the earth with his father's flute (J. N. B. Hewitt, *Bureau of American Ethnology, Twenty-first Annual Report*, 1903, pp. 234–5). In other words, the circling hero effects a concentration of winds, thus encompassing, or capturing, the breath of life. Cf. note 5, p. 334.

5 / The nahual, or nagual as it is usually spelled in English, may here mean nothing more than the hero's own soul, or conscience. Or it may hark back to some version of the story in which Quetzalcoatl, the morning star, is accompanied by his twin brother, Xolotl, the evening star. (In the crude variant given by Mendieta, the protagonist is simply Xolotl.) Quetzalcoatl claims to have taken the bones "forever," meaning that he intends to make man immortal. But see note 7.

6 / The crypt is a motif borrowed from uranic myths, where it is typically associated with the jealous stars who attempt to trap the sun or the morning star in order to prevent it from rising. (For another example, see *Popol Vuh*, Pt. I, ch. 7. For *Popol Vuh*, see p. 276.)

7 / This unhappy episode evidently explains the origin of human mortality—a problem that will be "solved" in Fragment E by the promise of immortality through art. For variant readings, see Mendieta, Bk. II, ch. 1, and "Histoyre du Mechique," ch. 7.

8 / Quilaztli and Cihuacoatl ("Serpent Woman") are names of the earth mother (or grandmother) as patroness of childbirth. (See Sahagún, Bk. VI, ch. 28.) Note the idealized coitus.

9 / All six names are epithets of Quetzalcoatl. See note 2. The title He-Who-Falls-Headlong undoubtedly refers to Quetzalcoatl as evening star. In the lines that follow, the newly created humans

are spoken of as "servants of the gods." That is to say: they bled for us, now we bleed for them (through ritual puncturing of the flesh). Here as elsewhere I have followed the time-honored custom of using the European term "penance" in connection with these acts. Yet they are probably not penances in the Christian sense of reparation for sin. Probably they are sacrifices, imagined as giving nourishment to the gods. In Fragment C, where the sister of Quetzalcoatl is addressed as "penitent lady," it should be understood that the epithet means "one who makes blood sacrifices."

10 / The colors of the ants, black and red, allude to a technique of imitative magic. By first identifying with black, then with red, the ritualist progresses symbolically from night to day, from death to life, or, by extension, from famine to plenty. In an Arapaho myth the hero revives corpses by first shooting black arrows into the air, then red arrows (G. Dorsey and A. Kroeber, *Traditions of the Arapaho*, 1903, p. 458). A fantasized food-conjuring ritual of the Cheyennes requires a black-painted youth and a red-painted youth, the former standing vigil through the night. At dawn, as the latter replaces him, food animals magically appear (George Grinnell, *By Cheyenne Campfires*, 1926, also 1962, p. 173). The underlying idea is that death is the necessary condition for life. It is the "black" quantity, therefore, that must be initially posited; the "red" quantity is then introduced in order to set an example for the "black." As the text has it, red shows black the way, i.e., the way to new life.

11 / Oxomoco and Cipactonal are the Aztec Adam and Eve. According to "History of the Mexicans as Told by Their Paintings" (ch. 2), Cipactonal was the first to use maize kernels in divination. (The anonymous author adds, "Indeed the woman *is* Cipactonal," by way of emphasizing his disagreement with a conflicting tradition. In Codex Borbonicus, for example, the name Cipactonal is appended to the figure of the man. See Lehmann 1938, p. 339.)

12 / The myth explains how agriculture became dependent upon the rain gods (which were supposed to have dwelled at all four cardinal points, represented by the colors blue, white, yellow, and red). The mysterious god Nanahuatl ("Afflicted with Syphilis" or "Covered with Sores") is chosen to play the indicated role perhaps because, as Seler imagined (1915, p. 186), he was the god of lightning and therefore empowered to split open the mountain. But if he is covered with sores, he is also feeble. In certain analogous myths, as J. E. S. Thompson has pointed out in his *Maya History and Religion* (1970), the old invalid faints at the crucial moment, and it is this that provides the rain gods with their opportunity.

Fragment B / The Ceremonial Fire

13 / Lehmann (1938, p. 365) supposes that the four-day birth may be meant to correspond with the second four days of the planet Venus's eight-day disappearance at inferior conjunction. If so, then the hero's birth coincides with the emergence of the morning star. See note 52 and figure 1.

14 / The sacred-almanac day Ce Acatl ("1 Reed") is the ideal, or ritualistic, date for the reappearance of Venus after inferior conjunction. Ce Acatl is therefore an epithet of the morning star. See note 13.

15 / Seler (*Gesammelte Abhandlungen*, Vol. IV, p. 154) locates Xihuacan "in the west," on the Pacific coast. (Cf. Lehmann 1938, p. 366.) The four hundred Mimixcoa are stars (see Seler, op. cit., pp. 64–98); the term "four hundred" means, figuratively, "innumerable." (The sand burial indicates the setting sun: see note 108.)

16 / The probable interpretation is that the "innumerable" stars of night have "murdered" the sinking sun, whose "corpse" they

have buried in the sands of the western sea. It then becomes the task of the sun's offspring, the morning star, to renew the diurnal cycle by rising up just before daybreak to disperse, or slay, the offending stars. But in the episodes that immediately follow, the narrator will begin to shift the symbolism away from the renewal of the twenty-four-hour day to the renewal of the fifty-two-year sacred fire.

17 / Although the prototypal image of the hero's father is no doubt the sun, in this variant the myth has been adapted to the cult of the god Mixcoatl ("Cloud Serpent"). The burial of the father in the temple of the god whom he represents is a poetic motif, recalling the actual custom of interring a king in the man-made "mountain," or pyramid temple, dedicated to a god he had served (see Ixtlilxochitl I, p. 41). But in Fragment C the "mountain" is said to be the temple of Quilaztli (the earth mother), suggesting that it represents the earth itself, through which the sun must pass in order to be reborn at dawn. The "mountain" also recalls the famous Hill of the Star, where the fifty-two-year sacred fire was customarily rekindled in Aztec times. (If we may return for a moment to Mixcoatl, it should be pointed out that the Milky Way, i.e., the nocturnal "cloud serpent," is generally supposed to be a manifestation of this deity. But in Codex Vaticanus 3738, the Milky Way is said to be Citlallatonac, whom I have identified with the sun in note 2. We may therefore conjecture that Mixcoatl is none other than the sun father himself.)

18 / Observe how the narrator subtly changes the identity of the antagonists, identified above as the four hundred Mimixcoa, thus shifting to a slightly different mythic ground. What follows draws heavily—yet creatively—upon the theme of the jealous elder brothers and the motif of the forbidden animals. (But for the sake of consistency the "brothers" are still identified as uncles. We must bear in mind that this myth is in a sense the continuation of an earlier myth in which Mixcoatl himself was the sun's child, who murdered his faithless brothers, the Mimixcoa—the term

Mimixcoa being simply the plural of *Mixcoatl*—and so restored the light of day. In our myth the Mimixcoa, returning from the dead, have avenged themselves, leaving Mixcoatl's son, Ce Acatl, with the perpetually unfinished business of turning the tables once again. Hence the paradigmatic brothers have here become uncles.) Now the mythic pattern calls for a family of four brothers, consisting of three elder antagonists (who stand for the "innumerable"—and faithless—star children of the paternal sun) and a despised youngest brother (the sun's favorite) who triumphs despite obstacles. The forbidden animals are simply an instrument by which the jealous elders discriminate against the youngest. All four brothers are hunters, but the fiercer, more prestigious game—bear, jaguar, wolf, eagle—is considered too difficult for the ineffectual youngest to obtain. Or so the elder brothers would like to believe. In one variant the bigger game is expressly forbidden. The youngest, then, is allowed to shoot only rabbits, snakes, deer, etc. It is by overcoming this discrimination that he is reborn, so to speak, as a hero. (For the myth of Mixcoatl as offspring of the sun, see *Legend of the Suns*, ff. 4, 5. For two important variants of the despised hero, see "Histoyre du Mechique," ch. 10, and "The Red Swan" in H. R. Schoolcraft's *Algic Researches*, 1839, Vol. II.)

19 / The uncles are taunting the hero. See note 18. But, as we shall see, the hero turns the situation to his advantage and, with the aid of the animals, succeeds nonetheless in lighting the fire on behalf of the sun. (As a mark of respect, the hero will use the term "my uncles" in addressing the animals.)

20 / In the actual "new fire" ceremony the flame was kindled with a block and drilling stick in the opened breast of a sacrificial victim.

21 / Without attempting to locate all the places named in this list of conquests, let it be noted that they describe—in terms of the political geography of Aztec times—a generally eastward trek

from the Valley of Mexico to Tlapallan (the "Red Place"), the mysterious land of the rising sun. At the same time it is entirely possible that the narrator has in mind the historical migrations of the militaristic Toltecs, some of whom pushed eastward into Yucatan around the turn of the first millennium A.D., there to rebuild the city of Chichén Itzá as an approximate replica of Tollan. Tlapallan may denote either the fabulous red land of the sun or, in some contexts (as perhaps here), the peninsula of Yucatan. The "water" at Acallan is probably the Laguna de Términos in the present-day state of Campeche.

22 / The five days of moribundity recall the five-stage journey to death. See note 86.

23 / The hero's cremation implies his rebirth as the morning star. The connection is made explicit in "Histoyre du Mechique," ch. 11, in Mendieta, Bk. II, ch. 5, and in Fragment C.

Fragment C / A Cycle of Transformation

24 / The word *chalchiuitl* may denote any precious or semi-precious green stone. In these texts it has been translated "emerald" or "jadestone." The mythical amazon Chimalma ("Shield Hand) usurps the role of the earth mother in several of the best-known versions of the Quetzalcoatl story. Codex Vaticanus 3738 turns this transfer into a dramatic incident, explaining that when the seminal "message'" came down from the sky, the frightened earth mother fainted, leaving Chimalma to take her place as the female parent of Topiltzin. In this source, too, the conception is regarded as immaculate—and the male parent is clearly identified with Citlallatonac ("Light-of-Day"). In other sources the male parentage is particularized to the cult of the local god Mixcoatl. See notes 17 and 18.

25 / The manuscript *Annals of Cuauhtitlan*, from which this myth

has been extracted, incorporates a count of years beginning with the year 1 Reed (A.D. 641) and continuing for the better part of a millennium—with every year named in order. The Quetzalcoatl story embraces the years 1 Reed (A.D. 850) through 1 Reed (A.D. 902), exactly completing an arithmetical calendar round of fifty-two years. We have then a typical case in which the ancient calendar, excellent chronometric instrument though it is, is used to achieve a purely mystical end. The enumeration of the Aztec years is the same as in the Maya system (see the explanation of Maya time counting, pp. 269–72 of this volume). The Aztec year bearers used in *Annals of Cuauhtitlan* are Reed, Flint, House, and Rabbit. Note that the possible pairings of the four year bearers and the thirteen numerals are exhausted after $4 \times 13 = 52$ years, at which point the calendar round begins anew. (Although the calendrics are in both cases the same, the Maya show a preference for the twenty-year katun as a basis for ceremonial renewal, while the Aztecs generally favor the fifty-two-year round.) Here the hero's life is equated both with the calendar round and—in a wholly fictitious manner—with the Venus cycle, which was supposed to commence on a day 1 Reed (Ce Acatl).

26 / The "ninth year" may allude to the ninth *day* following the disappearance of Venus as evening star, at which point the planet has "reached some awareness," i.e., it emerges as morning star. But the phenomenon of inferior conjunction is interpreted below in a quite different manner. See note 52. (It must be appreciated that allegorical constructs in Indian literature are often at odds with each other. The simple fact to remember is that there is no rule here against mixing metaphors.)

27 / The history of the politically insignificant Cuauhtitlan is of no real interest in itself, even though the succession of its kings forms the principal thread upon which these "annals" are strung. Observe, however, that the sketch of Huactli, while it is passed off as a historical sidelight, is in fact a mythic device—providing a foil for the great civilizer whose works will presently be

described. (A rude prior existence is one of the recurring motifs of the culture myth.)

28 / Just as the uncouth Huactli leads us to anticipate the culture bringer, the idolatrous Xiuhtlacuilolxochitzin suggests the need for a religious reformer. We shall see that the hero is an advocate of the higher religion, the cult of the supreme Spirit of Duality, which (in the eyes of the anonymous native compiler of this manuscript) ought rightfully to replace the worship of an old local god like Itzpapalotl. The author seems to view the native religion through Christian lenses, even resorting to Spanish for the opprobrious term *diablo* ("devil").

29 / The narrator contrives to get his hero to Cuextlan (the region of the Huaxtecs) in order to validate the important tradition that Quetzalcoatl originated in those parts. In the pictographic codices the god Quetzalcoatl is typically shown wearing Huaxtec attire.

30 / The compiler refers to one of his sources.

31 / The scrupulous compiler takes note of a contradictory tradition, evidently one of the many in which the fortunes of Tollan and Colhuacan are intertwined. (According to "Relación de la genealogía y linaje," Tollan was founded by migrating Colhuas. See also note 109.)

32 / Here we have the universal idea of the temple as an image of the world. (The four chambers correspond to the four world-quarters.)

33 / The priest-hero indulges in the common Indian practice of purifying the body by rubbing or whipping with coarse plant materials, sometimes violently, in order to make oneself acceptable to the gods. Cf. the flagellation with yucca leaves on the fifth day of the Night Chant. The cruciform branchlets of the sacred

fir (*Abies religiosa*) are emblematic of the four world-directions. (Mexicans still use them to decorate churches.) Here, of course, the boughs are idealized as "quetzal plumes."

34 / Again we have the four double names for the Spirit of Duality (see Fragment A and note 2). Tlallamanac Tlallichcatl may be rendered "Who-Gives-the-Earth-Solidity Who-Covers-the-Earth-with-Cotton," interpreted by León-Portilla in his *Aztec Thought and Culture* (pp. 29 ff.) as land base and cloud cover, i.e., earth and sky. Wrapped-in-Coal Wrapped-in-Blood, or Clothed-in-Black Clothed-in-Red, suggests the familiar antithesis: death and life.

35 / The Nahuatl names of these birds, followed by the English and Latin names in parentheses, are: quetzaltototl (quetzal, *Pharomacrus mocinno*); xiuhtototl (cotinga, *Cotinga amabilis*); tlauquechol (roseate spoonbill, *Ajaia ajaja*); zacuan (oropendola, *Gymnostinops montezumae*); tzinitzcan (trogon, *Trogonorus* sp.); ayocuan (Agami heron, *Agamia agami*). The identifications are problematical.

36 / The abjuration of human sacrifice and the worship of Ometeotl ("Spirit of Duality") are the salient features of Topiltzin's "new" religion, described again in similar terms by Sahagún (Bk. X, ch. 29, section 1). It is difficult to say whether these ideas are merely a projection of certain Aztec tendencies (see note 38) or whether there really existed a Toltec priest-king who, like the pharaoh Ikhnaton, made an unsuccessful attempt to reform his people's religion. Mexican studies in the mid-twentieth century have been characterized by a strong admixture of euhemerism, whose thrust is sometimes hard to resist. It is unquestionably true that the amber of the myth has preserved a certain number of historical flies. Yet it is equally true that the medium itself is paradigmatic—and hence ahistorical.

37 / The lore and terminology of Tlapallan ("Red Place") deserve

some elaboration. There are two Tlapallans: Old Tlapallan and Tlapallan proper, both referable to the crimson glow of the horizontal sun as it appears in either the east (Tlapallan) or the west (Old Tlapallan). Old Tlapallan is the seat of fecundity, the source place of agriculture and hence of communal life, technology, and civilization generally; it is the prototype of the mythical Tollan of Fragment C and, especially, of Fragment D. (According to Ixtlilxochitl the founders of Tollan were emigrants from Old Tlapallan; and in Tezozomoc's *Crónica mexicana* the name Tollan is corrupted to Tonalan, "Sun Place." Cf. Brinton, p. 83, and Seler, "Der Hauptmythus . . . ," p. 99. As for Tollan itself, the etymology need not concern us here—it is, or was, a mundane metropolis, like Rome or Jerusalem, unwittingly absorbed by the sponge of myth.) Tlapallan proper, or "new" Tlapallan as it might be called, is a derivative concept, applied to the "masculine" dawn as it mirrors the hue of its "feminine" counterpart in the west. By directing his flight toward Tlapallan, Quetzalcoatl seeks on one level to identify with the rising sun (and for this reason his destination is given in Mendieta's *Historia* as Tizapan, "White Place," white being the usual color associated with the "masculine" dawn); but on another level he seeks to merge with the "female" sun, returning symbolically to the seat of fecundity, which is Old Tlapallan, or, by reflection, Tlapallan. Both ideas, the "male" and the "female," are essential to the concept of rebirth. In Fragment D the female element appears to be emphasized (though in the final chapter a phallus is erected in the east as a symbol of revival); and Tlapallan itself is called Tollan Tlapallan, indicating that the hero is returning, symbolically, to Old Tlapallan. In the more "masculine" Fragment C we have the interesting trinomial Tlillan Tlapallan Tlatlayan, "Black-Place Red-Place Fire-Place," revealing the actual, or "structural," mechanism of rebirth. Black is the color of death, red the color of life; fire implies the cremation. The trinomial reads: "From death to life through the medium of fire." And this, of course, is what Fragment C is really about. Earlier in the fragment the destination is called Tlillan Tlapallan; finally it is called simply Tlatlayan, "The Burning Place."

38 / In Fragment C, as well as in Fragment D, the hero meets with a trio of antagonists comprising, chiefly, the god Tezcatlipoca, plus two additional powers included for the sake of rounding out the four-brother "family" (see note 18). In Fragment D the supplementary powers are Huitzilopochtli, the Aztec war god, and Tlacahuepan ("Human Log"), the "immovable" embodiment of human guilt; Tezcatlipoca himself is here called by the alternate name Titlacahuan ("He to Whom We Are Slaves"). In Fragment C the two assisting deities are, again, Huitzilopochtli (called by the poetic title Ihuimecatl, "A Lash of Feather Down," in allusion to his having been conceived of a mystical down) and Toltecatl, identified by Sahagún as a god of wine, used here (as is his counterpart in Fragment D) to implement the theme of guilt. But why Tezcatlipoca? (And why Huitzilopochtli?) The answer would appear to lie in the entrenched dualism of what might be styled, on one hand, a cult of the serpent, emphasizing fertility, wisdom, and the peaceful pursuit of the arts; on the other, a "jaguar" cult, marked by militarism and morbidity. By Aztec times the former had come to be represented essentially, though not wholly, by the spirit of Quetzalcoatl; the latter by Tezcatlipoca, the particular deity of the Nahuatl-speaking peoples and, specifically, a god of darkness and shadows. It was during the rule of the Aztecs that human sacrifice began to be practiced on a grand scale; but the "serpent" and "jaguar" alternatives had always coexisted in the Mexican mind and undoubtedly continued to do so even if the "jaguar" had temporarily gained the ascendancy. Looking back over the past, the latter-day Aztecs recalled that the deity Quetzalcoatl, whose cult had now been largely eclipsed, had once reigned supreme in Toltec days. And it is true enough that Tollan, for all its apparent militarism, had enshrined some form of the god Quetzalcoatl. Tollan, ca. A.D. 1100, had also yielded its superior culture and, through intermarriage, its

princely bloodline to the upstart Aztecs (who in later times were to regard their predecessors with a mixture of awe and accusation). Through myth, the decline of Tollan was now viewed as a personal defeat for Quetzalcoatl at the hands of the Nahua divinity Tezcatlipoca, assisted by the Aztecs' own special war god, Huitzilopochtli, and made possible in the first place by the presumed sins of the Toltecs. But the loss of Quetzalcoatl represented a tragedy as well as a victory, a tragedy at least for the suppressed "serpent" element, whose hopes were now invested in the dogma of eventual return. Thus developed a curious form of messianism—that of a dual personality divided against itself— quite unlike the Hebraic, or nativistic, messianism of the Yucatec Maya (see Cuceb) and more akin to the Christian variety. (The Quetzalcoatl myth has always fascinated Christians, not surprisingly. And it is perhaps for this reason that it has been so well preserved.) For comparisons with Iroquois dualism, see p. 111.

39 / The Aztecs, like many ancient peoples, considered the biliary system to be the seat of well-being. Compare the unwholesome gall spots associated with death in the Iroquois Requickening Address (pp. 144 and 146 of this volume).

40 / For another allusion to Maxtla and Toltec Mountain, see note 79.

41 / The honey, perhaps, is a voluptuary ingredient that will cause the hero to neglect his penances (i.e., neglect his obligations to his people), thus contributing to the destruction of society. Cf. Claude Lévi-Strauss, *L'Origine des manières de table*, 1968, p. 340.

42 / The chili-seasoned stew burns the hero's throat, causing him to crave drink—and perhaps making him sexually "hot," as we shall see below in the case of Huemac's daughter (Fragment D, "chapter" 5). (The Latin "et cetera" is indicated merely by "et" in the text.)

43 / *Tlatoyahualiztli* may mean "that which is poured, a drink, a portion," or, by extension, "a libation, a sacrament." If the latter meaning is intended (cf. Sahagún, Bk. II, app. 3), it is of course ironic. Four draughts were allowed; a fifth was considered the mark of a drunkard (Sahagún, Bk. X, ch. 29, section entitled "De los Mexicanos").

44 / The song presents a sunset image (see notes 56 and 83), the term *quetzal* here meaning simply "precious." The black- and gold-plumaged zacuan (see note 35) coupled with "redshell" yields the expected gold and red of the horizontal sun.

45 / Students of this text are generally agreed that incest is implied.

46 / Coatlicue: "She of the Serpent Skirt," an epithet of the personified earth.

47 / The crown of Quetzalcoatl, as shown in several of the ancient pictographic codices, contains two "thorns": the agave-leaf spike and the bone dagger, both implements of "penance," or sacrificial bloodletting.

48 / This curious incident calls to mind the four-day period of moribundity during which the planet Venus "dwelled in Mictlan" (see note 52). It corresponds to the hero's passage through Mictlan in the fourteenth "chapter" of Fragment D, to the burial of the father in Fragment B, and to the Katun's underworld descent in the Epilogue to the Cuceb. The myth *must* include either an underworld descent or an interment (a point that lends some credence to the nineteenth-century theory by which all such myths are related to the sun's nocturnal journey beneath the earth). From a strictly ethnographic point of view it should be noted that temporary burial followed by cremation is a widespread funerary practice.

49 / The celestial water: Chimalpahin calls it "the great water, the celestial water," i.e., the ocean, where sky and water meet (Lehmann and Kutscher, p. 11). The putting on of the finery is analogous to the "cruciform" rejuvenation at the close of Fragment D (see note 93). There, as here, the hero is preparing for his death, while on a mystical level he is being reborn. See note 90.

50 / The birds not previously identified in note 35 are: tozneneme (yellow-headed parrot, *Amazona oratrix*); allome (scarlet macaw, *Ara macao*); cochome (white-fronted parrot, *Amazona albifrons*). The cremation of the culture bringer in such a way as to make beautiful or useful things accessible to the world is a widespread motif. In a Bororo myth quoted by Claude Lévi-Strauss (*The Raw and the Cooked*, 1970, p. 93), culture heroes leaping into the fire are transformed into birds of gorgeous plumage, while from the ashes rise food plants and cotton. Edward Curtis (*The North American Indian*, Vol. XV, 1926, p. 122) records a California myth in which human knowledge issues from the exploding body of a cremated serpent.

51 / "The heart of the quetzal rose upward" (*in iyollo quetzaltototl in quitta*) could also be translated "the inner part of the precious penis rose upward." Cf. the symbolic phallus at the close of Fragment D and see note 93. To see the hero's penis is to know that he lives. In an Amazonian myth the hero descends to the underworld and attempts to join the dance of the dead. But the dead are not fooled. Seeing him, they cry, "It is a man! He shakes his penis [with the movements of the dance]!" (Curt Nimuendaju, *The Tukuna*, University of California Publications in American Archaeology and Ethnology, Vol. XLV, 1952, p. 117).

52 / It would appear that the eight-day transit of Venus through the underworld was thought of as a four-day period of dying, followed by a four-day period of rebirth or rearmament. See figure 1.

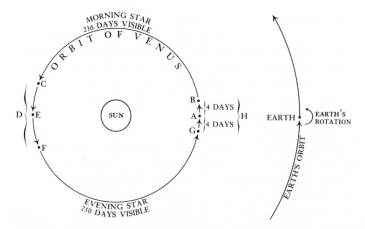

Figure 1 / The Synodic Period of Venus. A: Venus at inferior conjunction (invisible). B: Venus "emerges" as the morning star. C: The "death" of the morning star. D: Venus invisible for 90 days. E: Venus at superior conjunction (invisible). F: Venus "emerges" as the evening star. G: The "death" of the evening star. H: Venus invisible for 8 days

53 / The malignant influence of the morning star, especially upon its first appearance (issuing, as it were, from the evil realm of Mictlan, the Dead Land), is an important tradition in both Aztec and Maya religion. Generally speaking, however, it is not associated with Quetzalcoatl. Only here and in Mendieta (Bk. II, ch. 5), among sixteenth-century Mexican chroniclers, is the connection made.

Fragment D / The Fall of Tollan

54 / Book III of the Florentine Codex (from which this fragment has been excised) consists of fourteen chapters, the first two describing the gods Huitzilopochtli and Tezcatlipoca, the remaining twelve (chapters 3–14) devoted to the story of Tollan. The

chapter headings, composed in Nahuatl, are evidently the work of Fray Bernardino de Sahagún himself (the earlier Real Palacio version has them as marginal glosses in Spanish only), and for this reason they have customarily been deleted by literary anthologists wishing to present the purely native document. They are given here in full. (The word "chapter" appears in the text as *capítulo*, there being no Nahuatl equivalent.)

55 / This description evidently refers to the aged Quetzalcoatl. His reluctance to be seen in public and the misshapen face are described in Fragment C.

56 / Taken together, the first four of these "houses" correspond to the four-chambered temple of the world-quarters (see note 32). The turquoise and quetzal "house of beams" suggests the mythical house of the sun (similarly described in *Cantares mexicanos,* folio 36; see Garibay's translation and commentary in his *Poesía náhuatl,* Vol. III, pp. 25 and XXXII). I take the paragraph to mean that Quetzalcoatl's four-chambered house is in some sense an earthly replica of the house of the sun.

57 / Far-fetched as it may seem, Brinton was probably correct in identifying the swift-running Toltecs with light rays. The implied metaphorical link is the arrow in flight, a traditional emblem of sunlight but also the ideal measure of a runner's speed. See the parallel passage in "chapter" 11.

58 / The term *Anahuac* ("By the Water") may refer to the sea-coast, to the central lake district known also as the Valley of Mexico, or to the entire earth (according to Seler) imagined as a disc surrounded by water.

59 / Flower cacao—an aromatic chocolate (per Seler).

60 / The figure of winter, come to pay a call on the dying year.

61 / Montezuma used the same evidently formulistic expression—
"for five, for ten"—when he greeted Cortés (Sahagún, Bk. XII,
ch. 16).

62 / This would refer to the stock figure of the mentor, the
guardian of the afterlife, who conducts one through hell. But as
we shall see in "chapter" 12, the god Quetzalcoatl becomes his
own mentor. At the commencement of his journey into death
he will observe, "Truly I *am* old."

63 / The promise of renewed youth will be fulfilled in "chapter"
14. See note 92.

64 / "A report on the Huaxtec territory, dated 1579, states that:
'. . . they related that the idol Tezcatlipoca had killed the god of
wine (Ometochtli) with his consent and concurrence, giving out
that in this way he gave eternal life, and that if he did not die, all
persons drinking wine must die; but that the death of this
Ometochtli was only the sleep of one drunk, that he afterwards
recovered, and again became fresh and well.' "—Lewis Spence,
The Gods of Mexico, pp. 104–5. Torquemada (Bk. VI, ch. 24)
unequivocally states that Quetzalcoatl drank the potion in order
to render himself immortal.

65 / Toueyo means literally "Our Neighbor" and no doubt alludes
specifically to the proverbially licentious Huaxtecs (Sahagún,
Bk. X, ch. 29, section 8).

66 / As in many languages (but in English only as a rare gallicism),
the word in Nahuatl for "bird" (*tototl*) means also "penis."

67 / The Toueyo's amusing protest has been interpreted to mean:
"This is the manner to which we Huaxtecs are accustomed."
See note 65. And it may well be that the narrator, at least on a
superficial level, is dealing in ethnic satire. But it must be recognized that the humor is basically more general, even cosmic. In

effect, the Toueyo is saying, "But truly we humans are sexual (hence doomed) beings." For sexuality linked with doom, see notes 70, 74, and 79. See also p. 190.

68 / The English verb "to ditch" is exactly equivalent, in both its literal and applied meanings, to the Nahuatl *tlaltoca:* literally, "to put in the ground"; by extension, "to get rid of."

69 / The king uses irony to cover his embarrassment. The Toueyo is of course his own son-in-law.

70 / The story of the Toueyo is a sophisticated variant of the opossum legend (quoted below, see note 79), in which the sorcerer destroys the fabric of society by causing its women to bear a subhuman species. The implication here is that the sexy Toueyo will father a race of beasts. (If we read between the lines we may discover that the trouble, originally, is brought about by Huemac trying to keep his daughter for himself. Recall the opening lines of the fifth "chapter," where he prevents her from marrying. Note his interest in her genital tumescence, wittily described by the narrator as though it were a somatic plethora— p. 44. Here again we have an intimation of incest. See note 45. See also note 74.)

71 / One is reminded of the North American trickster tale catalogued as "hoodwinked dancers" in Stith Thompson's *Motif-Index.* An Arapaho version published by G. Dorsey and A. Kroeber (*Traditions of the Arapaho,* 1903, p. 60) includes the following details. Trickster, using Coyote as his herald, summons the various game animals to dance at the edge of a precipice. He instructs them to close their eyes as he sings and to leap forward on signal. They do. Trickster goes down to the base of the cliff and collects the carcasses for his dinner. It might in fact be argued that the entire Huemac saga as presented by Sahagún (Part II of Fragment D) is essentially a suite of trickster tales with the deity Tezcatlipoca representing the figure of the trickster in its

demonic aspect. The cavorting Quetzalcoatl (see note 94) evokes the playful, not the demonic trickster.

72 / A compiler's gloss? The parentheses appear in the Nahuatl text. The term *quetzalcoatl*, incidentally, is here used as an honorific title for the ruler of Tollan (presumably Huemac). Any Toltec king could be a "quetzalcoatl."

73 / "Sorcerer" refers to Titlacahuan, i.e., Tezcatlipoca, who in this "chapter" is aided by Tlacahuepan (also called Cuexcoch), who will be stoned to death, and Huitzilopochtli, the dancing manikin. (The trio was introduced at the beginning of the fourth "chapter.")

74 / According to Codex Vaticanus 3738, the immovable corpse represented the sins of the people—from which they were unable to escape. Undoubtedly, sexual sins are implied; and we may assume that the Toltecs are wrestling with the specter of incest (represented by a rotten log in so many Amerindian myths). To borrow the argument developed in Claude Lévi-Strauss's *L'Origine des manières de table*, the kind of sexual liaison hinted at in our "log" story suggests a marriage *too close* for comfort, whereas the beast marriage implied in the Toueyo episode (see note 70) suggests an alliance *too distant* for the propagation of the species. Either extreme must lead to the destruction of the social order, i.e., death on a cosmic scale (cf. note 79).

75 / The song and the text that follows incorporate a pun on the word *huepan*, the combining form of *huepantli*, "log." Toheupan reads "our log"; the name Tlacahuepan reads literally "human log." Note also the play on *tlaca*, the combining form of *Tlacatl*, "human." Tlacahuepan, as we have already been told in the fourth "chapter," is one of the three sorcerers come to plague Tollan. But here the word for sorcerer (*tlacatecolotl*) strikes the ear as "human owl." (The *tecolotl*, "owl," is synonymous with evil; hence a sorcerer is a "human owl.")

76 / *The log would ram them all, would run them over* must refer only to those pulling along a rope directly in front of the "log," where the "log's" forward momentum is maintained by a number of other teams pulling at slight angles on either side.

77 / Probably the white hawk stands for the sun (as it does in Algonkian myth). The white hawk plus the pierced head suggests a verbalized pictograph for "death of the sun." (The pierced head means "termination"; see Cuceb, entry for the sixth year. See also p. 236.)

78 / The "mountain," as elsewhere in this lore, would appear to stand for the earth. Here again we have a verbalized pictograph, reading "death of the earth."

79 / In other words, the end of the world—the inevitable conclusion to be drawn from the two omens "death of the sun" and "death of the earth" (see note 78). *Annals of Cuauhtitlan*, folio 10, also equates Tollan's fall with the death of the world, though there the event is couched in a different imagery: as he leaves the city, the victorious sorcerer boasts, "I played a trick on Maxtla, who lived on Toltec Mountain [i.e., in the sky] with his daughters, Quetzalquen and Quetzalxilotl, whom he kept like jadestones in a chest. I got them both with twins, such that each bore as offspring a pair of opossums. Likewise I played a trick on Cuauhtliztac, the keeper of Oztotempan ["In the Earth"], and on Cuauhtli, the keeper of Atzompan ["At the Water"]; it is I who destroyed them [i.e., I destroyed sky, earth, and water—the cosmos]." Or, alternately, "I destroyed the fabric of human society." See note 70 and the discussion of socio-cosmic models, p. 115. But why the opossum? The answer is that the opossum is the proverbial stinkard in Indo-America. On the cosmic level the sorcerer is putting an end to creation; on the comic level he is merely telling the Toltecs, "You stink."

80 / A rain of stones means barrenness, presumably brought about

by drought. (In Codex Vaticanus 3738, folio 7 verso, a stone is pictured with the label "sign of sterility.")

81 / This passage is a literary evocation of the drought rituals held in Aztec times at the little hill called Chapultepec (now a park in Mexico City), site of some famous springs sacred to the rain god Tlaloc. See Lehmann 1938, pp. 376–7. Paper flags smeared with rubber would have been carried as offerings to the god (Sahagún, Bk. II, ch. 20) and certain victims sacrificed at the altar.

82 / The sacrifice to Tlaloc (see note 81) would normally bring a return to life—symbolically, a replenishment of food. And so it does, but the food is inedible. The people have been "tricked."

83 / One is here reminded of the red and gold of the horizontal sun (see note 44). At night it conceals its "precious" light beneath the "mountain" of the earth (see note 108) or in caves (as suggested in *Cantares mexicanos*, folio 36; see Garibay's *Poesía náhuatl*, Vol. III, p. XXXII). According to *Historia Tolteca-Chichimeca*, "the entire treasure of Quetzalcoatl was sent eastward during the night" (Preuss and Mengin, p. 17). All of which lends support to Brinton's hundred-year-old thesis identifying Quetzalcoatl with solar light.

84 / The myth explains why these gorgeous birds, like the chocolate, do not (typically) occur in the dryish and rather chilly highlands inhabited by the Aztecs. (Cacao and tropical plumes were received from the east through trade.) This etiological overtone, however, is incidental to the main thrust of the imagery, which is calculated to link the hero's flight with the onset of winter. "A long time ago it was always winter, and towards the south always summer and all the beautiful birds lived there" (S. C. Simms, *Traditions of the Crows*, 1903, p. 282). Fragment D mixes seasonal metaphors (see also notes 60, 91, 92, and 93) with diurnal metaphors (see notes 56, 57, and 83).

85 / Anahuac would here mean the eastern seaboard. See note 58.

86 / With the hero's stop at Cuauhtitlan we begin a five-stage journey by puns, reminiscent of the punning migration narrative found in the Maya Codex Chumayel—which reads in part: "Then they came to Ticooh [*coh* means 'high-priced'], where they haggled for that which was dear. Ticoh was its name here. Then they arrived at Tikal [*kal* means 'to shut in'], where they shut themselves in." Etc., etc. (Ralph Roys, *The Book of Chilam Balam of Chumayel*, 1933, p. 71.) In the present case, however, the five stages represent a progression toward death. They are as follows: (1) the discovery of old age (at Cuauhtitlan), (2) the final testament (at Temacpalco), (3) the crossing of the Acherontic stream (at Tepanohuayan), (4) the renunciation of worldly effects (at Cozcahapan), and (5) the mystic sleep (at Cochtocan).

87 / The species that comes to mind is the Montezuma cypress (*Taxodium mucronatum*), known in the Nahuatl language as *ahuehuetl* ("old man of the water"). An apocryphal story has it that Cortés, fleeing the Aztec capital after temporary reverses, paused and wept beneath an ahuehuetl. J. G. Müller (paraphrased in Bancroft, p. 281) believed that the pelting of the tree might be a vestige of stone fetishism. The deity is indeed identified with stone in the opening lines of Fragment C (he enters his mother's belly as a swallowed emerald, or "green stone") and at the close of Fragment D (he erects a stone phallus as a memorial). Here it is as if the hero were setting up a more subtle kind of memorial, saying, "I am the stone, I am the tree." It may be worth noting that the analogous Iroquois hero is divided into two persons whose names are Flint and Sapling. In an interesting, if somewhat tenuous, argument, H. B. Alexander develops the idea that these two aspects, the stone and the tree, are symbolic of the earth in its (ice-hard) winter and (foliating) spring phases, hence in-

dicative of old age and rejuvenation. See his *The World's Rim*, 1953, pp. 57–9.

88 / For specific allusions to the fleeing Quetzalcoatl's entourage, see Fragment C (where he is accompanied by pages) and the fourteenth "chapter" of Fragment D (where his "dwarfs" and "hunchbacks" are mentioned).

89 / ". . . he stamped and imprinted his hands upon a rock, as though in very soft wax, to testify that he would accomplish all that he had promised . . ." (Ixtlilxochitl, *Historia chichimeca*, ch. 1).

90 / The sun has called him to Tlapallan (the red place, the land of the rising sun), meaning that his time has come to die. But his death becomes a transfiguration; he is in fact reborn (see notes 49, 63, and 93). In Fragment C the hero's death (by fire) is juxtaposed with his rejuvenation (he puts on youthful finery); in Fragment D his death (signaled by the call of the sun) is again juxtaposed with rejuvenation (according to the points of the cross, as discussed in note 93). The two pairings, "sun" with "cross" and "fire" with "finery," are brought into connection by an Arikara myth in which "sun" is paired with "finery," to the same effect: "[The old man's] father, the Sun, was coming after him to take him up to his home . . . The old man took his clothes that he used to wear in his early days, and put them on. He also painted himself . . ." (George A. Dorsey, *Traditions of the Arikara*, 1904, pp. 64–5).

91 / A retinue of dwarfs, or hunchbacks, was a mark of kingly prestige (Durán, "Ritos, fiestas y ceremonias," ch. 5). Here, however, the dwarfs may represent the numerous rain gods (the Tlaloques), or, by implication, the rain itself, congealed into snow—a final emblem of death (Spence 1923, p. 141; "History of the Mexicans as Told by Their Paintings," ch. 2).

92 / Here we have the "positive" companion to the "negative" image discussed above in note 91. Gazing eastward, the hero sees the traditional, snow-clad home of the Tlaloques (Poyauhtecatl, i.e., Mount Orizaba), white, as it were, with the water of life. At precisely this point the myth turns away from death and moves toward rebirth. (Observe how the color white is used similarly in the Night Chant, p. 345, note 60.)

93 / The following five "signs," transposed to topographic features, chart a cycle of death and rebirth according to the four points of the compass, taken sunwise from east to south to west to north and back again to east (the same five-step sequence used in Navajo ritual to symbolize rejuvenation: see p. 340, note 36). We begin at the "east," at dawn, with the childlike prankster and move "south" (the traditional direction of the adult warrior, associated with the Aztec war god Huitzilopochtli), where we find the field of ritual combat, the ball court (Quetzalcoatl was here vanquished by the night god Tezcatlipoca in Mendieta's version of the myth). In the "west," the direction of the sinking sun, the hero passes through the ceiba (a species often regarded by tropical American peoples as the tree of life; see p. 227), which becomes a portal to the realm of the dead (with the implication of rebirth; see note 97). In the "north," the traditional direction of death, he journeys to the underworld, returning once again to the "east" in the form of a symbolic phallus that reaffirms his generative power (see note 51). The topographic associations, following closely upon the withdrawal and promised return of rain (see notes 91 and 92), suggest the revival of the dead earth, i.e., spring.

94 / It would appear that the narrator refers to an old landslide scar grown over with magueys (whose fiber yields rope)—and that Quetzalcoatl, like other Indian heroes, was sometimes a trickster whose antics transformed the terrain. For a parallel passage, see George B. Grinnell, *Blackfoot Lodge Tales*, 1892, reprinted 1962, p. 143. See also E. Ahenakew, "Cree Trick-

ster Tales," *Journal of American Folklore*, 1929, p. 353.

95 / Symbolically a ball court. But topographically a canyon? See note 93.

96 / Ceiba: the silk-cotton, or kapok, tree (*Ceiba pentandra*). See note 93.

97 / Compare the parallel passage in "Histoyre du Mechique" (ch. 11): Quetzalcoatl fled to a wilderness "and shot an arrow into a tree and placed himself in the hole made by the arrow, and thus he died." I cite this in support of my literal translation of the passage at hand, which differs radically from the interpretative version suggested by Sahagún, viz., "And in another place he shot a ceiba *as though it were an arrow*, shooting it in such a way that it itself passed through the heart of *a second* ceiba, *thus forming a cross*." I propose that Sahagún arrived at this reading after conversations with native informants, who were aware that the tree of life was sometimes represented by a cross (see Ixtlilxochitl, Vol. I, p. 20) or that the entire context had something to do with the four world-quarters (see note 93), of which the cross is a conventional symbol. The cross, moreover, is an emblem of Quetzalcoatl himself. (In an Iroquois myth mentioned by Arthur C. Parker, *Seneca Myths and Folk Tales*, 1923, p. 59, the corpse of the sky father is laid within the tree of life; and life itself is created in an Algonkian myth by shooting arrows into an ash tree, from which newborn humans immediately emerge— Charles G. Leland, *The Algonquin Legends of New England*, 1884, p. 19.)

98 / An allusion to Mitla, the well-known archaeological site (including tombs) near Oaxaca.

99 / The Jungian psychotherapist Joseph L. Henderson reports having treated a patient who dreamed of a serpent raft as a prelude to "rebirth" after a traumatic menopause. The snake, he

believes, is an archetypal symbol of "rebirth after death" because, in nature, it appears to renew itself by shedding its skin. (See Henderson and Oakes, *The Wisdom of the Serpent*, 1963, pp. 39–40.)

100 / See note 54.

Fragment E / A Song of Survival

101 / The manuscript source indicates that this is a song for the teponaztli (a kind of tom-tom) and prefaces the text with the syllables "tico tico toco toto . . ." apparently setting the rhythm (or the melody?). There is no direct statement that it was to have been a theater piece; the reconstruction along dramatic lines is based entirely on internal evidence, following Garibay's lead. See his *Poesía náhuatl*, Vol. III. At the beginning of Act II the rhythm changes; and it will be readily observed, even in translation, that the lyric style is changed as well.

102 / The epithet Nacxitl derives from a root meaning "fourfold," applied to Quetzalcoatl as lord of the four directions.

103 / Topiltzin's loyal retainers ("our princes") remain behind in Cholula, there to carry on the Toltec traditions and, especially, the cult of Quetzalcoatl. (The city of Cholula did in fact preserve the religion of Tollan in Aztec times.) Meanwhile Topiltzin himself moves on to Poyauhtecatl and Acallan (see notes 92 and 21).

104 / Nonohualco is a rather vague name for the coastal region stretching through the modern states of Tabasco, Campeche, and Yucatan (Torquemada, Bk. III, ch. 7).

105 / The translation follows Garibay (*Llave del Náhuatl*, 1961, p. 235). The epithets allude to the female and male aspects of

solar light, respectively. The quechol (i.e., tlauquechol), or roseate spoonbill, is analogous to the Algonkian "red swan," the female sun of the western sky and the Golconda of the culture hero (see note 37). "Lord who pierces" refers to the male sun of the eastern sky, the archer whose arrows dispel the night. (See "The Red Swan" in H. R. Schoolcraft's *Algic Researches*, 1839, Vol. II.)

106 / In other words, my lord attired in quechol plumes, i.e., the western sun, has set. See note 105.

107 / Several sources, including Fragment C, mention Matlacxochitl as Topiltzin's royal successor. The idea here is that Matlacxochitl is remaining behind in Cholula to carry on in Topiltzin's name.

108 / The falling mountain and the rising sands are connected with the hero's perilous journey to Tlapallan, the eastern home of the sun. Both images suggest the problems faced by the nocturnal sun (with which the hero is identified) as it tries to work its way through the earth in time to reach the eastern horizon at dawn. We have already seen (in note 16) how the sun's entry into the underworld can be likened to a swallowing up by the sands of the western sea. And in the charming, if naïve, phraseology of Codex Vaticanus 3738 (folio 9) Quetzalcoatl en route to Tlapallan is obliged to pass beneath "certain mountains" that threaten to collapse and entomb him. The Navajo story of the hero-twins' journey to the house of their sun father provides an interesting parallel: along the way the heroes encounter "the rocks that crush" and "the land of the rising sands" (Washington Matthews, *Navaho Legends*, 1897, pp. 109–10).

109 / The name of Tollan is here embellished as "Tollan Nonohualco" as if acknowledging the tradition that it was once partly settled by the Nonohualcas (see note 104). According to *Historia Tolteca-Chichimeca*, Tollan was peopled jointly by the Colhuas

and the Nonohualcas, whose intramural feuding eventually led to the city's downfall. In Fragment C the name appears as "Tollan Colhuacan" (see note 31).

110 / Cinteotl: "Spirit of Maize."

111 / Tonan: "Our Mother," the personified earth.

112 / The correct reading of this stanza depends upon its double-edged puns. The secondary meanings are given in parentheses. (The primary images allude to Tlalocan, the watery abode of the rain god. According to *Legend of the Suns*, folio 8, the famine that accompanied the fall of Tollan was finally broken by the Tlaloques' presenting an ear of corn from the depths of the spring at Chapultepec. See note 81.)

113 / An undetermined species.

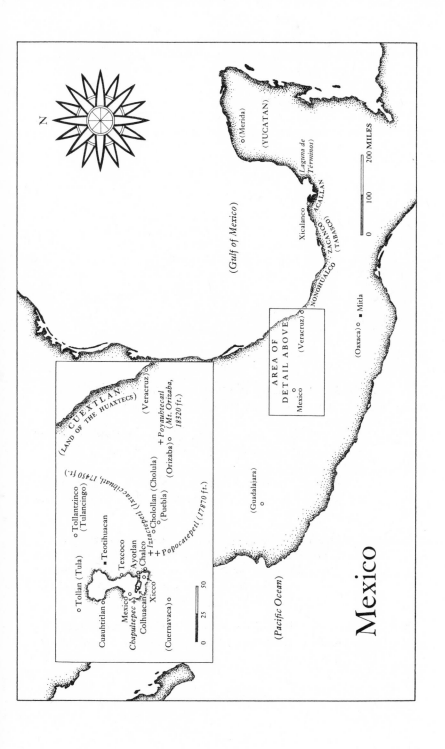

Mexico

(Pacific Ocean)

(Guadalajara) o

(Cuernavaca) o

o Tollan (Tula)
Cuauhtitlan o   o Texcoco
Mexico ○ o Ayotlan   o Teotihuacan
Chapultepec + ○ Chalco
Colhuacan o   ○
Xicco o

o Tollantzinco
(Tulancingo)

(Xtaccibuatl, 17450 ft.)

+ Iztaccihuatl
o Chololan (Cholula)
(Puebla)   (Orizaba) o

+ Popocatepetl (17870 ft.)

(Veracruz) o

(CUEXTLAN
(LAND OF THE HUAXTECS)

+ Poyauhtecatl
(Mt. Orizaba,
18320 ft.)

0   25   50

(Gulf of Mexico)

Xicalanco
CALLAN
Laguna de
Términos

ZACANCO
TABASCO)

NONOHUALCO

(Merida) o

(YUCATAN)

AREA OF
DETAIL ABOVE
(Veracruz) o
Mexico
o

(Oaxaca) o   ■ Mitla

0   100   200 MILES

1 / Sixteenth-century Nahuatl texts incorporating one or more variants of the Quetzalcoatl myth

Codex Chimalpopocatl (including *Annals of Cuauhtitlan* and *Legend of the Suns*): source of Fragments A, B, and C.

MS. Codex Chimalpopocatl. Museo Nacional de Antropología, Mexico, D.F. Facsimile published by Velázquez (see below).

Lehmann, Walter, *Die Geschichte der Königreiche von Colhuacan und Mexico*, 1938. Paleograph of the Codex Chimalpopocatl, with German translation and copious commentary. See §§ 54–157 (Fragment C), 1417–52 (Fragment A), 1555–87 (Fragment B).

Velázquez, Primo Feliciano, *Códice Chimalpopoca*, 1945. Facsimile of the Codex Chimalpopocatl with Spanish translation and notes.

Florentine Codex: source of Fragment D

MS. Florentine Codex. Biblioteca Laurenziana, Florence. Microfilm copy at the School of American Research, Santa Fe. (Earlier though less complete copies of the same material are the so-called Madrid codices, Real Academia de la Historia and Real Palacio, Madrid. A partial facsimile, including the Real Palacio text of the Quetzalcoatl myth, Fragment D, has been published by Francisco del Paso y Troncoso: *Fr. Bernardino de Sahagún / Historia de las cosas de Nueva España*, 1905–7. For Quetzalcoatl, see Vol. VII, 1906, pp. 215–40.)

Anderson, Arthur J. O., and Dibble, Charles E., *Florentine Codex*, 13 parts, 1950 et seq. Paleograph and English translation of the Nahuatl texts belonging to Fray Bernardino de Sahagún's monumental ethnography. For Fragment D, see Bk. III, ch. 3–14. (Note: Bk. I, ch. 5; Bk. X, ch. 29, section 1; and Bk. XII, ch. 3–5 are also of interest.)

Seler, Eduard, *Einige Kapitel aus dem Geschichtswerk des Fray Bernardino de Sahagún*, 1927. Paleograph and German translation. See pp. 268–92. (But the paleograph is faulty and must be used with caution.)

Cantares mexicanos: source of Fragment E

MS. *Cantares mexicanos*. Biblioteca Nacional de México, Mexico, D.F. Facsimile published by Antonio Peñafiel: *Manuscrito original existente en la Biblioteca Nacional*, 1904; for Fragment E, see folios 26 verso through 27 verso.

Garibay, Ángel M., *Poesía náhuatl*, Vols. II (1965) and III (1968). A selective two-volume edition of the *Cantares mexicanos:* reconstructed Nahuatl text, Spanish translation, notes. (Garibay's recension of Fragment E can be found in Vol. III, pp. 1–5.) Must be used with caution.

Schultze-Jena, Leonhard, *Alt-Aztekische Gesänge*, 1957. The first 57 folios of *Cantares mexicanos:* paleograph, German translation, notes. For Fragment E, see pp. 138 ff.

II / Other sixteenth-century Nahuatl texts

Lehmann, Walter, and Kutscher, Gerdt, *Das Memorial breve acerca de la fundación de la ciudad de Culhuacan . . . von Domingo de San Antón Muñon Chimalpahin Quauhtle-huanitzin . . .*, 1958. Chimalpahin's *Memorial Breve*. Paleograph, German translation, notes.

Preuss, Konrad Theodor, and Mengin, Ernst, "Die mexikanische Bilderhandschrift Historia Tolteca-Chichimeca," *Baessler-Archiv*, Beiheft IX, Teil 1, 1937. The anonymous Nahuatl manuscript called *Historia Tolteca-Chichimeca*. Paleograph, German translation, notes.

III / Sixteenth-century Spanish texts giving supplementary variants of the Quetzalcoatl

"Histoyre du Mechique, manuscrit français inédit du XVIᵉ siècle, publié par M. Édouard de Jonghe," *Journal de la Société des Américanistes de Paris*, nouvelle série, tome II, 1905. A sixteenth-century French translation of a lost Spanish original. See pp. 19 (a fleeting glimpse of Huemac), 26 (Ehecatl descends to the underworld), 27 (Xolotl nourishes a new race of men), 27–8 (Ehecatl procures pulque for the newly created men), 34–8 (myth of Topiltzin Quetzalcoatl).

Il Manoscritto Messicano Vaticano 3738, detto il Codice Rios, riprodotto . . . a spese di Sua Eccellenza il Duca di Loubat, per cura della Biblioteca Vaticano, 1900. The Codex Vaticanus 3738, or Codex Rios, known to Mexicanists as "Codex Vaticanus A." Sixteenth-century Italian translation of a lost Spanish original. See pp. 25–6.

"Historia de los mexicanos por sus pinturas," *Nueva Colección de Documentos para la Historia de México,* 1942. Also known as Codex Ramírez, Codex Zumarraga, or Codex Fuenleal. English translation by Henry Phillips, Jr., entitled "History of the Mexicans as Told by Their Paintings," in *Proceedings of the American Philosophical Society,* Vol. XXI, May 1883– Dec. 1884, pp. 616 ff. See pp. 616–22 (Tezcatlipoca and Quetzalcoatl take turns creating and destroying the world), 623–4 (brief account of Ce Acatl Quetzalcoatl).

Mendieta, Gerónimo de, *Historia eclesiástica indiana,* 1870. See Bk. II, ch. 1 (Xolotl descends to the underworld), ch. 5 (the flight of Quetzalcoatl), ch. 10 (Quetzalcoatl in Cholula).

Ixtlilxochitl, Fernando de Alva, *Obras históricas,* 2 vols., 1891–2. See Vol. I (*Relaciones*), pp. 11–73; Vol. II (*Historia chichimeca*), pp. 21–34. Ixtlilxochitl's Quetzalcoatl materials are rather poor. His work is chiefly valuable for its history of Tollan and for its version of the saga of Huemac (whom he calls "Topiltzin").

Torquemada, Juan de, *Monarquía indiana,* 3 vols., 1723. Worthy of being included among the sixteenth-century sources, even though compiled a little later. See Bk. I, ch. 14 (partly derived from a source used also by Ixtlilxochitl); Bk. III, ch. 7; Bk. VI, ch. 24 (derived from Sahagún), ch. 45 (derived from Mendieta).

Durán, Diego, *Historia de las Indias,* 2 vols., 1867 and 1880. The second volume has the "Ritos, fiestas y ceremonias," translated into English as *Book of the Gods and Rites* (1971): see ch. 1 (an account of Topiltzin Quetzalcoatl) and ch. 6 (the ritual of Quetzalcoatl).

"Relación de la genealogía y linaje de los Señores que han señoreado esta tierra de la Nueva España . . ." *Nueva Colección de Documentos para la Historia de México,* 1941.

IV / Translations, commentaries, criticism

Sahagún, Bernardino de, *Historia general de las cosas de Nueva España*, edited by Ángel M. Garibay, 4 vols., 1956, second edition 1969. Sahagún's own, free, Spanish translation of his famous Nahuatl texts. (The Nahuatl texts have been published with an English translation, under the title *Florentine Codex*. See Anderson and Dibble, above.) For a partial translation of Sahagún's Spanish, including Fragment D of Quetzalcoatl, see Fanny R. Bandelier, *A History of Ancient Mexico*, 1932, reprinted 1971.

Garibay, Ángel M., *Historia de la literatura náhuatl*, 2 vols., 1953–4. Useful survey of Nahuatl literature.

―――― *Épica náhuatl*, 1945 (second edition, 1964). Gives lengthy excerpts from the Quetzalcoatl myth and from the saga of Huemac (whom Garibay here identifies with Quetzalcoatl).

―――― *La literatura de los aztecas*, 1964. A small anthology of Nahuatl literature, including excerpts from the Quetzalcoatl.

Brinton, Daniel G., *American Hero-Myths*, 1882, reprinted 1970. Includes an extensive commentary on Quetzalcoatl, identifying the hero with sunlight.

Seler, Eduard, "Der Hauptmythus der mexikanischen Stämme und der Kulturheros von Tollan," *Gesammelte Abhandlungen*, Vol. IV, 1923. Seler's rebuttal to Brinton, in which he identifies the hero with the moon.

―――― "Die Sage von Quetzalcouatl und den Tolteken in den in neurer Zeit bekannt gewordenen Quellen," *Gesammelte Abhandlungen*, Vol. V, 1915. A commentary on Fragments A and B of Quetzalcoatl.

Bancroft, Hubert H., *The Native Races of the Pacific States*, Vol. III, 1875. Chapter 7 is a survey of nineteenth-century theories about Quetzalcoatl, including Brasseur's lost-continent hypothesis, Tylor's solar theory, and the still-useful interpretations of J. G. Müller.

León-Portilla, Miguel, "La historia del Tohuenyo: narración erótica náhuatl," *Estudios de la Cultura Náhuatl*, Vol. I, 1959. The story of the Toueyo (from Fragment D), translated into Spanish with notes and commentary.

———— *Pre-Columbian Literatures of Mexico*, 1969. An English-language anthology of Mexican and Mayan literature with running commentary. Includes excerpts from the Quetzalcoatl.

Kirchoff, Paul, "Quetzalcoatl, Huémac y el fin de Tula," *Cuadernos Americanos*, Vol. LXXXIV, 6, Nov.–Dic., 1955. An interesting attempt to reconstruct the history of Tollan during its last days.

Chadwick, Robert, "Native Pre-Aztec History of Central Mexico," *Handbook of Middle American Indians*, Vol. 11, 1971, pp. 474–504. Tollan is identified with Teotihuacan.

Cornyn, John Hubert, *The Song of Quetzalcoatl*, 1930. A reasonably faithful version of Fragment D. Englished in trochaic tetrameter after the manner of Longfellow's *Hiawatha*.

V / *Mexican religion*

Spence, Lewis, *The Gods of Mexico*, 1923. In the absence of a definitive general work on Mexican religion, Spence's old-fashioned treatment is still serviceable. His interpretation of Quetzalcoatl as a weather spirit is probably derived from J. G. Müller. See Bancroft, above.

Seler, Eduard, "Mythus und Religion der alten Mexikaner," in

Seler's *Gesammelte Abhandlungen*, Vol. IV, 1923. In five loosely related essays, Seler analyzes the cosmology, cosmogony, star lore, and hero worship of ancient Mexico.

————— "Einiges über die natürlichen Grundlagen mexikanischer Mythen," *Gesammelte Abhandlungen*, Vol. III, 1908. Seler searches the myths and the pictorial codices for traces of uranic symbolism. (Quetzalcoatl figures prominently as an avatar of the morning moon!)

Sáenz, César A., *Quetzalcoatl*, 1962. A tentative summary of the god-hero's attributes. Illustrated.

Caso, Alfonso, *The Aztecs: People of the Sun*, 1958. A simple but useful description of the ancient religious concepts.

Alexander, Hartley Burr, *Latin-American Mythology*, 1920, reprinted 1964. Includes a provocative survey of Mexican religion.

León-Portilla, Miguel, *Aztec Thought and Culture: A Study of the Ancient Nahuatl Mind*, 1963.

Burland, C. A., *The Gods of Mexico*, 1967. The author gives a popularized Jungian analysis of Quetzalcoatl, whom he views as "the picture of a complete human personality."

Séjourné, Laurette, *Burning Water: Thought and Religion in Ancient Mexico*, 1956. Includes a spiritualist interpretation of the Quetzalcoatl myth, in which it is argued that the planet Venus represents the human soul hungering for paradise.

VI / Language

Molina, Alonso de, *Vocabulario en lengua castellana y mexicana*, 1944. Molina's sixteenth-century lexicon, the principal authority in its field.

Siméon, Rémi, *Dictionnaire de la langue nahuatl*, 1963. An elegant nineteenth-century lexicon (incorporating Molina). The most complete Nahuatl dictionary.

Garibay, Ángel M., *Llave del Náhuatl: Colección de trozos clásicos, con gramática y vocabulario, para utilidad de los principiantes*, 1940, second edition 1961.

Swadesh, Mauricio, and Sancho, Madalena, *Los mil elementos del mexicano clásico*, 1966. An introduction to the study of Nahuatl.

The Ritual of Condolence

AN IROQUOIS CEREMONIAL

*"Now, we attach the Sun again
in its place for thee."*

INTRODUCTION

The Ritual of Condolence is an occasional ritual prompted by the death of a high chief—one of a supreme senate of fifty councilors representing the confederated Five Nations of the Iroquois and, symbolically, the whole of Iroquois society —the idea being that death has breached the great social "edifice," which the ritual now effectively mends, or restores. This it does, finally, by resurrecting the dead chief in the person of his successor.

Society is a woman. In the vivid imagery of the Condolence texts, "she" becomes the grieving widow whose eyes fill up with tears, whose throat and ears are clogged with ashes as she grovels among the dead coals in her darkened house. Death has stamped out her fire and scattered the firebrands who were her chiefs.

The figure of the bereaved "wife" points to the role of the woman as progenitress in a matrilineal society. It accords, moreover, with her real or imagined role as unifier of the social structure. Traditionally, the Iroquois have divided themselves into two halves, or moieties, a "senior" moiety synonymous with the Mohawk, Onondaga, and Seneca nations and a "junior" moiety comprising the Oneida and Cayuga. Women ideally marry "across the fire," that is, they take husbands from the opposite moiety, thereby tending to integrate the two sides. The Ritual of Condolence, figuratively speaking, addresses itself to the same task. It functions as a mutual exchange (of song and rhetoric) between participants representing the two opposing halves, recalling the actual exchange of marriage partners and with apparently the same intention of "binding up" society. The connection is openly expressed at the close of the performance when a speaker invites the visiting men to dance with women of the opposite moiety. This indicates, as William Fenton has observed, that the social order is restored.

Now the enemy of society is not merely death itself, but the *cult* of death. The death of a kinsman may lead one into a state of depression, or "insanity," symptomized perhaps by an excessive veneration of the corpse (and cannibalism?), conducive to thoughts of suicide or, alternately, murder. If suicide, then yet another member will be lost. If murder, then the morbid cycle may be reinduced among the kinsmen of the new victim, producing the vendetta, or blood feud, that inevitably rends the fabric of society. By organizing themselves into a great polity (as distinct from the moiety and clan divisions upon which the polity is superimposed), the Iroquois have attempted to thwart this cult of death. The polity is known variously as the confederation, the league, the work, or the Great Peace. In theory it safeguards the life of the people; and while it is evidently a secular institution, the people regard it as sacred.

According to legend the great league was conceived by the hero Hiawatha, who had himself been afflicted by a morbid state of mind. One day, so the story goes, he noticed the reflection of a new face in the surface of the water. Not recognizing it as his own, he looked up and saw peering over his shoulder the beautiful figure of his second self, a seemingly real personage to whom mythmakers have given the name Deganawidah ("the Thinker"). It was Deganawidah who persuaded Hiawatha to give up the practice of cannibalism and to become, moreover, the advocate of a Great Peace. Having reformed himself, Hiawatha proceeded to reform his people.

Hiawatha's teachings are said to have taken root first among the Mohawks. (He himself is believed to have been a Mohawk.) One infers that the principal Mohawk chieftain, Tehkarihhoken ("Of Two Minds"), had doubts about the league initially, but was ultimately convinced. Next the Oneida were converted, and together with the Mohawk they formed the league's first link. The Cayuga, Onondaga, and Seneca followed suit. In order to win the crucial support of the Onondaga, at that time the most powerful of the five nations, the reformers are said to have repeatedly and unavailingly approached the evil Onondaga ruler, Atotarho. (In the version of the story recorded by Horatio Hale, Atotarho is portrayed as a sorcerer who subjects Hiawatha to a series of misfortunes, eventually putting him to flight. It is during this exile, then, that he encounters Deganawidah and begins to work for the league.) Finally, in the words of a typical Iroquois metaphor, Hiawatha "combed the snakes from Atotarho's hair" and the Onondagas were taken in. (Note the similarities between Hiawatha/Deganawidah and Huemac/Quetzalcoatl, each representing the flesh and the spirit; and between Hiawatha/Atotarho and Quetzalcoatl/Tezcatlipoca, each typifying the hero and the sorcerer. The essential difference between Hiawatha and Quetzalcoatl as messianic figures is that the former has returned, while the latter remains in exile.)

Having agreed to form a confederation, the five nations, or

rather a select group of representatives including Hiawatha, Atotarho, and other leaders, met in conference to choose a senate of fifty high chiefs. In accord with various cultural and political necessities the chieftainships were apportioned unequally: the Mohawks and Oneidas got nine apiece (so that each of their principal "families" had one chief); the Onondagas were given fourteen (as a sop to the recalcitrant Atotarho), the Cayugas ten, and the Senecas eight.

Upon the death of a chief, his successor inherits not only the position but also the name. In this manner the fifty founders are mystically kept alive. And so there will always be a chief called Hiawatha, one who is Atotarho, etc.

For the purposes of ritual, the moiety that has sustained the loss will play the role of the grieving woman, the mourner. The opposite moiety becomes the comforter (though of course, in a larger sense, both sides are mourners). The program consists of an elaborate interweaving of five prescribed texts, administered in the spirit of a "mutual embrace":

The Eulogy, or Roll Call of the Founders. The roll call works its way through the ritual in the manner of a prolonged incantation, as if rebuilding the great "edifice," unit by unit. Each of the fifty founders is named in a precisely calculated sequence, punctuated by repetitions of a four-line refrain in such a way that the chant yields a verbal diagram of Iroquoia as a whole. In the words of native informants, it "puts the house in order." With reference to figure 2, I will here briefly attempt to show how the Eulogy expresses the idea of wholeness on the political level, on the social level, as a model of the Iroquois homeland, and, perhaps, as a model of the natural world. Note that the fifty chiefs are grouped in nineteen "classes," indicated in the figure by the letters A through S, each class being a political unit superficially related to the counseling system of the tribe to which it belongs. In the Mohawk "house," classes A and B sit as brothers on the same side of the fire, facing class C. Class A is the "chairman" who introduces the topic for discussion; the matter will then be thrown back and forth "across the fire" by B and C until unanimity is reached. The Oneida counsel among themselves in virtually the same manner. But as we progress from tribe to tribe, the tripartite method of the Mohawks is gradually transformed; and by the time we have reached the house of the Seneca, it has become a near-perfect moiety system. Here each class is regarded as a pair of cousins, facing one another across the fire, throwing their discussions back and forth without the controlling influence of a third party (although it is probable that class P at least partially fills this role). The Cayuga system is something of a hybrid. The two chiefs of class O function as "doorkeepers"; it is they who introduce the topic, while class M and class N toss it to and fro across the fire, announcing their decision to class L, the "firekeepers," who, if they do not concur, send the matter back for further debate (see Shimony). The details of the Onondaga system are not clear; but it would appear to be more like the Cayuga than the Oneida (see Parker, p. 33). On the intertribal level, the Mohawk, Onondaga, and Seneca sit together as brothers on one side of the great fire, facing the opposite moiety—as, for example, during a performance of the Condolence ritual, though in the administrative councils of the league the arrangement was somewhat different. (There the Onondaga would sit to one side as "firekeepers," with the principal chief of that nation, Atotarho, no. 19, sometimes recognized as the presiding sachem.) Now compare figure 2 with the map on page 179. Notice that the political geography of Iroquoia coincides with the sequence of chiefs as named in the Eulogy. The Mohawks are the keepers of the "eastern door." The

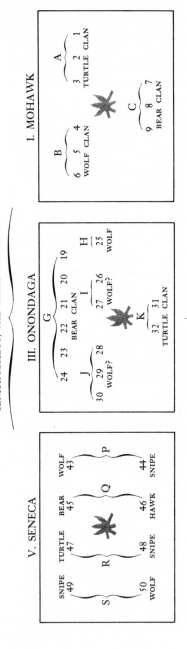

Senecas are said to guard the "western door," while the centrally positioned Onondagas, as mentioned above, are "firekeepers." Returning to the political structure, we may see that it is really a societal plan in disguise. Each class, at least in theory, corresponds to a totemic clan, or pair of clans, which may in turn be divided into "families," or "households." Ideally, each family owns a chieftainship, so that the council of fifty as a whole may be taken to represent the far-flung social structure in all its various parts. Whether or not this structure can be made to read as a cosmic model, following the suggestion of Lévi-Strauss, there are certain ideas, or rather clues, that bear noting. The difficulty is that we do not, apparently, have enough ethnography to determine what the

Figure 2 / The Roll Call of the Founders (read from right to left). MOHAWK: 1. Tehkarihhoken, 2. Hayenwatha (Hiawatha), 3. Shadekarihwade, 4. Sharenhhowane, 5. Tehyonheghkwen, 6. Owenheghkohna, 7. Tehhennaghkarihne, 8. Aghstawenseronttha, 9. Shaghskoharowane. ONEIDA: 10. Odatseghdeh, 11. Kahnonkwenyah, 12. Tehyohhakwendeh, 13. Shononghseseh, 14. Thonaeghkenah, 15. Hahtyadonnentha, 16. Tehwahtahontenyonk, 17. Kahnyadaghshayen, 18. Honwatshadonneh. ONONDAGA: 19. Wathadotarho (Atotarho), 20. Onehseaghhen, 21. Tehhatkahdons, 22. Skaniadajiwak, 23. Aweakenyat, 24. Tehayatkwayen, 25. Hononwirehdonh, 26. Kawenenseaghtonh, 27. Hahhihhonh, 28. Hohyunhnyennih, 29. Shotehgwaseh, 30. Shahkohkenneh, 31. Sahhahwih, 32. Skahnahwahtih. CAYUGA: 33. Tahkahenhyunh, 34. Jihnontahwehheh, 35. Kahtahgwahjih, 36. Shonyunhwesh, 37. Hahtyahsenhneh, 38. Tehyuhenhhyunhkoh, 39. Tehyuhtohwehgwih, 40. Tyawenhhehthonh, 41. Hahtonhtahhehhah, 42. Teshkahhea. SENECA: 43. Skahnyahteihyuh, 44. Shahtehkahenhyesh, 45. Sahtyehnahwaht, 46. Shakenhjohnah, 47. Kahnohkaih, 48. Nishahyehnenhhah, 49. Kanonhkehihtawih, 50. Tyuhninhohkawenh. (Principal sources for the seating arrangement and clan affiliations shown in the diagram: Hale 1883, Shimony 1961, Fenton 1950, Hewitt and Fenton 1945)

Iroquois system was originally intended to express. Vicissitudes over the centuries may have slightly jostled the societal patterns, the confederation of the Five Nations itself has evidently confused the picture, and in the course of history the symbolism of the totems has been obscured, if not lost. Yet, inasmuch as other Indian societies have constructed totemic, or clan, systems that in some way present a cosmic model—an image of the universe—it is not inconceivable that the Iroquois have done the same. Let us imagine that there are not one but two world views involved: the triadic Mohawk and the dualistic Seneca. The three Mohawk clans, the Wolf, the Turtle, and the Bear, may be imagined as representing sky, water, and earth, respectively; or, expressed in slightly different terms, heaven, earth-surface, and underworld. (A similar societal model for ancient Mexico could be postulated using the evidence adduced on p. 88, note 79.) The Seneca system, on the other hand, suggests a simple opposition of earth and sky (note in figure 2 that for the most part land animals are paired with birds). The late Iroquoianist J. N. B. Hewitt would appear to have had something similar in mind when he proposed that the junior moiety of the confederated Five Nations as a whole represented the "mother principle," while the senior moiety stood for the "father principle."

At the Wood's Edge. It is the "wood," or the "great forest," that separates the two moieties. In a chant of welcome, the orator for the mourning moiety gives thanks that the opposite half has arrived safely at the edge of the mourners' clearing. Now the ritual can begin. (In effect, the speaker here acknowledges the coming together of the two halves of society, concluding with a roll call of the widely dispersed villages, which he draws together in a triadic pattern according to the classic Mohawk totems, Wolf, Turtle, and Bear.

Obviously this chant, and perhaps the entire Ritual of Condolence, must be traced to a Mohawk origin.)

The Requickening. A speaker for the comforters addresses himself to ailing society (represented by the mourning moiety), whom he treats as a patient to be lifted from the throes of grief and morbidity. In a series of fifteen formulas, or "articles," he restores the senses of the groveling, grief-stricken "widow," whose eyes, ears, and throat had been clogged with tears and ashes (articles 1, 2, 3); he restores her body (article 4) and her dwelling place (article 5); he rescues her from the darkness of grief by restoring the sun (articles 6, 7, 8); he properly inters the corpse of the dead chief (article 9); he reintegrates the social order by dissolving animosities (article 10), by rekindling the council fire (article 11), and by exhorting the chiefs to honor their women and their warriors (article 12); he forbids the dangerous "insanity" of grief (article 13) and demands that in case of future death the stricken moiety come for healing to the ritual (article 14); finally he appeals to the mourners for a new candidate to replace the dead sachem (article 15). In an unusual burst of enthusiasm Hewitt writes: "The psychological insight of the framers of this wonderful ritualistic address is without question unsurpassed in any other composition of its kind in any other literature of the world."

The Hymn. This anthem, or "hymn," in praise of the socio-political order is regarded by the Iroquois as the most sacred of their songs. Hale's well-known translation reads:

    I come again to greet and thank the League;
    I come again to greet and thank the kindred;
    I come again to greet and thank the warriors;

> I come again to greet and thank the women;
> My forefathers—what they established—
> My forefathers—hearken to them!

But in performance each of the six verses gives rise to an extended vocalise, repeated by an assistant singer, then repeated again by the entire moiety singing in unison. The Hymn is sung by the comforters before the main portion of the Requickening. Then, when the Requickening has been completed, the Hymn is returned by the mourners—but with slight changes so that it now appears as if the dead chief himself is giving answer.

Over the Great Forest. A chanter for the comforters prepares for the day when yet another death shall occur. His words are a valediction against morbidity, "thrown over the great forest" from one moiety to the other, calling to mind the legendary conversion of Hiawatha. (Significantly, the hero is referred to in this chant as "Deganawidah.") In an extended three-part rhetorical figure, the too-fascinating corpse is pulled down from the sky platform to the earth-surface and thence to the underworld, where a "swift current" carries it out of sight.

In former times the ritual was handed down orally, evidently with the aid of pictographs and mnemonic strands of wampum, although native ritualists (using an orthography borrowed from missionaries) had begun to write out the texts as early as the mid-1700's. A century later the philologist Horatio Hale was privileged to study a more or less complete set of these texts at the Six Nations Reserve near Brantford,

Ontario, and subsequently published the first English translation in his classic work of 1883 (*The Iroquois Book of Rites*), complete with Mohawk paleograph and copious commentary.

Hale was unable to present the Condolence in proper order, however, having not as yet witnessed an actual performance (a shortcoming for which he substantially compensated in his paper of 1895). Moreover, his skimpy Requickening text now appears to have been little more than a sketch, made by copyists who had not mastered their material or who deliberately chose to epitomize it. For whatever reason, Hale's version falls short of the fully developed Requickening Address of Chief John Arthur Gibson, translated by Hewitt and published in final form in the *Journal of the Washington Academy of Sciences* for March 1944. Accordingly, the translations offered below are Hale's, except for the Requickening, which is Hewitt's. Program details, including a number of interpolated and supplementary speeches, have been drawn from Hale, Beauchamp, Hewitt, and others, but principally from William Fenton's "An Iroquois Condolence Council for installing Cayuga chiefs in 1945," based on a Condolence witnessed at the Six Nations Reserve, mentioned above, where the league still survives ceremonially and in microcosm.

The reconstruction gives preference to the earlier sources, relying upon the more recent observations of Fenton wherever necessary. Those glosses clearly indicated as such by Hale, Hewitt, or Fenton have been printed in italic (as have reconstructed phrases in the second half of the Eulogy). As for the pronunciation of Iroquois names, the following rules may be observed: consonants and consonant combinations are as in English (except for the guttural, breathy *gh*, similar to the German *ch* as in *ach*, or the Spanish *j*), vowels as in Spanish or Italian, with frequent nasals as in French: *an* is sounded as in the French *danse*, *on* as in *bon*, and *en* as in the subverbal

English negation, *unh-unh*. The syllable is not nasalized, however, if the *n* is followed by a vowel, e.g., in the word *Kanesadakeh*. A double *n* means that the preceding vowel is nasalized, while the following syllable begins with the normal sound of *n*. Doubled vowels have the same sound as the single vowel, but prolonged. The stress is on the penult.

As a general caution, Iroquois words should be pronounced more toward the throat than toward the lips, avoiding the typical explosiveness of English consonants. The consonants *k* and *g*, as well as *t* and *d*, are interchangeable.

In Hale's orthography the familiar Hiawatha becomes Hayenwatha (pronounced virtually the same), Deganawidah becomes Dekanawidah (pronounced the same), and Atotarho appears in the variant form Wathadotarho.

THE RITUAL OF CONDOLENCE

With ritual texts translated from the Mohawk Iroquois by Horatio Hale and from the Onondaga Iroquois by J. N. B. Hewitt; with supplementary texts translated by William N. Fenton; and with descriptions of ritual procedure paraphrased by John Bierhorst, after Hale, Fenton, Hewitt, and others

PARTICIPANTS[1]

THE TWO BROTHERS, collectively the eighteen high chiefs of the two "younger" nations, the Oneida and the Cayuga. With respect to the opposite moiety (the three "elder" nations), they may be styled "offspring," or, more properly, "nephews." Normally their number is nineteen, nine Oneidas and ten Cayugas. But in the hypothetical case here offered as an occasion for ritual, one has lately died: the first of the Cayuga chiefs, Tahkahenhyunh, in whose memory the Two Brothers become "mourners."

THE THREE BROTHERS, collectively the thirty-two high chiefs of the three "elder" nations, apportioned as follows: nine Mohawks, fourteen Onondagas, eight Senecas. In ceremony the "younger" moiety will address them as "my adonni," literally "my father's clansmen," often freely translated "my uncles" or even "my fathers." Under the proposed circumstances the Three Brothers consider themselves "unscathed" or "clearminded" ones. They will comfort the "mourners," "requicken" them, and install a new chief in place of the deceased Tahkahenhyunh.

I / The Summons

Tahkahenhyunh is dead. A courier representing the mourners passes through the forest, bearing the black strand of wampum called "tears," crying out as he enters each clearing:

Kwa!

—three times, signifying the death of a high chief. The wampum reads: "Tahkahenhyunh calls for a council." Attached is a small tally stick, notched to show the number of days remaining until the day of ritual.[2]

II / Journeying on the Trail

The thirty-one chiefs of the Three Brothers, accompanied by matrons, warriors, and others, assemble in the forest about a mile distant from the principal Cayuga village. At the appointed hour, shortly after noon, the singer rises and begins the Eulogy:[3]

> Now listen, ye who established
> The Great League. Now it has become old.
> Now there is nothing but wilderness.
>
> Ye are in your graves who established it.
> Ye have taken it with you, and have placed it
>   under you,
> And there is nothing left but a desert.

There ye have taken your intellects with you.
What ye established ye have taken with you.
Ye have placed under your heads what ye
    established—the Great League.[4]

*The procession begins to move in double file, headed by the
singer and a crier, the two abreast, followed by chiefs, matrons,
warriors, et al. The singer continues without interruption:*

Now, then, hearken, ye who were rulers and
    founders: Tehkarihhoken!
Continue to listen! Thou who wert ruler,
    Hayenwatha![5]
Continue to listen! Thou who wert ruler,
    Shadekarihwade!

Refrain / That was the roll of you,
     You who were joined in the work,
     You who completed the work,
     The Great League.

Continue to listen! Thou who wert ruler,
    Sharenhhowane!
Continue to listen! Thou who wert ruler,
    Tehyonheghkwen!
Continue to listen! Thou who wert ruler,
    Owenheghkohna!

Refrain / That was the roll of you,
     You who were joined in the work,
     You who completed the work,
     The Great League.

Continue to listen! Thou who wert ruler,
    Tehhennaghkarihne!
Continue to listen! Thou who wert ruler,
    Aghstawenseronttha!
Continue to listen! Thou who wert ruler,
    Shaghskoharowane!

(*Refrain*)

As he completes the roll of the nine Mohawk founders, the singer yields to the crier, who calls:

My offspring!

—a signal of approach to the waiting mourners. Now the singer resumes the Eulogy (with a digressive tribute to the Mohawk and the Oneida, the "father" and "son" who established the League's first link):

Ye two were principals, father and son,
Ye two completed the work, the Great League.
Ye two aided each other, ye two founded the
    House.

The roll of the nine Oneidas:

Now, therefore, hearken! Thou who wert ruler,
    Odatseghdeh!
Continue to listen! Thou who wert ruler,
    Kahnonkwenyah!
Continue to listen! Thou who wert ruler,
    Tehyohhakwendeh!

Refrain / That was the roll of you,
        You who were joined in the work,
        You who completed the work,
        The Great League.

    Continue to listen! Thou who wert ruler,
        Shononghseseh!
    Continue to listen! Thou who wert ruler,
        Thonaeghkenah!
    Continue to listen! Thou who wert ruler,
        Hahtyadonnentha!

                  (*Refrain*)

    Continue to listen! Thou who wert ruler,
        Tehwahtahontenyonk!
    Continue to listen! Thou who wert ruler,
        Kahnyadaghshayen!
    Continue to listen! Thou who wert ruler,
        Honwatshadonneh!

                  (*Refrain*)

The Oneida roster is complete. Again the crier calls:

        My offspring!

*The singer resumes, beginning the roll of the fourteen Onondagas
("brothers" to the Mohawks, therefore "uncles" to the just-named
Oneidas):*

These were his uncles: now hearken! Thou who
    wert ruler, Wathadotarho:[6]
Continue to listen! These were the cousins:[7]
    thou who wert ruler, Onehseaghhen!
Continue to listen! Thou who wert ruler,
    Tehhatkahdons!
Continue to listen! These were as brothers[7]
    thenceforth: thou who wert ruler,
    Skaniadajiwak!
Continue to listen! Thou who wert ruler,
    Aweakenyat!
Continue to listen! Thou who wert ruler,
    Tehayatkwayen!

(Refrain)

Then . . .

But as the party reaches the clearing the Eulogy is broken off.

III / Welcome at the Wood's Edge

Alerted by the call of the clearminded crier, the mourners come out from their longhouse to the edge of the village clearing, where they now stand in several ranks behind a welcoming fire. As the Three Brothers approach the fire, the mourners' orator steps forward and delivers the chant called "At the Wood's Edge."[8]

Now today have I been greatly startled by your

voice coming through the forest to this opening.
You have come with troubled mind through all
obstacles. You kept seeing the places where they
met on whom we depended, my adonni. How then
can your mind be at ease? You kept seeing the
footmarks of our forefathers; and all but
perceptible is the smoke where they used to
smoke the pipe together. Can then your mind
be at ease when you are weeping on your way?

Great thanks now, therefore, that you have safely
arrived. Now, then, let us smoke the pipe together.
Because all around are hostile agencies which are
each thinking, "I will frustrate their purpose."
Here thorny ways, and here falling trees, and here
wild beasts lying in ambush. Either by these you
might have perished, my adonni, or here by floods
you might have been destroyed, my adonni, or by
the uplifted hatchet in the dark outside the house.
Every day these are wasting us; or deadly invisible
disease might have destroyed you, my adonni.

Great thanks now, therefore, that in safety you
have come through the forest. Because lamentable
would have been the consequences had you
perished by the way, and the startling word had
come, "Yonder are lying bodies, yea, and of
chiefs!" And they would have thought in dismay,
what had happened, my adonni.

Our forefathers made the rule, and said, "Here
they are to kindle a fire; here, at the edge of the
woods, they are to condole each other in few

words." But they have referred thither all business
to be duly completed, as well as for the mutual
embrace of condolence. And they said, "Thither
shall they be led by the hand, and shall be placed
on the principal seat."[9]

The chant ends with a roll call of the ancient villages:[10]

Now, therefore, you who are our friends of the Wolf
clan: Karhetyonni, *The Broad Woods;*
Oghskawaseronhon, *Grown Up to Bushes Again;*
Geadiyo, *Beautiful Plain;* Onenyodeh, *Protruding
Stone;* Deseroken, *Between Two Lines;*
Tehodijenharakwen, *Two Families in a
Longhouse, One at Each End;* Oghrekyonny;
Teyoweyendon, *Drooping Wings.* Such is the
extent of the Wolf clan.

Now, then, thy children of the two clans of the
Tortoise: Kanesadakeh, *On the Hill Side;*
Onkwiiyede, *A Person Standing There;*
Weghkerhon; Kahkendohhon; Thogwenyoh;
Kahhekwake. Such is the extent of the Tortoise
clan.

Now these, thy brothers of the Bear clan:
Deyaoken, *The Forks;* Jonondeseh, *It Is a High
Hill;* Otskwerakeron, *Dry Branches Fallen to the
Ground;* Oghnaweron, *The Springs.* Now these
have been added lately: Karhowenghradon,
Taken Over the Woods; Karaken, *White;*
Deyohero, *The Place of Flags;* Deyosweken,

Outlet of the River; Oxdenke, *To the Old Place.*
Such is the extent of the Bear clan.

These were the clans in ancient times.

*The clearminded now produce the first three strands of the
Requickening wampum, draping them over a horizontal pole held
up by a pair of forked stakes. An orator for the Three Brothers
takes up the first strand and (addressing the mourners) intones
the contents thus:*

THE FIRST ARTICLE / TEARS, OR ONE'S EYES

Oh, my offspring, lo, verily, this present day,
such as is this day in kind and aspect, He Himself,
He the Finisher of Our Faculties, He the Master
of All, has made. Even He has prepared the light
of this day, such as it is.[11]

Now therefore, they who are customarily called
the Three Brothers are journeying along the path
of the Ritual as it was prepared for us by our
forefathers upon whom our minds rested in
confidence.

It is that, therefore, that brings their persons
here, the calamity, so hopeless and dreadful,
which has befallen thy person, this one
(*indicating*), thou whom I have held in my
bosom, thou noble one, the two of you who are
the Two Brothers.

It is that, therefore, as to that,[12] verily, this
present day, I thrust aside the door-flap from the
place where thou art lying as an object that is black;
it is that in the midst of great darkness thou art
sitting too prone in grief, thy back alone visible
in the thick darkness. Thou whom I have weaned.

It is that, therefore, that[13] I shall stoop low there
at the edge of thy ash-pit, grasping my knees, and
that, therefore, I shall utter such words that I shall
with them soothe and appease by caresses any
displeasure of thy guardian spirit.

It is that, therefore, that I come for the sake of
my Offspring.

It is that, therefore, that this present day, we, thou
and I, seat ourselves side by side, and that, therefore,
it is here in the very midst of very many tears.

It is that, therefore, that the cause of it, indeed, is
the dreadful thing that has stricken thy person, this
one (*indicating*), thou noble one whom I have
been wont to hold in my bosom.

It is that, therefore, that now today has been
caused to be vacant the seat of husk matting, the
place whereon he who was a co-worker with thee,
and upon whom rested the eyes of the wise minds
in full confidence, was wont to be seated.

It is that, therefore, that[13] has caused it to be so,
the being that is demonic in itself, the being that is

faceless because its lineaments were unknown to
our ancestors, the Great Destroyer that it is,
which every day and every night roams about
with its weapon couched, yea, uplifted, at the
very tops of our heads, wherein it and its kind
desire it, and so they severally boast, "It is I, I will
destroy all things, even the Commonwealth of
the League."

It is that, therefore, that there it delivered a vital
stroke whereby it snatched away from thee one in
whom thou didst trust for words of wisdom and
comfort; and now in his turn it has borne him
away, it may be indeed, to the place unknown.
Now, therefore, today, thou dwell amidst many
tears.

It is that, therefore, Oh, thou my offspring, thou
yaanehr, *thou Federal Chief*,[14] are not thy Father's
blood-kin, the Three Brothers, making their
preparations? And now, therefore, let them say,
"Now do we pass our hands through thy tears in
sympathy; now, we wipe away the tears from thy
face, using the white fawn-skin of pity."[15] Now,
therefore, let them say, "We have wiped away thy
tears." Now, therefore, in peace of mind, thou
wilt continue to look around thyself, enjoying
again the light of the day. Now, also, thou wilt again
behold what is taking place on the earth, whereon
is outspread the handiwork of the Master of All
Things.[16] Now also thou wilt again see thy
sister's sons and daughters, *thy nephews and
nieces*,[17] as they move about thy person, even to

the least of them, the infants. Now, thou wilt see
them all again.

Now, therefore verily, thou wilt again do your
thinking in peace, this one, my offspring, thou
yaanehr, thou whom I have been wont to hold in
my bosom.

Enough, therefore, verily, that even for one brief
day, also in peace, mayst thou do thy thinking.

Thus, perhaps, let them do, the Three Brothers,
who had been so called ever since the
establishment of their affairs, *since the institution
of the Great League.*

Now, therefore, do thou know, this one, my
weanling, that now the Word, *the attesting
wampum,* of thy adonni is on its way hence to
thee.

*A messenger for the orator takes the strand just "read" and carries
it across the fire to the opposite side, where it is draped over a
horizontal pole belonging to the mourners. The clearminded
orator now takes the second strand:*

THE SECOND ARTICLE / EARS, OR HEARING

Oh, my offspring, there is a different matter, and
we will say as we continue to speak that it
comes to pass where a great calamity has befallen
one's person that the passages of the ears become

obstructed and the hearing is lost. One then hears
not the sounds made by mankind, nothing of what
is taking place on the earth.

It is that, therefore, that this dreadful thing has
indeed befallen thy person, thou my weanling,
thou, you Two Brothers, thou yaanehr, *thou
Federal Chief.*

Is it not then true that what has befallen thy
person is so calamitous that it must not be
neglected? Indeed, now thou hearest nothing of
the sounds made by mankind as they move to and
fro about thy person, nor anything of what is
taking place on the earth. Now, therefore, let the
Three Brothers say, "We have made our
preparations, and so we proceed to restore thy
person by removing the obstacles obstructing
the passages of thy ears." Now, therefore, thou
wilt again hear when one will address words to
thee on whatever matter it may be, words which
may be directed to thee personally, thou
yaanehr, and next in order, the sounds made by
thy sister's sons and daughters, *thy nephews and
nieces,* moving around thy person. Now, thou wilt
again hear all things, also all that is taking
place on the earth, all these things thou wilt again
hear. And, now, also thou wilt be able to hear
clearly when we Three Brothers address you
ceremonially in the Chief Place.[18]

It is that, therefore, that we do this that even for
one brief day, also in peace, mayst thou do thy

thinking, thou, my offspring, thou yaanehr, thou,
my weanling.

Thus, perhaps, let them do, the Three Brothers,
who had been so denominated ever since the
establishment of their affairs, *since the institution
of the League.*

Now, therefore, do thou know, this one, my
weanling, that now the Word, *the attesting
wampum,* of thy adonni is on its way hence *to
thee.*

*As the messenger delivers the second strand, the orator continues
with the third:*

THE THIRD ARTICLE / THROAT

Oh, my offspring, there is still another matter to
be considered now, and we will say, as we
continue speaking, that it comes to pass where a
great misfortune has befallen a person, where the
Great Destroyer has been harshly cruel, that the
throat of the flesh-body becomes sorely
obstructed, so that then it is plainly to be seen
that the vitality of the person's life has become
lessened, also that of the mind of that person.

Verily, therefore, this has happened to thy
person, this one (*indicating*), my offspring, thou
yaanehr, thou whom I have been wont to hold in
my bosom.

Is it not then the fact that what has befallen thy
person is so dreadful that it must not be
neglected? Is it not true that thy flesh-body has
become choked up? Now, verily, thou canst
breathe only with great difficulty, also thou art
not able to say anything except in distress. Now,
therefore, surely the powers of thy life are
greatly weakened by it.

Now, then, verily, let the Three Brothers declare:
We have now made our preparations, and now,
therefore, we remove from thy throat of thy
flesh-body again the throttling obstructions.

Now, verily, again thou wilt breathe with ease
and comfort, and now, too, thou wilt again move
thy members with ease. Now, too, thou wilt
again speak with pleasure when soon we, thou
and I, will mutually greet each other in the Chief
Place.

It is that, therefore, that we do this, that even for
one brief day, and also in perfect peace, mayst
thou do thy thinking, thou my offspring, thou
yaanehr, this one (*indicating*), whom I have been
wont to hold in my bosom.

In this manner, perhaps, let the Three Brothers,
so denominated ever since the time they had
established their Commonwealth, do this.

Now, therefore, my weanling, know it, that the
Word, *the attesting wampum,* of thy Father's
Kinsmen is on its way hence *to thee.*

This is the sum of our words at this place.

When the third strand has been delivered, an orator for the mourners confirms all three articles by reading them back across the fire, repeating the speeches verbatim, but prefacing each with the words "You said."[19] This done, he makes some such announcement as the following:

Now have we completed it. The preliminary words are over. We both have rubbed down each other's bodies. Everything on our side is now ready; they shall take you by the arm and lead you to the principal bench, and there shall one seat you in the place where the entire business will be carried to a conclusion, as many matters as remain for us. Thus the appointed warrior chief will take you by the arm there and he will place you where benches have been prepared for you.[20]

Two of the mourners, designated "warrior chiefs," stand abreast facing the village. The singer and the crier for the clearminded fall in directly behind them, followed by the remainder of the chiefs and their party. The "warriors" give the signal:

Now let us proceed.[20]

As they begin to move, the singer resumes the Eulogy, picking up where he had left off. (He is nearly halfway through the roll of the fourteen Onondaga founders, with eight more to go. See above.)

Then his son: he is the great Wolf. There were
combined the many minds! *Now hearken!*
Thou who wert ruler,[21] Hononwirehdonh![22]

Refrain / That was the roll of you,
   You who were joined in the work,
   You who completed the work,
   The Great League.

  Continue to listen! These were his uncles, of the
   two clans[23]: *thou who wert ruler,*
   Kawenenseaghtonh!
  Continue to listen! Thou who wert ruler,
   Hahhihhonh!

            (Refrain)

  Continue to listen! These were as brothers
   thenceforth: *thou who wert ruler,*
   Hohyunhnyennih!
  Continue to listen! Thou who wert ruler,
   Shotehgwaseh!
  Continue to listen! Thou who wert ruler,
   Shahkohkenneh!

            (Refrain)

  This befell in ancient times. They had their
   children, those the two clans.
  He the high chief: *now hearken! Thou who wert*
   ruler, Sahhahwih![24]
  This put away the clouds:[25] he was a war chief;
   he was a high chief—acting in either office:
   continue to listen! Thou who wert ruler,
   Skahnahwahtih!

            (Refrain)

The procession passes through the village and into the council
house. Seats are taken as the singer completes the Eulogy, pacing
back and forth in the house.[26] *(He precedes the Cayuga roll with*
an interpolated apostrophe to the dead chief, Tahkahenhyunh,
"son" to the above-named Onondagas.)

> Then his son. Know that she, *society*, is grieving.
> > They are mourning in their minds when he
> > did pass away, he on whom we depended.
> > He carried away with him the minds of them
> > who subsist on the stump—as the tree puts
> > forth suckers. Now thou deceased one
> > hearken![27] Thou who wert ruler,
> > Tahkahenhyunh!
> With his brother: *now hearken! Thou who wert*
> > *ruler*, Jihnontahwehheh!

Refrain / That was the roll of you,
> > You who were joined in the work,
> > You who completed the work,
> > The Great League.

> > *Continue to listen! Thou who wert ruler,*
> > > Kahtahgwahjih!
> > *Continue to listen! Thou who wert ruler,*
> > > Shonyunhwesh!
> > *Continue to listen! Thou who wert ruler,*
> > > Hahtyahsenhneh!

> > > > > > > *(Refrain)*

> > Then they who are brothers: *now hearken! Thou*
> > > *who wert ruler*, Tehyuhenhyunhkoh!

Continue to listen! Thou who wert ruler,
    Tehyuhtohwehgwih!
Continue to listen! Thou who wert ruler,
    Tyawenhhehthonh!

                             (*Refrain*)

Continue to listen! Thou who wert ruler,
    Hahtonhtahhehhah!
Continue to listen! Thou who wert ruler,
    Teshkahhea!

                             (*Refrain*)

*The Eulogy ends with the roll of the eight Seneca founders,
collectively "uncle" to the above-named Cayugas:*

Then his uncle: *now hearken! Thou who wert
    ruler,* Skahnyahteihyuh!
With his cousin: *continue to listen, thou who
    wert ruler,* Shahtehkahenhyesh!

                             (*Refrain*)

Continue to listen! Thou who wert ruler,
    Sahtyehnahwaht!
With his cousin: *now hearken! Thou who wert
    ruler,* Shakenhjohnah!

                             (*Refrain*)

Continue to listen! Thou who wert ruler,
    Kahnohkaih!

With his cousin: then *hearken! Thou who wert
ruler*, Nishahyehnenhhah!

(*Refrain*)

Then, in later times, they made additions to the
great mansion. These were at the doorway,
they who were cousins. These two guarded
the doorway: *now hearken! Thou who wert
ruler*, Kanonhkehihtawih!
With his cousin: *continue to listen! Thou who
wert ruler*, Tyuhninhohkawenh![28]

Refrain / That was the roll of you,
You who were joined in the work,
You who completed the work,
The Great League.

Now we are dejected in our minds.

IV / The Council

*Stretching a curtain (formerly of hides or bark matting) in front
of the Two Brothers, the clearminded sing the first five verses of
the Condoling Song, or Hymn:*[29]

I come again to greet and thank the League;
I come again to greet and thank the kindred;
I come again to greet and thank the warriors;

I come again to greet and thank the women.
My forefathers—what they established!

*The curtain is lifted. A representative of the Three Brothers
begins the chant called "Over the Great Forest," pacing to and
fro before the assembly.*

Hail, my grandsires! Now hearken while your
grandchildren cry mournfully to you—because
the Great League which you established has
grown old. We hope that they may hear.

Hail, my grandsires! You have said that sad will
be the fate of those who come in the latter times.

Oh, my grandsires! Even now I may have failed
to perform this ceremony in the order in which
they were wont to perform it.

Oh, my grandsires! Even now that has become
old which you established—the Great League. You
have it as a pillow under your heads in the ground
where you are lying—this Great League which
you established; although you said that far away
in the future the Great League would endure.

*The chanter returns to his place among the clearminded. The
curtain is hung again and the Three Brothers sing the final
(sixth) verse of the Hymn:*

My forefathers—hearken to them!

The curtain is removed. The chanter intones certain "laws" of the League (*comprising the second and final portion of* "*Over the Great Forest*"):

Hail, my grandsires! Now hear, therefore, what
they did—all the rules they decided on, which
they thought would strengthen the House. Hail,
my grandsires! this they said: "Now we have
finished; we have performed the rites; we have
put on the horns."[30]

Now again another thing they considered, and
this they said: "Perhaps this will happen. Scarcely
shall we have arrived at home when a loss will
occur again." They said, "This, then, shall be
done. As soon as he is dead, even then the horns
shall be taken off. For if invested with horns he
should be borne to the grave," oh, my grandsires,
they said, "we should perhaps all perish if
invested with horns he is conveyed to the
grave."[31]

Then again another thing they determined, oh,
my grandsires! "This," they said, "will strengthen
the House." They said, if anyone should be
murdered and *the body* be hidden away among
fallen trees[32] by reason of the neck being white,[33]
then you have said, this shall be done. We will
place it by the wall in the shade.[34]

Now again you considered and you said: "It is
perhaps not well that we leave this here, lest it
should be seen by our grandchildren; for they
are troublesome, prying into every crevice. People

will be startled at their returning in consternation, and *the children* will ask what has happened that this *corpse* is lying here; because they will keep on asking until they find it out. And they will at once be disturbed in mind, and that again will cause us trouble."

Now again they decided, and said: "This shall be done. We will pull up a pine tree—a lofty tree —and will make a hole through the earth-crust, and will drop this thing into a swift current which will carry it out of sight, and then never will our grandchildren see it again."[35]

Now again another thing they decided, and thought, this will strengthen the House. They said: "Now we have finished; we have performed the rites. Perhaps presently it will happen that a loss will occur amongst us. Then this shall be done. We will suspend a pouch upon a pole, and will place in it some mourning wampum—some short strings—to be taken to the place where the loss was suffered. The bearer will enter, and will stand by the hearth, and will speak a few words to comfort those who will be mourning; and then they will be comforted, and will conform to the great law."[36]

Now, then, thou wert the principal of this Confederacy, Dekanawidah, with the joint principal, his son, Odatseghdeh; and then again his uncle, Wathadotarho; and also again his son, Tahkahenhyunh; and again his uncle,

Skahnyahteihyuh; and then again his cousin,
Shahtehkahenhyesh; and then in later times
additions were made to the great edifice.[37]

*The chanter yields to the clearminded orator, who resumes the
Requickening Address. The remaining strands of wampum—one
for each article of the Requickening—lie draped over a horizontal
cane set up on the Three Brothers' side of the house. The orator
takes up the fourth stand:*

THE FOURTH ARTICLE / WITHIN HIS BREAST

Oh, my offspring, now there is still another
thing that ever occurs wherever and whenever a
great calamity has befallen a person; verily, this
affliction comes when the being demonic of itself,
the Faceless One, the lineaments of whose face
our ancestors failed to discern, the Great
Destroyer, puts forth excessive ferocity against
one.

It is ever true that the organs within the breast
and the flesh-body are disordered and violently
wrenched without ceasing, and so also is the mind.
Now, verily, therefore, there always develop
yellow spots[38] within the body. Verily, now, the
life forces of the sufferer always become
weakened thereby. This ever takes place when the
Great Destroyer puts forth excessive ferocity
against one in causing such great affliction.

Oh, my offspring, thou art now such a sufferer.

Oh, my offspring, verily, in this manner too thou
hast suffered this affliction, this one (*indicating*),
thou yaanehr, *thou Federal Chief.*

Is not what has befallen thee then so dreadful that
it must not be neglected? For, at the present time,
there are wrenchings without ceasing within thy
breast, and also within thy mind. Now truly, the
disorder now among the organs within thy breast
is such that nothing can be clearly discerned. So
great has been the affliction that has befallen thee
that yellow spots have developed within thy body,
and truly thy life forces have become greatly
weakened thereby; truly thou dost now suffer.

It is that, therefore, that in ancient times it thus
came to pass that the hodiyaanehshon, *the Federal
Chiefs,* our grandsires, made a formal rule, saying,
"Let us unite our affairs; let us formulate
regulations; let us ordain this among others that
what we shall prepare we will designate by the
name Water-of-pity, which shall be the essential
thing to be used where Death has caused this
dreadful affliction, inducing bitter grief."

And so, in whatever place it may be that such a
tragedy will befall a person, it shall be the duty
of him whose mind is left unscathed by it to take
up and make use of the Water-of-pity, so
denominated by us, by taking it in hand, and
then pouring it down the throat of the one on
whom the great affliction has fallen; and, it shall
be that when the Water-of-pity shall have

permeated the inside of his body, it will at once
begin the work of reorganizing all the many
things there which have been disarranged and
disordered by the shock of the death, not only in
his body but also in his mind; and it will also
remove utterly all the yellow *gall* spots from his
throat and from the inside of his body.[39]

Oh, my offspring, this great tragedy has befallen
thee too. Do thou know it, therefore, that now the
Three Brothers, so called from the beginning, have
made their preparations. Now, verily, therefore,
they take up the Water-of-pity and now, then, let
them say, "We now pour into thy body the
Water-of-pity." Oh, my offspring, it shall,
therefore, come to pass when this Water-of-pity
settles down in thy body it shall at once begin the
work of restoring to order the organs which have
been disarranged and disordered in thy body, and
will bring order to thy mind also; all things will
be restored and readjusted, and also all the yellow
spots in thy body will be severally cleared away
from thy body; now, therefore, all things shall be
in good condition as to the powers of thy life.
Then, therefore, there will be health and comfort
in thy life.

Thus, therefore, for one brief little day mayst
thou think thy thoughts in peace, thou noble one,
thou yaaṅehr, whom I have been wont to hold in
my bosom.

In this manner, then, perhaps, let the Three

Brothers, so denominated ever since they
established their Commonwealth, expedite this
matter.

Now, therefore, do thou know it, thou noble one,
thou whom I have been wont to hold in my
bosom, thou yaanehr, *thou Federal Chief*, that the
Word, *the attesting wampum*, of thy adonni is
now on its way hence to thee.

*A messenger takes the attesting wampum and brings it over to
where it is received on a cane set up by the Two Brothers. The
remaining strands are read across to the mourners in like manner:*

THE FIFTH ARTICLE / THE BLOODY HUSK-MAT BED

Now, oh, my offspring, there is still another
matter to be considered at this time.

It is this, that it invariably comes to pass, where a
great calamity has befallen a person, that a trail of
blood is smeared over the husk-mat couch of that
person; now invariably, of course, that one's
place of rest is not at all pleasant—sitting
cross-legged in wretchedness.

Thus, therefore, art thou stricken in thy person in
this very manner, oh, my offspring, whom I have
been wont to hold in my bosom, thou noble one,
thou yaanehr, *thou Federal Chief*. Is not then
what has befallen thy person so dreadful that it

must not be neglected? Now, at this time is there
not a trail of blood smeared over thy husk-mat
couch? Today, thou dost writhe in the midst of
blood.

Now, therefore, do thou know it, that the Three
Brothers have made their preparations, and now,
therefore, let them say it, "Now, then, we wipe
away the several bloody smears from thy
husk-mat resting place. Moreover, we have
employed the skin of the spotted fawn, *the words
of pity and comfort*, to wipe away the bloody
trails."

It will, moreover, come to pass that on whatever
future day that our minds shall be parted, one
from the other, and that when thou wilt return
to thy mat, it will be in the fullness of peace, and
it will be spread out in contentment, when thou
wilt again sit cross-legged in thy resting place.[40]

Thus, therefore, may it be that for one poor brief
day, also in peace, thou mayst carry on thy
thinking in contentment, this one (*indicating*),
thou noble one, thou yaanehr, *thou Federal Chief*,
whom I have been wont to hold in my bosom.

In this manner, perhaps, let the Three Brothers,
so denominated ever since their Commonwealth
was completed, do this.

Now, therefore, do thou know it, oh, my

offspring, that the Word, *the attesting wampum*,
of thy adonni is on its way hence to thee.

THE SIXTH ARTICLE / THE DARKNESS OF GRIEF

Now, oh, my offspring, there is still another
matter to be considered at this time.

It is this, that where a direful thing befalls a
person, that person is invariably covered with
darkness, that person becomes blinded with thick
darkness itself. It is always so that the person
knows not any more what the daylight is like on
the earth, and his mind and life are weakened and
depressed.

This very thing, then, has befallen thee, my
weanling, thou noble one, whom I have been
wont to hold in my bosom.

Is not then what has befallen thy person so direful
that it must not be neglected? Now, therefore, at
this time thou art become thick darkness itself in
thy grief. Now, thou knowest not anything of the
quality of the light of day on the earth.

Now, oh, my offspring, do thou know it, that
now the Three Brothers have made their
preparations, and now, therefore, let them say,
"Now therefore, we make it daylight again for

thee. Now, most pleasantly will the daylight
continue to be beautiful when again thou wilt look
about thee whereon is outspread the handiwork
of the Finisher of Our Faculties on the face of the
earth."

Thus, therefore, for one brief little day mayst
thou think thy thoughts in peace, thou noble one,
thou yaanehr, my weanling.

In this manner, then, perhaps, let the Three
Brothers, so denominated ever since they
established their Commonwealth, effect this
matter.

Now, therefore, do thou know it, my offspring,
thou noble one, thou whom I have been wont to
hold in my bosom, thou yaanehr, *thou Federal
Chief*, that the Word, *the attesting wampum*, of
thy adonni is on its way hence to thee.

THE SEVENTH ARTICLE / THE LOSS OF THE SKY

Oh, my offspring, now there is another matter to
be considered at this time.

It is that, then, that where a great calamity has
befallen a person it invariably comes to pass that
the sky is lost to the senses of that person;
invariably he does not know anything of what is
taking place in it.

Verily, my offspring, this very thing has befallen
thy person, thou noble one, thou yaanehr. Verily,
then, is not what has befallen thy person not to be
neglected? Now, therefore, the sky is completely
lost to thy view. Now, thou dost know nothing
of what is taking place in the sky.

So, now, therefore, do thou know it, that now the
Three Brothers have made their preparations, and
now then let them say, "Now, then, we beautify
again the sky for you. It shall now continue to
be beautiful. Now, thou wilt do thy thinking in
peace when thy eyes will rest on the sky. The
Perfector of Our Faculties, the Master of All
Things, intended that it should be the source of
happiness to mankind."

Thus, therefore, for one brief little day, also in
peace, mayst thou do thy thinking, thou noble
one, thou yaanehr, my offspring.

In this manner, perhaps, let them do it, the Three
Brothers, so denominated ever since they had
established their Commonwealth.

Now, therefore, do thou know it, my offspring,
that the Word of thy Father's blood-kin is going
hence to thee.

THE EIGHTH ARTICLE / HIS SUN IS LOST

Oh, my offspring, now there is still another matter for serious thought. Thus it invariably comes to pass where a great calamity has befallen a person that the Sun is lost to that person's senses. Then such a person knows nothing about the movements of the Sun, nothing of its drawing nearer and nearer to him; he is then in darkness.

This very thing, therefore, has happened to thee, my weanling, thou noble one, thou yaanehr. The Sun is now lost to thee. Verily, then, is not what has befallen thy person not to be neglected? No more art thou aware of the movements of the Sun, nothing of its drawing nearer and nearer to thee.

So, now, therefore, do thou know it, that the Three Brothers have made their preparations. Now, then, let them say it, "Now, we attach the Sun again in its place for thee; that then shall come to pass, when the time shall come for the dawning of a new day, that verily thou shalt see the Sun when it shall come up out of the horizon, when, indeed, our Elder Brother, *the Sun*, who lights up the earth shall come over it."

Thus, then, my offspring, thy eyes shall rest on it as it draws ever closer to thee. That, therefore, when the Sun shall reach, or place itself in mid-heaven then around thy person rays or haloes of light will abundantly appear. Then, indeed, shall

thy mind resume its wonted moods; then also wilt
thou remember the many things of whatsoever
kind they may be, pertaining to the welfare of
thy people, thy children, and thy grandchildren,
matters, indeed, in which thou hadst been toiling.

Thus, then, may it be, that for one brief little
day thou mayst do thy thinking in peace, thou
noble one, thou yaanehr, thou my weanling.

In this manner, therefore, let the Three Brothers,
so denominated ever since the institution of their
Commonwealth, do this.

Now, therefore, do thou know it, my offspring,
that the Word of thy adonni is on its way hence
to thee.

THE NINTH ARTICLE / THE HEAP OF CLAY ON THE GRAVE[41]

Oh, my offspring, now, again, there is another
matter for consideration. Now, this other thing
concerns the course of action caused in a case
where a great tragedy has stricken a person,
where it occurred with outrageous harshness, for
invariably the mind of that person is simply
tossed and tormented on the grave of him in
whom he fondly trusted.

So then this selfsame thing has happened to thee,
thou noble one, thou yaanehr. Now, it is that thy

mind is simply lying there on the grave of the
one whom thou didst trust. Is not what has
befallen thee so serious that it must not be
neglected? So, therefore, do thou know it, that
the Three Brothers have completed their
preparations, and let them say, "We now level the
rough ground over the grave of him in whom
thou didst fondly trust." Now, then, they place
over it a fine slab of wood, and now too they pull
up several kinds of grasses which they will cast
on it for, truly, there are two different things that
always take place during the days and during the
nights; one is that it may become very hot, but
now it will then not reach into the place where
his corpse lies; the other is that it may rain
heavily, but now it will then not reach the place
where his bones lie. And so the bones of him on
whom thou didst fondly trust shall rest
peacefully and undisturbed.

THE TENTH ARTICLE / TWENTY IS THE PENALTY FOR HOMICIDE[42]

And, more than this, we now restore thy land to
orderliness, and now the Three Brothers say, "We
have pity for your lost homeland. Now, we rush
forward, throwing ourselves here and there, in
that we may now gather together again thy other
bones, so widely scattered as they have been by
the Being Malefic in Itself, the Being that is
Faceless—the Being that is the Great Destroyer—
Death."

More than this, that our departed grandsires made
a ruling, in that they said that twenty *strings of
wampum* shall be the value of this, at that price
did they fix it, *the price of a death by murder,*
in that they denominated it by this: That it shall
be valued at twenty *strings*; they declared that
one shall bind their bones thereby.[43]

Do thou know it, furthermore, this one
(*indicating*), my offspring, that now, do not the
Three Brothers take that up now?—and that now,
completing their preparations, let them say it,
"Now, we bind thy bones one and all, restating
the value of twenty on them."

Now then, my offspring, thou wilt again do thy
thinking in peace in the future. Thus, therefore,
let it be, that for one brief little day thou mayst
do thy thinking in peace and contentment.

In this manner, therefore, let the Three Brothers,
so denominated ever since they had established
their Commonwealth, do this.

And, now, my offspring, do thou know it, that the
Word of thy adonni is on its way hence to thee.

THE ELEVENTH ARTICLE / THE COUNCIL FIRE

Now, another thing: That our grandsires, now
long dead, and in whom our minds rested in trust,

decreed, because they did not know its face, the
face, indeed, of that Being that abuses us every
day, every night, that Being of Darkness, lying
hard by the lodges where it is black night, yea,
that Being which here at the very tops of our
heads, goes about menacing with its couched
weapon—with its uplifted hatchet—eagerly
muttering its fell purpose, "I, I will destroy the
Work—the Commonwealth," they decreed, I say,
that therefore they would call it the Great
Destroyer, the Being Without a Face, the Being
Malefic in Itself, *that is, Death.*

More than this it has already done; it has put
forth its lethal power there in thy frail lodge of
bark, this one (*indicating*), my weanling, my
offspring, thou noble one, and so snatching
therefrom one on whom thou didst depend for
words of wisdom and kindly service.

And so now, at this very moment, there is in that
lodge of bark a vacant mat because of this stroke.

And, in striking this cruel blow, it scattered the
Firebrands, *thy Chiefs,* widely asunder from the
place where thou art wont to kindle thy *Council*
Fire, and, now, more than this, the Great
Destroyer has danced exultingly, stamping that
hearth underfoot.

Thou sittest there now with bowed head; thou
no longer dost meditate on anything whatsoever
of thy former affairs—wherein thou wast laboring

for thy niece and for thy nephew, *for the men
and the women of thy people;* yea, for thy
children, and also for thy grandchildren, who run
about thy sides, and for these also who are still
swathed to cradleboards, and also for those
children who, still unborn, whose faces, still
underground, are coming toward thee; yea, for
these warriors and for these women; that is the
extent, indeed, of the solicitude and vigilant care
which were in the hands of him, thy uncle—*thy
mother's brother*—who has departed, while he
labored for their daily welfare, and who at this
moment is floating away far homeward.

So, now, do thou know it, this one, thou yaanehr,
my offspring, thou noble one, that the Three
Brothers have perfected their preparations, and
so let them say it, "Now, we gather again the
scattered Firebrands, *thy Chiefs,* and now, indeed,
do we rekindle the *Council* Fire for thee. And
now, in fact, verily, the smoke shall rise again, and
that smoke will be fine, and it will even pierce the
sky."

So, now again, the eyes of the peoples—alien to
us, perhaps—shall see again, also, the full number
of our Council Fires.

Now, again, indeed, we raise thee up to full
stature, erect among thy people. We also cheer
up thy mind. More than this, we again set thee
in order around the place where we have
rekindled the Fire for thee, my offspring.

Let the Three Brothers, furthermore, say it, "Do thou again transact the business upon which thou wert hitherto engaged promoting the welfare of the posterity of thy families."

Thus, furthermore, let it be so, that for one poor short day, thou mayst continue to think in peace, thou yaanehr, my offspring, thou noble one, my weanling.

In this manner, then, shall they now perform this duty of requickening, the Three Brothers, so denominated ever since their affairs had been completed.

Lastly, more than these things, do thou know it, thou yaanehr, my weanling, thou noble one, that the Word of thy adonni is now going hence to thee.

THE TWELFTH ARTICLE / WOMAN AND WARRIOR

Now, there is another thing to be considered today. It is that wherein the Perfector of Our Faculties who dwelleth in the sky did establish this matter in that He desired that He should have assistants everywhere, even down to the earth, that these latter assistants shall devote their solicitous care to the number of matters which pertain especially to the earth and which I have ordained, He says, one and all.[44]

It is that, in fact, that first among others, He
caused the body of our mother—*the woman*—to
be of great worth and honor. He purposed that
she shall be endowed and entrusted with the
duties pertaining to the birth—*the becoming*—
of men, and that she shall, in the next place, circle
around the fire in preparing food—that she shall
have the care of all that is planted by which life
is sustained and supported, and so the power to
breathe is fortified; and moreover that the
warriors shall be her assistants.

So that, too, is a great calamity, that it may be
the Great Destroyer will make a sudden stroke
there in the ranks of our mothers, and that he will
thus snatch away one there, so that her body shall
fall. The evil of this misfortune is that a long file
of expected persons shall fall away, which, indeed,
would have come in the manyfold lines of grandchildren who would have been born from her in
the future.

In that case, moreover, her assistants, the
warriors, will then just stand around listlessly,
but grieving.

For, now, that one on whom they so much
depended is now, very probably, floating away
to the homeland, and now the minds of all those
who still remain have fallen low *in grief.*

So now, moreover, the Three Brothers, having
perfected their preparations, do say, "Let us

comfort them now and raise up their minds."
And that, indeed, shall happen—they will now
again devote themselves to their cares and their
duties.

More than this, now, thou yaanehr, thou noble
one, my offspring, thou hast a nephew and a
niece,[45] that is to say, the warriors and the
women. They are and shall be thy immediate care.

And that more than this, thou yaanehr, thou noble
one, thou shalt and must give a full hearing to
whomsoever will speak to thee for counsel or for
service. That, too, let the Three Brothers say,
"Do ye heed and obey one another." It is, in fact,
a grievous thing, should it be that thou, noble
one, should cast over thy shoulder whatsoever
word is spoken to thee.

That mood of mind may have place only when
the time is near in which the feet of thy people
will hang over the abyss of the sundered earth.[46]
There is no one dwelling beneath the sky who has
the power to come out therefrom, when that shall
have come to pass. Furthermore, this great
responsibility rests both upon thee and upon thy
niece and thy nephew—that ye listen to and obey
one another.

Thus, too, let it be done, that for one poor short
day, thou mayst continue to think in contentment,
my offspring, thou noble ruler, whom I have been
wont to hold in my bosom.

In this manner then, perhaps, let them do it, the
Three Brothers, so denominated ever since they
were in the prime growth of their affairs.

Now, more than this, do thou know it, this one
(*indicating*), my offspring, thou noble ruler,
whom I have been wont to hold in my bosom,
the Word of thy adonni is on its way hence to
thee.

THE THIRTEENTH ARTICLE / ANYTHING CAN HAPPEN ON EARTH, EVEN INSANITY

Now, another thing, I say. That, verily, it is a
direful thing for the mind of him who has
suffered from a grievous calamity to become
insane, that, in fact, the powers causing insanity
are immune from everything on this earth, and
have the power to end the days of man, and that
it may be caused by the lack or falling away of
the mind.

That, more than this, do thou know it, my
offspring, whom I have been wont to hold in my
bosom, that the Three Brothers have now
perfected their preparations, and now, furthermore, let them say it, that "We forbid thee in this
matter. We caution thee, let not the minds of thy
people become insane from grief; let the matter,
instead, remain in perfect peace."

Thus, furthermore, let it be that for one poor

short day thou mayst continue to think in contentment and peace, thou noble ruler, my offspring, whom I have been wont to hold in my bosom.

In this manner, then, perhaps, let the Three Brothers, so denominated ever since they were in the prime of their affairs, do it thus.

Now more than this, do thou know it, this one (*indicating*), my offspring, thou noble ruler, whom I have been wont to hold in my bosom, the Word of thy adonni is on its way hence to thee.

THE FOURTEENTH ARTICLE / THE TORCH OF NOTIFICATION

Now, another thing I say. That when our grandsires, who have departed this life, conjoined their affairs, they made a decree, saying: "Here we place two rods together, and therein, moreover, we fix a torch between the two rods. We, every one of our council fires, own this torch equally. Moreover, this torch shall be one of the essential things wherever be the place in which a direful thing may occur.

"If it so be, that one will see what may cause them death then that person shall take this torch and that person shall indeed start at once through the Lodge of the League, and in such manner shall he

go that in the shortest possible time that person
shall pass the Lodge of the League, and all the
council fires shall have notice of the message, even
that very night.

"And it shall be done in such manner that there
shall be *no traces*—no forms—of lying down on
the path." Now, more than this, the Three
Brothers say, "Now we again put the torch
between the two poles, and we also now put back
there the small pouch containing the Short
Wampum, *the black strand of notification*, which
we equally own."[47]

Thus, furthermore, let it be, that for one poor
short day, thou noble ruler, my offspring, thou
mayst continue to think in contentment.

In this manner, then, perhaps, let them do it, the
Three Brothers, so denominated while they were
in the prime of their affairs.

Now, furthermore, do thou know it, thou noble
one, my offspring, their Word, *the attesting
wampum*, is going hence to thee.

These are the number of words, then, that the
Three Brothers desired to address to thee, this one
(*indicating*), my offspring, thou noble ruler,
whom I have been wont to hold in my bosom.
Now, more than this, we do expect that all our
words, thus addressed to thee, have come to pass,
for thy peace and welfare.

Now, more than this, do thou know it, this one
(*indicating*), thou yaanehr, my offspring, thou
noble ruler, whom I have been wont to hold in my
bosom, the Word, *the attesting wampum*, of thy
adonni is on its way hence to thee.[48]

THE FIFTEENTH ARTICLE / THE APPEAL FOR THE CANDIDATE

Now, another matter let us consider this day.
Thou must give strict attention to the words,
thou yaanehr, my offspring, whom I have been
wont to hold in my bosom.

Now, again I have set in order all thy affairs.
Now furthermore, the Three Brothers have been
noticing that the mat whereon thy co-worker was
wont to rest has been caused to be vacant.

Moreover, that they upon whom our forefathers
depended for wisdom and guidance, in uniting
their affairs, decreed, saying: "It matters not,
indeed, on which side of the Council Fire there is
a loss, it shall be possible, and it shall be urgent
that they shall again set the candidate's face
fronting the people; that they shall again raise
him up, that they shall again name him, and that
also he shall again stand upright in front of the
people."

More than this, thou yaanehr, my offspring, thou
noble ruler, the Three Brothers are on the

ceremonial path; and so now let them say it, "Do
thou now point out to us the one who shall be
our co-worker."

Thus, now, thou yaanehr, my offspring, thou
noble ruler, do thou know it; we Three Brothers
have completed the ceremony.

Now, then lastly, that which gave us notice of this
matter, *the black strand of notification*, now goes
hence to thee.[47]

Also, do thou know it, thou yaanehr, my
offspring, thou noble ruler, that immediately now
the Three Brothers shall rise to depart homeward;
and there, moreover, at the forest's edge, they
will lay down their pouches for the night.

There it is.

*As the orator has indicated, the Three Brothers now rise to leave,
paying tribute to the ancient custom whereby visiting delegations
withdraw after having made a proposal to the host council. But
the mourners waive the requirement—saying,* My uncles, we ask
you to kindly remain until further notice. That is all.—*and the
clearminded resume their seats.*

*For the last time the curtain is stretched. The mourners "re-
turn" all six verses of the Hymn, but with slight variations in the
wording of the first four, so that it appears as if the dead chief
himself is giving answer:*[49]

> The League has come again to greet me;
> The kindred come again to greet me;

The warriors come again to greet me;
The women come again to greet me.
My forefathers—what they established—
My forefathers—hearken to them!

The curtain is lifted. The mourners' orator returns, with wampum, the fourth through fifteenth articles of the Requickening Address. It is now nightfall or shortly thereafter.

V / The Investiture

When the last of the Requickening strings has gone back across the fire, the orator for the mourners (or hosts) will advise the clearminded (or visiting) chiefs:

You now have the completed words of both of us, the number of my father's kinsmen.

And now it will be possible to show his face right here before the crowd. Now one will raise him to a standing position in front of the chiefs and also one shall call his name, which is that of the dead chief. Now another thing: one will place him in the vacancy. Now, moreover, my father's kinsmen, you shall think that events have transpired here just as you specified when you did say, "Now show us the new man who will be our co-worker from now on." Therefore, be alert, for this is the real thing! Now you shall take a good look at him. For we are now going to show you your future colleague![20]

The long-awaited moment has arrived. In his paper of 1946, Fenton writes: "Although others besides myself . . . knew who was going to be the chief, no one let on, and the tension built in five hours of ceremonial reached a climax. The building over-flowed with anxious humanity . . ." Now the matron who "owns" the title of the deceased chief rises and moves toward the man who has been nominated by his fellow clan members to fill the vacant office. She takes his arm and, raising him to a standing position, leads him before the hosts' speaker, who presents him to the assembly:

Now all of you look here, for he is standing here before you, the one who was appointed by the owner of the title which reposes in that continuing lineage, the Bear Clan, whose bench was made empty where their late great one used to sit. And further, this one who came and stood there in front of you is the one whom they are crowning with antlers and henceforth you all shall denominate him Tahkahenhyunh.[20]

The speaker holds in his hand a string of white wampum to be kept by the woman whom the matron designates as "guardian" for the chief. The "guardian," whose duty will be to serve as the chief's cook on ceremonial occasions, comes forth and stands with the speaker. A man designated "chief's deputy" also stands. The speaker presents them both to the opposite moiety, sending the white wampum across the fire for confirmation. When the visiting chiefs have signified their approval and returned the wampum, a speaker for the visiting chiefs releases the Two Brothers, saying:

Now that together we have finished the work and all is clear between us, you and I are free.[20]

The hosts' speaker replies:

Now then, my father's kinsmen, together you and I have

finished everything. Therefore you shall be informed that the Two Brothers have prepared a feast. Accordingly the time being shall be devoted to this. And so let us eat together for a while. As soon as our meal is finished then the time shall be devoted to rejoicing together because the new one has been elevated that he may strive for the welfare of ongoing generations of our families. Now then we all shall rub antlers, you chiefs: *we shall dance.* Now, moreover, it is up to the crowd to have a good time.

So now, my father's clansmen, I now let escape from my hands our womenfolk. Accordingly you shall use them properly. Don't anyone treat them too roughly! (*This remark elicits laughter.*)

So now another thing. Time may also be devoted to something else. Perhaps one of you may have had a dream. Then in that event let us amuse our minds with dreams.[50]

1 / Since about 1715, when they adopted the Tuscarora (a related tribe formerly of North Carolina), the Iroquois have styled themselves the "Six Nations." A few non-Iroquoian groups, including certain Delawares and Tutelos, were also adopted. But as these tribes never attained full ceremonial privileges, it is sufficient here to consider only the five original members: Mohawk, Oneida, Onondaga, Cayuga, and Seneca. It may be of interest to note that the senior moiety included the most populous nation (Seneca), the most powerful (Onondaga), and the one perceived as most ancient (Mohawk).

2 / The summons is described in a seventeenth-century account quoted by Beauchamp (1895). Nowadays, at the Six Nations Reserve, the dead chief's deputy drives to the home of the firekeeper of the opposite moiety, shouting the death cry from his car window as he passes the other houses (Shimony). Cf. Parker, pp. 40, 108–9.

3 / Such has been the practice over the past hundred years. In earlier times, however, the clearminded chiefs and their followers chanted the Eulogy day after day on the trail as they made their

way toward the home village of the deceased (Hewitt and Fenton 1945).

4 / In order to call attention to the triadic phrasing of the original text, Hale's translation of this brief exordium has been broken into lines and stanzas. Actually each "stanza" should be a doublet of triples, regularly interlarded with repetitions of the familiar *haii haii* ("hail, hail!"). Following Beauchamp (1907), the first "stanza" reads:

> Hail, hail! Hail, hail! Now listen! Hail, hail! Hail, hail!
> You who completed the work! Hail, hail! Hail, hail!
> The Great League!
> Hail, hail! Hail, hail! Now it has become old. Hail, hail!
> Hail, hail! Now indeed. Hail, hail! Hail, hail! It is a
> wilderness again.

5 / The name Hiawatha may be translated "He Who Seeks the Wampum Belt," emphasizing the hero's role as peacemaker, or treaty-maker. It may also be translated "He Who Combs," i.e., he who combs the snakes from Atotarho's hair. See note 6.

6 / Atotarho ("Ensnarled"): the famous magician-chief from

whose head Hiawatha combed the "snakes" of evil thought.

7 / The kinship term seems to indicate a political relationship within the Onondaga council. Generally speaking, "brothers" sit together on the same side of the fire, while "cousins" face each other on opposite sides, as do "fathers" and "sons" or "uncles" and "offspring." In the case of the Onondagas, where ethnographic data are scanty, there has been no attempt to show these political relationships in the diagram (figure 2), preference being given to the presumed original clan affiliations, following Hale 1883.

8 / In performance the chant reminded Fenton (1946) of high Anglican Mass, the orator taking a fresh breath before intoning each line:

Now-today,
Have-I-been-greatly-startled,
By-your-voice-coming . . .

9 / The "few words" mentioned in the opening sentence of this paragraph allude to the first three articles, or Part I, of the Requickening, which is presently to be delivered here at the wood's edge. The remaining twelve articles, or Part II, are spoken of as the "mutual embrace of condolence" (or the "rubbing down of each other's bodies," as Fenton has it). The words "thither" and "principal seat" refer to the council house, where later the two moieties will reciprocally administer this "embrace of condolence," which is considered the main business of the day.

10 / Few of the twenty-three villages in this ancient roll call can be located with any certainty, nor was Hale able to translate all of the names. See Hale 1883; and Parker, pp. 27–8. (The Turtle is spoken of as "two clans," indicating a subdivision more pronounced in some of the nations than in others. The Turtle is "off-

spring" to the Wolf, but the Bear is the Wolf's "brother," indicating a moiety division with Wolf and Bear on the senior side and Turtle on the junior side. Hale supposed that these three were the original Iroquois clans.)

11 / The speaker alludes to the Iroquois god Teharonhiawagon, but in an exordial manner perhaps borrowed from missionaries. Cf. Hale 1883, p. 148.

12 / "It is that therefore as to THAT [i.e., the calamity mentioned in the preceding paragraph], [that] verily this present day I thrust, etc."

13 / Hewitt's peculiar construction "It is that, therefore, that . . ." must be read with the stress on "therefore." For example: "It is that THEREFORE that I shall stoop low." A simpler, if less faithful, rendering would be: "Moreover, I shall stoop low." In cases where the subject of the sentence has been inverted, the syntax unquestionably borders on the awkward. For instance: "It is that THEREFORE that has caused it to be so, the being that is demonic in itself." In other words, "Death, moreover, has caused it." But bear in mind that the style of the Requickening is "intermediate between speaking and singing" (Hale 1895). The skillful reader who wishes to capture its lofty, incantatory tone—or any reader who takes the trouble to practice—should find this version more than congenial.

14 / The Iroquois high chief, one of the council of fifty, has been styled by different writers as Federal Chief, lord, noble one, chief, sachem, senator, etc. Iroquois variants of the term are sayaaneh, yaanehr, royaner.

15 / The fawn-skin is merely a figure of speech.

16 / See note 11.

17 / "Thy sister's sons and daughters": a stylized expression meaning "thy clansmen," or, especially, "the posterity of thy clan." (In a matrilineal society a man must look to his sister's offspring to carry on his clan name.)

18 / The term "Chief Place" refers to the council house.

19 / The manner in which the wampum is returned (reported by Beauchamp, 1907, p. 385) suggests mere confirmation rather than reciprocity. Yet the ethnography as a whole makes it plain enough that the Requickening benefits both sides—a principle forcibly demonstrated in the Condolence witnessed by Fenton, where the first three articles were delivered *by the mourners,* then returned by the comforters. Cf. Hale 1895, Hewitt 1944.

20 / Source: Fenton 1946.

21 / From here on out, the Eulogy text as received by Hale appears to have been set down in skeletal form, no doubt for the sake of economy. I have taken the liberty of supplying, in italic, the phrases that I presume are missing.

22 / This important Wolf-clan chief, who forms a class by himself, was keeper of the wampum records for the Five Nations; hence the expression "There were combined the many minds!" He is considered a "son" to the chief named before him. See note 7.

23 / "Uncles of the two clans" evidently refers not only to the two chiefs of this class but also to the three members of the following class. Hale found that the chieftainships of the two classes were held by the Deer and Eel clans, respectively, but conjectured that all five had originally belonged to Wolf (as shown in figure 2). They are "uncles" to the above-named Hononwirehdonh. See note 7.

24 / Some ritualists believe that Sahhahwih ("He Bears a Toma-
hawk in His Belt") is merely an alternate title for Skahnahwahtih
("Over the Creek"), the chief described in the following line.
If so, there can be but forty-nine chiefs, not fifty. Probably the
idea stems from the peculiar nature of Skahnahwahtih, who
appears to be a dual personality, a war chief and a high (or peace)
chief at one and the same time (Parker, p. 52). The distinction
is an important one. A high chief is not ordinarily empowered
to lead war parties. A war chief, on the other hand, does not
ordinarily vote in the councils of the league. (Thus the league is
equated with peace.) See Hale 1883, Fenton 1950.

25 / I.e., he put away the clouds of war. One might conclude that
Sahhahwih-Skahnahwahtih had been a war chief who converted
to the cause of peace. See note 24.

26 / Or, at the entrance to the council house, the Eulogy may
be interrupted and performed again in its entirety from the beginning (Fenton 1946, p. 115). Cf. Beauchamp 1907, p. 378.

27 / The interpolated passage "Know that she, *society*, is grieving.
. . . thou deceased one hearken!" has been supplied from Fenton
(1946, p. 116).

28 / Hale (1883, p. 164) suggests that when new tribes were
received into the confederacy, these last two chiefs had the
formal office of "opening the doorway" to the newcomers. See
note 1.

29 / The Hymn, or rather the manner in which it is used, creates
an aura of mystery. It would seem that the living chiefs—on one
level—are communicating with their dead colleague, for whom the
Hymn is supposed to be a "song of farewell" (Fenton 1946, 1957).
Toward the close of the program, when the mourners respond
in kind, it is imagined that the dead chief himself is returning the
greeting. "This is evidently done to secure the departure of the

ghost in peace" (Hewitt 1917). But the Hymn may also be understood as a message of sympathy, extended by the comforters to the mourners (in which case the second line has been interpreted to read, "I come again to greet and thank the *dead chief's* kindred"—Hale 1883, pp. 64, 150). The mourners' reply then serves as the expected acknowledgment, cast in the form of a reciprocal greeting; while the stretched curtain symbolizes the darkness of grief (Hale 1895), or even, specifically, the widow's veil (Beauchamp 1907, p. 378). In context, however, the Hymn must be viewed at least partially as an epitomization of the chant called "Over the Great Forest," with which it is interwoven. The final verse of the Hymn ("My forefathers—hearken to them!") seems calculated to draw the hearers' attention to the "laws" about to be recited (per Hale 1883, p. 64); and the curtain itself must now be taken to symbolize the "great forest" that divides the two moieties (Hewitt, "Ethnological Researches Among the Iroquois and Chippewa," 1927). But bear in mind that the Hymn is often sung outside the ritual. Broadly speaking, its anthem-like verses combine to glorify both the league and the kinship system (whose essential components are the "warrior," i.e., the man, and the woman) upon which the league necessarily is based.

30 / The chanter looks ahead to that time when the fifty chiefs, having completed the Condolence and invested their new colleague with the horns of office, shall once again be faced with a death.

31 / Today the "horns" are merely a figure of speech. The point here is that the corpse must not be allowed to take away the badge of office. Rather the "horns" must be passed on to an appointed successor. (This is the first of the three laws.)

32 / "Hidden away among fallen trees": a figurative expression alluding to the long-abandoned custom of platform burial (per Simeon Gibson, cited by Fenton, 1946, p. 118).

33 / "By reason of the neck being white": an obscure phrase, the significance of which had already been lost by Hale's time. (A quite different, and in my opinion dubious, reading of this entire passage is offered in Fenton's introduction to the 1963 reprint of Hale's book.)

34 / So the corpse is to be taken down from its lofty platform (from which it was wont to pounce, vampire-like, upon the living; see Fenton 1946, p. 118) and placed at ground level, resting against the wall. But this is no solution either. For a description of the morbid funerary practices attached thereto, see Hale (1883, pp. 72–3).

35 / Note the orderly progression of the corpse from sky to earth-surface to underworld. (The banishing of the corpse is the second of the three laws.)

36 / In other words, the grief of the victim's kinsmen shall be verbally assuaged. There shall be no excessive veneration of the corpse. (Thus the third and final law.)

37 / In conclusion, the chanter invokes the hallowed founders, but naming only the principal chief (or chiefs) of each national roster and substituting, understandably, the title Dekanawidah where Tehkarihhoken might have been expected. The kinship terms refer to the intertribal relationships as set forth in the Eulogy (the Oneida is son to the Mohawk; the Onondaga, being brother to the Mohawk, is uncle to the Oneida; etc.), except for the cousinage of the two Seneca chieftains, which is, of course, intratribal.

38 / Yellow, or gall-colored, spots are supposed to result from an inward bitterness caused by grief. The allusion is evidently figurative, but Fenton notes that such spots are in fact associated with " 'gall trouble,' for which the Iroquois regularly take emetics in springtime." See Hewitt (with Fenton) 1944.

39 / The "Water-of-pity" is reminiscent of actual Iroquois medical practice. "The midwife drops an infusion of poplar bark down the baby's throat to purge its bowels," writes Fenton, "and the council of animals cure the good hunter by dropping the sacred Little Water medicine down his throat and revive him." See Hewitt (with Fenton) 1944, p. 72.

40 / Hewitt's translation of this paragraph as given in his paper of 1944 is hopelessly unclear. I have consequently substituted his earlier reading (Hewitt 1916).

41 / This refers to the mound of freshly upturned earth over a new grave.

42 / The tenth article assumes that the dead chief was murdered, a circumstance evidently common enough in days gone by. In recent performances this article has been omitted.

43 / The bereaved family is entitled to exact a price of twenty wampum strings from the murderer or his relatives, so satisfying the desire for revenge and avoiding the otherwise inevitable blood feud. The payment "binds their bones": that is, it keeps them alive, keeps them from becoming future murder victims.

44 / See note 11.

45 / See note 17.

46 / The speaker envisions the end of the world. Cf. J. N. B. Hewitt, "Iroquoian Cosmology," *Twenty-first Annual Report of the Bureau of American Ethnology*, 1904, pp. 175–6, and *Forty-third Annual Report of the Bureau of American Ethnology*, 1928, p. 480. See also p. 190.

47 / The reference here is to the wampum called "tears," sent by the mourners to the clearminded as a summons to the ritual.

48 / The wampum representing the fourteenth article is not to be confused with the black string of notification.

49 / I here invert each of the first four lines of Hale's Hymn, according to the information given by Fenton (1946, p. 121). See note 29.

50 / Source: Fenton 1946. On the subject of dreams, see Cuceb, entry for the ninth year and accompanying commentary under *comes the telling of destinies*, p. 243.

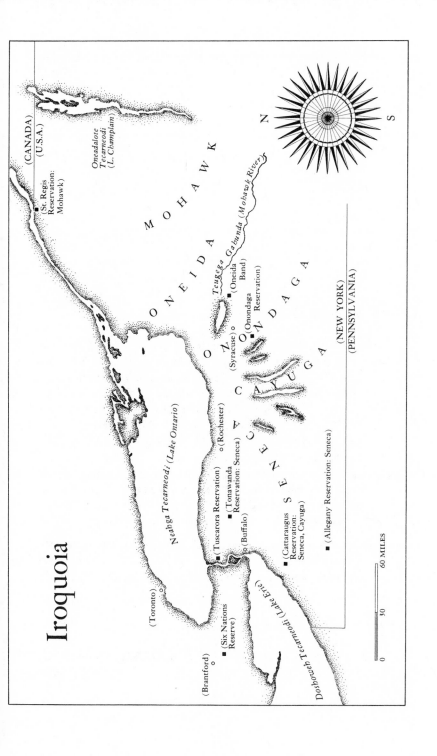

Iroquoia

(CANADA)
(U.S.A.)

Oneadalote Tecarneodi (L. Champlain)

■ St. Regis Reservation: Mohawk

M O H A W K

O N E I D A

Teugega Gahunda (Mohawk River)

■ (Oneida Band)

O N O N D A G A

■ Onondaga Reservation

N

○ (Syracuse)

C A Y U G A

S E N E C A

(NEW YORK)
(PENNSYLVANIA)

Neahga Tecarneodi (Lake Ontario)

○ (Rochester)

■ (Tuscarora Reservation)

■ (Tonawanda Reservation: Seneca)

■ (Cattaraugus Reservation: Seneca, Cayuga)

■ (Allegany Reservation: Seneca)

○ (Buffalo)

(Lake Erie) *Doshoweh Tecarneodi*

■ (Six Nations Reserve)

○ (Brantford)

○ (Toronto)

N

S

0   30   60 MILES

BIBLIOGRAPHY

I / Primary sources

MS. *Okayondonghsera Yondennase* ("Ancient Rites of the Condoling Council"). Missing? The Mohawk MS. of Chief John
"Smoke" Johnson (Six Nations Reserve, Brantford, Ontario),
transcribed by Hale for his *Iroquois Book of Rites* (see
below). Hale also consulted a similar text owned by John
Buck of the Six Nations Reserve. William Fenton (private
communication) is reasonably certain that neither of these
MSS. is now extant. As for Hale's transcription, it was
probably consumed in the Wellesley College Library fire of
1914. The only record of it that I have been able to discover
is a notation among Hewitt's personal papers (per Fenton)
to the effect that it had been deposited at Wellesley.

MS. 856, National Anthropological Archives, Smithsonian Institution, Washington. The Onondaga text of Chief John Arthur
Gibson's Requickening Address, recorded by J. N. B. Hewitt.

II / Condolence texts in translation

Hale, Horatio, *The Iroquois Book of Rites*, 1883, reprinted 1963 with an introduction by William N. Fenton. Hale's English translation is accompanied by a Mohawk paleograph, a Mohawk-English lexicon, textual commentary, and a series of introductory essays on Iroquois culture and history.

Hewitt, J. N. B., edited by William N. Fenton, "The Requickening Address of the Iroquois Condolence Council," *Journal of the Washington Academy of Sciences*, March 15, 1944, pp. 65–85. Published by Fenton after Hewitt's death.

Hewitt, J. N. B., "The Requickening Address of the League of the Iroquois," *Holmes Anniversary Volume*, 1916, pp. 163–79. Hewitt's first draft, superseded by his paper of 1944 (see above).

III / Ethnography pertinent to the Ritual of Condolence

Fenton, William N., "An Iroquois Condolence Council for installing Cayuga chiefs in 1945," *Journal of the Washington Academy of Sciences*, April 15, 1946, pp. 110–27.

Hale, Horatio, "An Iroquois Condolence Council," *Proceedings and Transactions of the Royal Soc. of Canada*, Second Series, Vol. I, section II, 1895, pp. 45–65.

Beauchamp, William M., "Civil, Religious and Mourning Councils and Ceremonies of Adoption of the New York Indians," *New York State Education Dept. Bulletin*, 402 (*N.Y. State Museum Bulletin* 113), 1907, pp. 341–451.

——— "An Iroquois Condolence," *Journal of American Folklore*, Vol. 8, 1895, pp. 313–16.

Fenton, William N., *The Roll Call of the Iroquois Chiefs*, Smithsonian Miscellaneous Collections, Vol. III, no. 15 (publication 3995), 1950. Also issued as *Cranbrook Inst. of Science Bulletin* 30.

———— *American Indian and White Relations to 1830,* 1957.

Hewitt, J. N. B., and Fenton, William N., "Some mnemonic pictographs relating to the Iroquois condolence council," *Journal of the Washington Academy of Sciences,* Oct. 15, 1945, pp. 301–15.

Hewitt, J. N. B., "Ethnological Studies Among the Iroquois Indians," *Smithsonian Miscellaneous Collections,* Vol. 78, no. 7, 1927, pp. 237–47.

———— "Ethnological Researches Among the Iroquois and Chippewa," *Smithsonian Miscellaneous Collections,* Vol. 78, no. 1, 1927, pp. 114–17.

———— "Some Esoteric Aspects of the League of the Iroquois," *Proceedings of the Nineteenth International Congress of Americanists Held at Washington, Dec. 27–31, 1915,* 1917, pp. 322–6.

Parker, Arthur C., *The Constitution of the Five Nations,* New York State Museum Bulletin, no. 184, 1916. Reprinted in *Parker on the Iroquois,* edited with an introduction by William N. Fenton, 1968.

IV / General ethnography and theory

Morgan, Lewis H., *League of the Ho-dé-no-sau-nee, or Iroquois,* 1851. Morgan's book is still the best general account of the Iroquois. The 1962 Corinth paperback edition has an introduction by William Fenton.

Shimony, Annemarie A., *Conservatism Among the Iroquois at the Six Nations Reserve,* Yale University Publications in Anthropology, no. 65, 1961.

Lévi-Strauss, Claude, "The Logic of Totemic Classifications" (chapter 2 of Lévi-Strauss's *The Savage Mind,* 1966). A provocative attempt to uncover the "masterplan" of totemic classification. Iroquois references.

Wallace, Anthony F. C., "The Rituals of Fear and Mourning" (chapter 4 of Wallace's *The Death and Rebirth of the Seneca,* 1970).

Harris, Marvin, "Law and Order in Egalitarian Societies" (chapter 16 of Harris's *Culture, Man, and Nature,* 1971).

Speck, Frank G., *The Iroquois: A Study in Cultural Evolution,* 1945, second edition 1955, reprinted 1969.

Foley, Denis, "The Iroquois Condolence Business," *Man in the Northeast,* Spring 1973. The Ritual of Condolence is shown to be part of a larger framework embracing burial rites and treaty conferences.

Weinman, Paul L., *A Bibliography of the Iroquoian Literature,* New York State Museum and Science Service Bulletin, no. 411, 1969.

Cuceb

A MAYA PROPHECY

". . . *comes the wind, the rain,*
comes the telling of destinies."

INTRODUCTION

Cast like a horoscope under the spell of celestial omens, the ritual epic called Cuceb assumes the form of a prophecy, which in turn masquerades as a book of years.

The prophecy, at least in part, is the messianic vision of a priest seeking his people's deliverance from an alien ruling class, the so-called Itzá, whose Mexicanized cohorts and mercenaries dominated the affairs of Yucatan during the last few hundred years prior to the Spanish Conquest. Together with apocalyptic portents—fire, flood, swarming insects, the shaking of the earth and the darkening of the skies—the prophet imagines the intervention of the great god Itzam Na, appearing as Amayte Ku ("Angular Lord"), come to expel the Itzá and restore the land to its rightful inheritors.

With due regard for tradition, he associates his vision with one of the 7200-day ritual periods—called katuns—by which Maya prophecy, like Maya history, was customarily measured. Accordingly, he sees a katun's worth of suffering under the rule of the Itzá, to be completed by the ending, or "turn," of the katun, bringing with it a reign of "goodness" and restitution.

The doctrine, and even the ritual, of the katun cult are the foundation upon which the prophecy rests. The central figure is a time god, the deity known as Lord of the Katun, who both *represents* the 7200-day period and in a sense *is* that period; for roughly twenty years (i.e., 7200 days) the Katun presides over the destiny of the world, but as his tenure draws to a close he suffers a loss of vitality, becoming corrupted by the sins (of the human community?) which are believed to gather within his body and to visibly alter its appearance ("The Katun begins to limp" reads a line from one of the ancient texts). And so in the due course of time the old lord degenerates into an unappetizing brute upon whom, in the person of a human surrogate, the priesthood may inflict certain tortures and even death in order to punish the accumulated guilt and make way for the incoming, or new, Katun.

To say that the prophet uses the old Katun as a metaphor for the predicted fate of the Itzá would not be quite correct, but the two are nevertheless neatly parallel—up to a point.

Though reviled as a scapegoat, the Katun is yet a god. When the ritual is stripped away, he reveals himself as a mystical traveler, circling the earth in an epic journey through space and time, bearing on his shoulders the *cuch*, or "burden," of destiny; and though the journey ends in death, the god himself, or rather the human surrogate, enjoys a kind of transfiguration, rising up to a paradise somewhere within the sky.

Possibly the name Cuceb (KOO-keb), translated "that which revolves," is a veiled reference to the life cycle of the katun lord; and probably the Katun is best considered not as a one-time god to be dispatched and replaced, but as an eternal being who is killed and resurrected repeatedly; thus the god embodies both a scourge and a hope.

Customarily, however, the Katun is spoken of in terms of a recurring series of thirteen lords, each presiding over his own

period of 7200 days and each with his own symbolism and
astrological associations. The Cuceb, specifically, is cast as a
prophecy for the fourth Katun in the series, the one whose
name is 5 Ahau. It links the flagitious rule of the enemy Itzá
with the waning influence of Lord 5 Ahau and looks forward
to the coming of the fifth lord in the series, Lord 3 Ahau,
whom the prophet closely identifies with the above-mentioned
Amayte Ku. As the katun "turns," so are the plagues, the
drought, and the bloodshed turned back upon the Itzá. The
Maya, who had been forced to seek refuge in the wilderness
during Katun 5 Ahau, now return to the "well" and "grotto"
of civilization, while the Itzá depart "in their misery" to live
"among trees, among rocks."

Superficially the text reads like a string of twenty-one individual prophecies, corresponding to the twenty-one years
during which a Katun 5 Ahau might presumably fall. But it
would be erroneous to assume, as some have, that such a dating
scheme is to be taken literally. What we have in fact is a
single unified prophecy, measured piecemeal against the katun's
passing years, whose names, like the tolling of a bell, follow
one upon the other with a rhythm and sequence all their own.
Even though a section of text may begin, "In the year 7 Cauac
such-and-such an event will occur," the reader must not be
deceived into thinking that the event has any *necessary* connection with the year whose name is 7 Cauac.

As a further embellishment, the prophet slips in a count of
tuns. That is, in addition to the count of the 365-day years, he
marks the passage of each twentieth part of the katun, i.e., the
period of 360 days known as the tun. And true enough, in so
doing he does occasionally note some ritualistic detail that
might be associated with the particular tun in question. But
in general, and despite exceptions, this double tolling of years
and tuns must be taken as a kind of ornamentation, running

along the periphery of the work (to change the comparison) like a serial frieze of months or seasons.

Beneath the quintessentially Mayan trappings—the katun cult and the rich calendrical symbolism—and juxtaposed with the seasonal cycle of decay and rejuvenation, is yet another, perhaps more deeply rooted cyclical pattern, one that is perceived by Indian mythmakers throughout the Americas as both a glory and a tragedy. Roughly speaking, it may be characterized as the ascent of ignorant man to a state of culture, accompanied by the tightening of societal (and sexual) bonds, a concomitant loss of innocence, a sense of guilt, the expectation of punishment, and an eventual reckoning in the form of natural or supernatural catastrophes, reducing the world once again to a state of wilderness. Countless myths of both simple and relatively complex Indian cultures concern themselves with this cycle or at least with one or two of its stages. At every step along the way the prospect for humanity, if hopeful, is also dire. The serpent who symbolizes the acquisition of knowledge in many of the myths is sometimes beneficent, sometimes malign. In the great myth cycle of the Iroquois, for example, the preculture state is supposed to have existed in a world above, where a woman said to be the first bride is sexually enticed by a dragon. As a result of her temptation, the sky opens and she finds her feet "hanging down into the chasm"; as she slips into the real world of society and culture, the serpent himself hands her the requisite corn and the homemaking utensils (Bureau of American Ethnology, *Forty-third Annual Report*, p. 480, and *Twenty-first Annual Report*, p. 224). Later, when the day of reckoning has arrived, when a sufficient number of sexual or social wrongs have been committed, the serpent may return to claim his own and the dangerous events of primal days may be reenacted. With this in mind, the Iroquois composer of the Ritual of Condolence, contemplating a serious breach of the social ethic, harks back to the origin myth and warns of a future time when "the feet of the people," like the feet of the first bride, "will hang over the abyss of the sundered earth" (see p. 160). Similarly the malign serpent of the Cuceb, Chac Uayeb Xoc, who is both water monster and fire dragon (but who must not be confused, at least not at this level, with the serpentine manifestations of the supreme god Itzam Na), comes in the end to claim the guilty Itzá. See pp. 211, 219, and 233. (In the Cuceb, as already suggested above, we have the interesting and quite common psychological phenomenon of guilt projected onto an enemy tribe. It is the hostile Itzá, not the persecuted Maya, who must take the final blame, who endure the wrath of Chac Uayeb Xoc, and who are forced out into the wilderness. Thus the economy of the Maya "psyche" is preserved—that is, the guilt is taken care of—with a happy, if illusory, ending for the beleaguered "patient.") But this is not to say that the Cuceb is a culture myth in disguise, merely that certain aspects of its symbolism, if their significance is to be fully grasped, must be seen in context with the entire fabric of native American mythology. If space permitted, the subject could be pursued at greater length, starting perhaps with a renewed consideration of the Quetzalcoatl myth, especially Fragments C and D, in which the doomed hero is a culture bringer—and not overlooking Fragment D, "chapter" 5, in which the sexual guilt of the Toltecs is projected onto a representative of the alien Huaxtec tribe. The reader is left to draw his own conclusions.

Not counting the inscriptions in stone—which belong in a

class by themselves—the literature of the pre-Conquest Maya survives principally in four hieroglyphic codices and in the several Latin-script compendia known as the Books of Chilam Balam. Of the hieroglyphic books, only the one residing in Paris, the so-called Paris Codex, contains anything that might resemble a prophecy such as the Cuceb, and inasmuch as the glyphs have not been deciphered, even this is a wild conjecture. The Chilam Balam books, on the other hand, comprise a modest treasury of literature that is both interesting and accessible: three epic prophecies (of which the Cuceb is the finest), about a dozen minor prophecies, a migration history of the Itzá, rituals, prognostics, personal memoranda, fragments of old songs, certain "chronicles," and other items.

Written in phonetic Maya, using the alphabet learned from Spanish missionaries, these native bibles are the secret compilations of Yucatec priests, prepared during the early colonial period in defiance of a general ban against non-Christian teachings. Copied and recopied throughout the sixteenth, seventeenth, and eighteenth centuries, they eventually fell into disuse and were either lost or spirited out of Yucatan by antiquaries. Of those that survive, the most valuable are the Chilam Balam of Chumayel, the Chilam Balam of Tizimin, and the Chilam Balam of Mani. (The Cuceb is preserved in the Tizimin and, with minor variations, in the Mani. Though rooted in pre-Conquest sources, the Cuceb as we have it obviously belongs to the colonial period—and contains certain allusions to Christianity which I will attempt to explain in the commentary following the text.)

Bristling with puns and archaisms and marred by copyists' errors, the Chilam Balam books have been generally approached with the greatest of caution, mixed at times with abject resignation. It would almost be fair to say that without the painstaking labor of the late Ralph L. Roys, the best of this material would still be wrapped in mystery. Credit should also be given to the distinguished Mayanist Alfredo Barrera Vásquez, and other names might be mentioned as well; but Roys's work, despite imperfections, comes the closest to establishing a standard.

Roys's English translation of the Cuceb, published in 1949, though convincingly accurate on the whole, unfortunately lacks the clarity of his earlier and much better known *Book of Chilam Balam of Chumayel*. By contrast, the pioneering Spanish version of Alfredo Barrera Vásquez and Silvia Rendón, published a year earlier, reads marvelously—yet advances more than a few interpretations with which it is now difficult to agree. Accordingly, the translation presented here is essentially the work of Roys—but largely recast from available paleographs and with due attention to the Spanish of Barrera and Rendón. The paleographs I have used are the Tizimin (with Mani variants) published by Roys and the Mani as published by Ermilio Solís Alcalá in his *Códice Pérez*. I have also used a photographic copy of the Mani, or Codex Pérez, Cuceb obtained from the Peabody Museum at Harvard. The entire text of the Cuceb has been included, even the copyists' interpolations and even the glyphs that adorn the Mani version, reproduced (after Roys) in approximately the same positions in which they appear in the manuscript.

Words and phrases printed in italic are strictly glosses, either my own or those borrowed from Roys or from Barrera and Rendón, added to facilitate the reading of what is otherwise a quite literal translation. Many of the glosses are simply translations, either etymological or sometimes rather free, of the Maya term immediately following (or preceding).

For simplicity's sake, Maya consonants may be pronounced as in English, the vowels as in Spanish or Italian, with the following exceptions: *x* has the value of *sh*, hence *Uxmal* (OOSH-mal); *c* is invariably hard, as in *Cuceb* (KOO-keb); double vowels, as in *caan*, are simply prolonged (hence *caan* and *can* are virtual homonyms); *u* before a vowel has the value of *w*, hence *cauac* (CAH-wahk); a consonant written with an apostrophe is to be followed by a glottal stop, as in *t'ul*, which may be approximated by sounding the consonant explosively, or by adding a quick catch in the throat, roughly *tuh-HOOL*. The accent is on the penult unless otherwise indicated.

CUCEB

Translated from the Maya by Ralph L. Roys,
revised by John Bierhorst

FIRST YEAR / 13 KAN

13 Kan as it falls on 1 Pop: taken is the idol of the
katun of 5 Ahau—in the year 1593. On 15 Tzec it
speaks its name and here I declare the coming
charge.

On the day that the katun is taken, the katun's
face and the point of its change will be Mayapan.
Then will the child of the quetzal, the child of
the *green bird* yaxum, descend. In its time will
the offspring of woman, the offspring of man, be
devoured: the skulls will be heaped in its time.
The dawning, the vigil, the great tearing down of
the walls *will come. And then* will the trunk of
the ceiba be covered with seals.

Owing to its complexity, the Cuceb has not been annotated with num-
bered notes, which would have proved so numerous as to mar the text.
Instead, the reader will find a commentary keyed by phrase, beginning
on p. 223.

It will be then that the water sources are dry. It
will be then that T'ul Caan Chac, *Chac of the
Dripping Sky*, stands over the muddy water,
stands erect at the end of the water. Mourned will
be that which is written in the heart of the
plumeria. In its time, in its katun would it be—
would another power come over Ah Chaante,
Beholder, Kinich Chaante, *the Sun-Eyed Beholder*,
and it shall be born in the sky.

With the passing of 13 Kan would it be. Between
the years 1593 and 1594 would it fall.

SECOND YEAR / 1 MULUC

1 Muluc is seated: and then will the mountains,
one to another, speak over the surrounding earth,
over Ah Uuc Chapat, *Seven Centipede*. The
charge will be seven, seven the surcharge during
its second tun. Breechcloths are lost, mantles
lost to the childless generations. Their bread
will be snatched away, the water snatched out of
their mouths. Mandata.

THIRD YEAR / 2 IX

2 Ix: a time of sudden violence, a time when fire
will flare in the heart of the province. The earth
will burn, the sky will burn: a time when the

stored provisions are used, a time when the skies
are implored. Lost is the bread, lost the food.

The screech owl will cry, the horned owl will
cry at the crossing roads, throughout the earth,
throughout the sky. The wasps will clamor *and
swarm. And then* will they clamor—the miserable
ones—in the rule of Ah Bolon Yocte, *Lord
Nine Strides*, Ah Bolon Kanan, *Lord Precious
Nine.*

Fallen is the face of the savannah land, fallen the
face of the walled enclosure. *Yet* a time will there
be when he that remains is removed, when Buluc
Ch'abtan, *Eleven Breast of Creation*, son of Ah
Uuceb, shall rule in the land, shall rule in the
province. This is the time. It shall occur, at the
edge of the sea.

Chac Mumul Ain holds open his jaws, Chac
Uayeb Xoc holds open his jaws. In its time will
the wasps be heaped upon that which remains of
the water, upon that which remains of the food.
Three folds of the katun *now* would it be, in the
third tun—in the time, in the reign of Lord Katun
5 Ahau. Mandata.

FOURTH YEAR / 3 CAUAC

3 Cauac: the time when they will go out from
their well, from their grotto. They beg for their

food. They roam through the night, begging for
water. Where will they drink their water? Where
will they eat at least leavings of bread? Ah Uucte
Suy, *Seven Screech Owl*, Ah Uucte Chapat, *Seven
Centipede*, will startle their hearts unaware. And
still in its time would it be, in its katun: would
they of the well, *would they* of the grotto, *seek*
among trees for their food, among rocks for their
food. To the plumeria they point. Their bread it
would be, of plumeria their bread in *the time of*
its rule.

Then would he take up his burden. The third tun
would it be; and yet there would be Lord 13 Ahau
Buluc Ch'abtan, *Lord 11 Ahau, Lord 9 Ahau.*
Comes the removal of the burden *of 5 Ahau*, the
end for him—below and on high. 5 is his burden;
he departs from his reign.

This is the time of 3 Cauac. Maṇḍata.

FIFTH YEAR / 4 KAN

4 Kan: the time of the waning of Katun 5 Ahau.
In its time, in its katun, the skulls shall be
gathered; a humming of flies would there be at
the crossroads, at the resting places, and at the
four corners beside the four roads; and upon his
passing, the screech owl will cry, the horned owl
will cry—the dove will cry. Ulu!

Comes the commanding of Chac Uayeb Xoc,
Great Demon Shark. The trees will sink, the
stones will sink. Ah Uuc Chuuah, *Seven Scorpion,*
comes forth in its time: the face of the earth will
burn, and the frogs will croak at noon in their
wells.

The command will be loosened in 4 Kan when
another power comes over the white jaguar, over
the red jaguar, over Masuy, when in the fifth tun
of Lord 5 Ahau comes Buluc Ch'abtan to
pronounce the word of the day, the word *that
will rise* from the painted signs. *And with it* the
quelling, *the exceeding in number,* comes over the
host of Ah Itzá. Thus his command, he seeks his
burden, and they shall be gone.

Then will the son of the day, the son of the night,
declare his command. Comes a time when the
burrowing opossum and the red jaguar will bite
one another, when also in 4 Kan a new rule
arrives; and the sky will move and resound, the
earth will move and resound, as the sun and the
earth come together within the province, within
the navel of the katun. Then will he be seated,
then will the benefits be his, in his time and in
his katun.

SIXTH YEAR / 5 MULUC

5 Muluc: the time when he passes on, when his

eye will be pierced and he vomits that which he swallowed, so it is said, and gives up his surcharge.

In Katun 5 Ahau is the time, in 5 Muluc the time, when there will be bread *yet* farther from the province.

In its rule would be water, his rule alone, *if* he were to yield his command, *if* the burden were shifted. Harsh his command. Alone does he rule. He stands at the muddy water, stands erect at the *end of the* water. Of sin is their drink by day, by night, at the *shrinking* pools and everywhere over the earth at that time and at once when it rules.

Then at that time comes a noise at the well, at the grotto, for then would it happen to them, the Itzá; in its time they depart in their misery, depart from the well, from the grotto; and they shall go out among trees, among rocks. Thus would it be, would it be declared, to him who remains in the time, who remains in the katun. Mandata.

SEVENTH YEAR / 6 IX

6 Ix: the time when the bird, *the prophecy,* of the katun shall be composed, a time of penance: removed are the breechcloths, *removed* the mantles; the time of Ahau Can, *Lord Serpent, the time of* the seizing of the jewel from Chac Bolay

Ul, *Great Predator Lord;* the time when he shall
be set in the sky, *shall Ahau Can,* and he shall
observe the holder of the mat, the holder of the
throne, when he vomits that which he begged,
which he swallowed, which passed through his
throat; when the children of Maax Cal, *Monkey
Speaker,* turn traitor: for *the monkey* Maax Kin,
the monkey Maax Katun, specter of the earth, has
loosened their breechcloths. Such his command.
Red his breechcloth. From the north did he come,
from the west did he come; *then* were they sold,
were the children of Uuc Suhuy Sip, in his time,
in his katun. Of sin is his word, of sin is his mouth.

Comes a time when the drum will resound on
earth and the rattle on high, when the bird, *the
prophecy,* of the katun shall be composed; the
katun will turn: comes a violent tearing, a ripping:
the skies will be parted, the clouds will be parted,
suddenly, at once, in the face of the sun, in the
face of the moon.

Of no use, of no profit, are you the motherless,
you the fatherless, in the fold of the end of the
katun. Lost will be that which you knew, which
was known of you. Comes a time when the dry
leaves are heaped above you; gone are your
breechcloths, your mantles; gone is your mask,
gone your home. Mandata.

EIGHTH YEAR / 7 CAUAC

7 Cauac, 1 Pop, in the time of the seventh tun:
the time of the fold, the time when the soot is
removed from *the monkey* Maax Kin, from *the
monkey* Maax Katun; a mounding of skulls *would
there be.*

Comes a time when the red jaguar's back will be
gouged; a time when his teeth will be broken, a
time when the kinkajou's claws will be pulled.
The bread does he covet, he covets the water: he
puts down his knee, he puts out his foot and the
palm of his hand; and his face shall be maddened
in *the time of* its reign. Buluc Ch'abtan arises:
he departs *from his reign. And then* in that time
is extinguished the fire of him that remains of
Ah Itzá. Up to three folds of katuns *now* would
it be.

NINTH YEAR / 8 KAN

8 Kan, 1 Pop, in the eighth tun would it be, in
Katun 5 Ahau would it be: a time when they will
be crouched at their caves. The mountain will
burn, the valley will burn. Fire will flare in the
great sucte trees; and the sandy banks of the sea
will burn, and the *seeds of the calabash* Sicil will
burn and the *calabash* Kum will burn; and also the
Macal, *yam*, will burn. At Ichcaansihó, *Birth of
Its Face in the Sky*, will the flame of the katun be

drenched, will the burdens of Ah Itzá, *he of Itzá*,
be gathered upon him and he receives the harsh,
the painful charge. The living rock will crack;
the tinamou cries out, the deer will cry out. On
the white savannah will Ix Kan Itzam T'ul, *She
the Yellow Iguana of Dripping Water*, be
scattered, and it shall appear to *the wise ones*
Ah Nitob, Ah Maycuc, upon the savannah. In its
time will the breechcloths be white, will the
mantles be white, in the katun of the lost ones, in
the misfortunes of life.

In its time comes the wind, the rain, *comes* the
telling of destinies. *Comes* the rule *in its* time,
comes the rule: Buluc Ch'abtan. In the eighth tun
would it be, would it come to pass. Mandata.

TENTH YEAR / 9 MULUC

9 Muluc, 1 Pop: then will the name 5 Ahau be
declared; will Ah Uuc Yol Sip, *Lord Seven Heart
of Error*, declare his command. In its time will
be strength, will be much youthful vigor. In its
time will the aged engender, the aged conceive.
Everywhere over the land in that time prevails the
command of *the monkey* Maax Kin, the monkey
Itzá; come the weeping faces, the fleshless faces:
covered with blood are the roads, are the resting
places *beside the roads*, to the north, to the west.
The eyes are uplifted, the neck outstretched
toward Ahau Can, *Lord Serpent*.

Then will the stick be raised, the stone be raised, *raised* over the mother, *raised* over the father, for Ah Uuc Yol Sip, *Lord Seven Heart of Error*, for sevenfold rashness, for sevenfold greed. *For* then in its time comes the truth of the katun: punishment for guilt is its face, is the face of Ix Chaante, *Beholder*, fulfilling its law in its reign. Then over its face in the sky, the face of the youth, will another descend, crossing over the night, crossing over the day. In its ninth tun *would it be*. Mandata.

ELEVENTH YEAR / 10 IX
Part I

10 Ix, 1 Pop, in the time, in the reign—in the katun—of 5 Ahau. The heavenly fan, the heavenly bouquet, the bouquet of the ruler, descends *from the skies*. Then will he point with his finger, will he be established, will he be declared, will he be erected; and on that day, possessing his rule, his cup, and his throne, his mat and his seat, would he be seated; Amayte Ku, *Angular Lord*, would he be; and he at his food would be seated. The command shall be taken, taken the cup, taken the bowl; for he is declared *in his rule* at the time of the setting in place of the stone, at the time of the change of the mat and the change of the throne. And they will go out to the land of trees, to the land of rocks, at the pronouncement of his law and his teaching.

A *new* cup is created that he may have drink.
And on that day when his eyes are unbound, the
cup will be brackish, brackish the drink, at the
time of the setting in order of the mat *for* Yax
Bolay Ul, *New Predator Lord:* not for his mouth
is there plentiful water. Then P'iltec receives his
donation. The serpents are linked at the tail, at
the tail will the beasts be linked; thus would it
be, would it come to pass in its time. He takes the
fire, *does* Ah Uuc Yol Sip, *Lord Seven Heart of
Error:* his time is of forcible seizure, of greed:
dried are the waters.

Then removed is the last of the mat, the last of
the cup. Comes the rule of the knee of *the priest*
Ah Kin, the green-*mantled* knee of Ah Coctun
Numya, *Knife of Ill Fortune and Pain.* Angular is
the face of the lord; to him is it granted: to him
the remainder of the throne, to him the remainder
of the mat, to him the sky. So *would it be at*
the gazing of Buluc Ch'abtan, so would he
comfort the soul of Ah Siyahtun Chac.

Suddenly at once would it be in its time, in the
time of the turn *of the katun, the time of* the
weeping of Ahau Tun, *Lord Jade*, Ah Niy Pop,
Chief Ruler, and of Ah Masuy. Comes the
dawning, the descent of Ah Kinchil, *Lord
Sun-Eye*, Ah Chac Chibal, *Great Lord of
Affliction.* Then is the time of the coming of
misery to him who remains of Ah Itzá, here in the
province of Mayapan, *Banner of the Maya,*
fulfilling the end, *fulfilling* the time. Mandata.

ELEVENTH YEAR / 10 IX
Part II

 10 Ix it would be; at the end of the tun would it
be; a time when they run with their shields on
their backs, a time when the trunk of the ceiba
is covered with seals; and they that remain will be
hanged. A time when Ah P'iltec *comes forth to*
receive his donation: then from the poor will he
take it; from the wretched he takes his donation,
for then at the four crossed roads does he take
his donation, at the four resting places *beside
the four roads.* In its time will the charge of the
mountain descend to Masuy: here will it happen,
at Mayapan, *Banner of the Maya*, in Mani, in
May Ceh, *Deer Hoof*, in Xau Cutz, *Turkey
Claw.* Here is the passing of all things, here it
shall happen: an end shall arrive; in its katun the
redbird, the redtail, will dance in the dust at the
grotto, upon the savannah; and he shall arise.

Here shall it happen, for these are the birds, the
augury, of Halach Uinic, *the chief.* Then the ix
uixum, the bird of the rulers, will hop and turn
in the air, fulfilling the command of *Ah* Buluc
Am, *the diviner*, called Montezuma. Here it is
ended at May Ceh, *Deer Hoof;* here is the passing
of all things; and it shall be said: "Here did it
happen, here passed the Itzá." To them was it
spoken by Montezuma, the jewel of Itzá, for
his was the name given Ah Buluc Am, *the
diviner.*

So would it be, still in its katun. So would it
happen, for this is the katun when Hapay Can,
Sucking Serpent, arrives. In its time they prepare
for the end: perching in swarms, the quail will
cry out from the branch of the ceiba. *Comes* the
end of his begging, the end of his greed, *the end
of* the reign of Lord 5 Ahau. Then will the cup
be turned mouth up, the mat established; *taken*
are your breechcloths, *taken* your mantles,
taken your dress, according to the command of
the *tenth* tun. And they shall come forth from the
well, from the grotto. Mandata.

TWELFTH YEAR / 11 CAUAC

11 Cauac, 1 Pop, in the eleventh *tun:* still in the
reign of Ah Cakin Pop, *He of the Two-Day Mat*,
Ah Cakin Dzam, *He of the Two-Day Throne*,
would it be.

Set in its place is the cup of the Weeping Mask,
of the masked Bacab, Ah Cantzicnal, *He of Four
Corners*, at the seating of the tun in the eleventh
tun of the katun. Then Ah Cantzicnal, *He of
Four Corners*, Ah Can Ek, *He of Four Darkness*,
Ah Sac Dziu, *He the White Cowbird*, comes
forth in its time. In its time, in its katun, will
Ah Cantzicnal, *He of Four Corners*, take that
which is his; and as Ix Tol Och, *Mummer
Opossum*, he appears in its time, preparing the

wine of the katun; on 11 Xul it would be. Then
will another word come forth, another teaching,
and prayers to Ku Caan, *Sky Lord;* a time when
the sky will be favorable, a time when the serpents
are linked *at the tail, one to another.* New
breechcloths are taken, new mantles. A new
lord of the mat, of the throne, *will there be,* and
his face shall appear in the sky. In its reign comes
the loss of the rule of the katun; *and then* will
he follow the road of the jaguar, the serpent, *the
road of* Chac Bolay Ul, *Great Predator Lord.*

A time will there be when they, the Itzá, prepare
one another in the heart of the forest, in the heart
of the thicket; a time when the soul of *Ah*
Siyahtun Chac will cry aloud. The days of the
katun are misery; misery of ill fortune will they
endure, they the children of Ah Itzá, the
descendants of day, the descendants of night.
Comes a swarming of wasps in its time at the edge
of the trees; at the edge of the thicket; a swarming
of bees, of the Red Demon Bees, upon the
numberless white ones. Mandata.

THIRTEENTH YEAR / 12 KAN

In the time of 12 Kan, 1 Pop, in the twelfth tun:
then at that time will the word of the day be
declared. The descendants of day, the descendants
of night will tell their true destinies one to
another.

On earth, in the sky, would it be. In the twelfth
tun would it be. The sky will burn, the earth will
burn. An end to greed! What then might not
occur? Drought. And prayers to *One Lord,*
Hunab Ku. The ruler will weep; the years of
drought will be seven; the living rock will crack;
the nests of the birds will burn; and the branch of
the sucte tree will burst into flames—on the open
savannah, and in the ravines.

Then they return to their well, to their grotto.
Then will they take the provisions they've
stored. Now will the offering be made by *the
priest* Ah Kin, by the green-mantled knee;
thirteen are his surcharges, knotted his girdle;
angular the face of *the priest* Ah Kin. Now they
return to their well, to their grotto again; their
prayer is received at the grotto; and he shall be
killed on his heap of stones, shall the holder of the
mat, the holder of the throne. An end to greed, an
end to tribute. They return to their well, to their
grotto again.

Then will there be a new reign, a new teaching,
according to the word of the priest Chilam Balam.
Just as it may be, so it may not be. Yet they shall
see it behind and before, they the descendants of
Ah Itzá in their misery—it comes—when it comes
to pass, in the land of Sacnicteil, *White Plumeria,*
Mayapan, *Banner of the Maya,* Cuzamil, *Place of
the Swallows,* when it comes to them at the mouth
of the well, at the mouth of the grotto, and upon
the savannah. Comes a time when the walls are

destroyed and the house thrown down, when *destruction* comes over the lords of the land, the hooded ones, lords of the hills.

The monkey Maax Kin, the monkey Itzá, would there be—at once—to declare the command of the fatherless, motherless. *Yet* would it be in its time, in its katun: the word, the law, of him that remains, the seed of Itzá. In the time of Lord 5 Ahau, in its twelfth tun, would it be.

In its time comes the drinking of wine, *comes* the power of the katun; the wooden mask shall laugh. The cup is established, established the bowl and established the seat. In the katun of Lord 5 Ahau, in its twelfth tun would it be. Mandata.

FOURTEENTH YEAR / 13 MULUC

In the thirteenth tun is 13 Muluc on 1 Pop. 1 Oc would be the day when the *power of the* mat, of the throne, descends.

In the thirteenth *tun* would it be, in the time of the joint rule, in the remaining time of his rule in the sky. Great is the cup, great is the bowl, that they may consume together the water they've begged, the crumbs that remain of the bread, consuming together the remains of that which they've begged. In the time, in the katun, of 5 Ahau would it be. And he had come forth to the

seat in his rule, had *Great Slime Crocodile*, Chac
Mumul Ain, in the katun of Ho Habnal Tok,
Five Sharpened Flint.

Here would it happen, in Chacnacultún,
Ichcaansihó, *Place of the Great Piled Stone, Birth
of Its Face in the Sky*, in Saclactun, *Place of the
White Stone*, beside the savannah, in the heart of
the land. Comes a time when the katun will point
with his finger, *point* to the realm of *Ah* Itzá;
there would it happen, beside the savannah.

Then will he seek out the son of the day, the son
of the night. So may it happen, so may it not
happen. This is the word—*the word* for you,
you the motherless, the fatherless ones. Mandata.

FIFTEENTH YEAR / 1 IX

In the fourteenth *tun* would it be: *1 Ix* on 1 Pop:
in the fourteenth tun. In its time, in its katun,
Ah Xixteel Ul, *the Furrowed Lord*, Chac Uayeb
Xoc, *Great Demon Shark*, will appear: and then
will the fire be set; by the tail will the shark be
set, will he thus be set, will *the shark* be set in the
sky, in the clouds. It shall be seen, everywhere.
Covered is the face of the sun, covered the face
of the moon. In the fourteenth tun would it be.

Death will the wooden mask give to Xiuit for his
insolence to his mother, his insolence to his father,

for the insolence of his lineage of offspring, of youths. Gone are the remaining *chiefs* Halach Uinicob: no more shall they be. An end to the loss of our precious stones. Gone are *the chiefs,* taken by Chac Uayeb Xoc, *Great Demon Shark.* Comes the misery, the heaping of skulls: *of no use,* of no profit, are they in the time of the katun, the time of its rule. An end to the last of the race of Itzá. Not in the west, not in the north will they find one another; the beasts of the hills shall be bitten. It shall be done. In the fourteenth tun would it be.

Comes the misery of the time, the misery of the katun; the Xulab *ants* shall descend, *the bees* Chac Uayeb Cab shall descend to break into the grotto, the well.

Fallen is the charge of the *chief* Halach Uinic, as declared in the sacred paintings, the painted signs of the priests.

Then did they see it in the surcharge of the katun; then was it seen: the falling of the charge of the katun, the sinning of 1 Ahau; then was it read in the Book of Seven Generations by *the priest* Ah Tep'an Ciz, *Enveloped in Stench,* and by Ah Buluc Am, *the diviner.* In the fourteenth tun would it be.

Then will the Batabs, *They of the Ax,* be lost; and the *chief* Halach Uinic will fall from his rule. In the fourteenth tun would it be.

SIXTEENTH YEAR / 2 CAUAC

In the fifteenth *tun would it be*, in the time of
Lord 2 Cauac on 1 Pop, at the end of the law of
Lord 5 Ahau: the Katun paces itself *to
completion*: the knife descends, the penis descends;
the cord will appear and the arrow appears. In its
fifteenth tun would it be.

Comes the tearing out of the eyes of him who
clings to the chair, who exults in his rule, who
usurps, who extorts; then will the jade no longer
be crushed, the precious stones no longer be
crushed; the time when the arrows come
gathered in sheafs; *when* Kinich Chaante, *the
Sun-Eyed Beholder*, appears, so-called Kinich,
Sun-Eyed.

Comes Buluc Ch'abtan; *and* he shall be gone; then
affliction shines down on the *ruling* intruders,
lords of the land, the hooded ones, lords of the
hills; nor does he take tribute from those who
would follow the proper road.

Comes the time of the sudden death: this is its
slavery: *it strikes*, it fells; it fells *and beats down,
drawing* vomits of blood.

Comes the binding of the burden of *another*
Katun; in the katun of 5 Ahau would it fall.
Comes the retribution to Ah Itzá in the first of

the katun, the first of its years: bound to the tree
is *the Madness of the Time,* Co Kin, *the Madness
of the Katun,* Co Katun: nor would he go free in
the day, nor go free in the night, would Co
Katun: his heart would be turned.

And then will the emblem of Ah Cantzicnal, *He
of Four Corners,* the Bacab, be taken: he comes
to fulfill its command: in its time would it be,
in the time of 2 Cauac. The earth will shake.
Comes the headlong descent of the katun, the
katun of Mummer Opossum. The weakening *will
come,* the pursuit, the mocking of the Katun.

He shall understand it if there be a priest, if his
soul is unspoiled. Mandata.

SEVENTEENTH YEAR / 3 KAN

In the sixteenth tun, in the time of Lord 3 Kan
on 1 Pop would it be, would the burden be bound
on the Katun. Bound are the eyes of the lords of
the world in its reign. *But* the Katun shall not be
mocked in the time of 3 Kan.

Spots are removed from the red jaguar, white
jaguar; claws shall be drawn, teeth shall be drawn
from the jaguars of Ah Itzá. None shall there be.

Great rains in its time, great winds shall there
be; and the face of the god shall come forth to

the mat, to the throne; for they had gone out
among trees, among rocks, revering his image.

Gone is the cup, the chair; gone the mat when
Lord 3 Ahau takes the road. Comes another law,
another rule: changed are the priests at the
changing of the katun: comes the change of the
cup, the change of the bowl, the change of the
rule; comes the counting, the molbox, *the closure;*
comes another law, comes another reign.

To the north, to the west, still in its sixteenth
tun would the rule of the katun prevail in the land.
Behind us, before us, still in the reign of Lord 5
Ahau would it be.

EIGHTEENTH YEAR / 4 MULUC

In the seventeenth tun on 4 Muluc: the coming of
the time when the katun attaches *itself to another,*
the time when a coming together of katuns is
made *that* would bury the Katun; the time of the
white rain, the weakness, the cruel years. *Three
Heaper of Skulls,* Ah Ox Kokol Tzek, will sweep
through the province, will gather the skulls.
Excessive suns will lay waste the land. *There is*
sudden death. Days of hunger and days of thirst.
The water will fail, the springs and the veins in
the earth grow dry. Bloodied are the roads,
bloodied the rest houses: bewailed are the flies
at the gates of the towns. Buluc Ch'abtan,

Bulucte-ti-Chuen, is his face in its rule. The god
will weep, the world will weep. They remember
their mother, their father. Death will they suffer
for three folds of katuns, lost, dispersed in the
forests, the thickets, by the order of thirst, by
command of the sun.

So would it be in the seventeenth tun, so it appears
in the painted signs of the Book of Seven
Generations, as read by the priest Chilam Balam,
reading the roll of the katun, and the priest Napuc
Tun, and the priest Hun Uitzil Chac of Uxmal:
made known from the painted signs of the anahte,
the book of the prophet, according to the law, by
the one who perceived it, *the prophet* Ah Kauil
Ch'el, when he saw how the charge would fall.
So was it spoken by Chilam Balam, *as ordered* by
Hunab Ku, *One Lord*, Oxlahunti Ku, *Thirteen
Lords*. So would it happen. Fighting, hardship, a
tribute of cloth would it be by command of the
painted signs. Perhaps it would be, perhaps it
would not be: here at the tree of the chapat, *the
centipede;* or if not, upon bread, or on water: for
great is the punishment of guilt, the command
of the katun: it appears in the signs of the katun,
appears in the anahte, *the book of the prophet*.

Here would it be in the north of the land, in the
south of the land, here in the city of Mayapan,
Banner of the Maya: Ah Uuc Chapat, *Seven
Centipede*, will make himself fearful; Ah Uuc Yol
Sip, *Seven Heart of Error*, will make himself
fearful. Mandata.

NINETEENTH YEAR / 5 IX

At the coming of the charge in the time of Lord 5
Ix, in the eighteenth tun, is the *final* agony, *the
end* of the katun. In its time will the burden be
bound on Lord *3* Ahau, when Ah Cap Uah Tun,
the Commander of Tuns, will arrive, will enslave,
with his *excess of* misery. The wooden drum will
cry out: it will speak in *the thunder*, the heart of
the rain. It is truly the time when the Mummer
Opossums will bite one another; the time of the
change of the law, of the seating, by order of
Seven Bird, Ah Uuc Tut.

The law of the eighteenth *tun* would it be, when
the Itzá will travel the land, destroying homes,
when the wax image travels. But his rule will
end in the midst of the rain: he gives up his
office, his waning rule is consumed. Comes a
reign of goodness: changed is the cup, changed
is the mantle; the wooden mask shall be beaten.

In 11 Ahau they contend for the mat: the masks
of wood will face one another. *And then will he*
laugh, will the mask of metal, pointing the finger
at him who was two days sweet, *who was* three
days powerful.

Then will they stray from their well, from their
grotto; then will the stepchildren make
themselves ready. They search, crouched on their

shins with bowed heads, for water. Thus is it
ordered, for then will the Itzá go wandering in
misery, in thirst, seeking their places, *seeking* new
grottos.

The sky will resound, the earth will resound; the
red wild bees will buzz at their wells, at their
grottos; the wooden mask turns back to mock the
red evil, *to mock* the white evil: *as* Ah Maben
Tok, *Knifed in the Chest*, will he be, *will he be*
displayed in the katun. Mandata.

TWENTIETH YEAR / 6 CAUAC

6 Cauac in tun nineteen is the time when the
struggling arrives. Sudden death would there
be in its time, in its year, and in truth would
they wound one another, would Ah Uucte Suy
and *He of the Great Rotten Stench*, Ah Chac
Mitan Ch'oc, at the beat of *the drum*, the shell
drum, of the katun.

Here would it happen, at the edge of the sea, *to*
Ah Masuy, *in* Tz'itz'omtun, *Place of the Hoof-
Pointed Stones*, *to* Chac Hubil Ahau, *Great
Conch Lord*, *in* Sihomal, *Place of Amoles*.

Comes the time in which that which was loose will
be tightened by Kukulcan, the katun when the
shaker of the rattle will sit on his buttocks,

shaking the rattle of the katun, calling out for his
tribute, beckoning with his hand, in the
nineteenth tun, at the shaking of the rattle of the
katun.

At the beckoning command they draw near, in
the thunder, the heart of the rain. From the
weeping ones, sprung from the lust of creation,
the lust of begetting, he takes his donation. *Yet
even* if he shall be seen, he shall not declare his
command in its time.

In the year 6 Cauac the tree of the sacred clown
will arise: comes compassion: Amayte Ku,
Angular Lord, is its face; the *green bird* yaxum
spreads over the ceiba; and they that remain in
the katun—the hunchback, the mask—shall be
overthrown, *for* they shall come first and behind
shall come Chac Uayeb Xoc, *Great Demon Shark*.

Then would Ah P'iltec come forth to receive his
donation: then in the west comes the jostling of
one by another, the biting of one by another.
Gone is the rule of *Lord* 5 Ahau. The thrice-
greeted one is established.

In the *nineteenth* tun, in its rule, in its reign,
would it fall. Comes the seizure. It happens. This
is the surcharge of the katun. Mandata.

TWENTY-FIRST YEAR / 7 KAN

7 Kan would it be in the time of its ending: a
time when the road of the katun is taken by the
lord of the mat, by the lord of the throne.

Compelled by misery, compelled by need, he
gives up his cup at the close of the katun.
Compelled by hunger, he sets up Ah Uaxac Yol
Kauil, *Eight Heart of Food*. Comes the time, the
katun, when his rule is renounced. From the sky
it will come; the earth will open; and the sky will
turn back: there is fear for food. In the west, in
the east is his seat in his reign. Then will his
burden, his rule, be drawn to its close, fulfilling
the charge of the katun. Bound are his eyes; lost
his throne, lost his mat; and with them is lost the
command, the greed, of the katun. 7 Kan is the
time: the poison is summoned; there is bread in
the katun. The knife will be summoned.
Summoned the bread, summoned the food. Thus
to the greed of the katun. 7 Kan is the time.
Mandata.

13 Oc would be the day of the pacing off of the
katun; 4 Cauac would be the turn of the fold of
the katun, the time when he gives up his mat and
his throne. Comes the change of the cup and the
mat; comes the change of the throne and the
reign, and the fall of the charge of Lord 5 Ahau.

And he will look back to the time when he took
his donation. Gone is his cup, gone is his mat,
gone is the bearer of his command. And he will
rise up to a different world with its ceiba trees,
ceiba groves. Thus would it be, only thus is
completed the charge of the katun. Thus shall it
happen in Mayapan, *Banner of the Maya*,
Cuzamil, *Place of the Swallows;* then again the
true lineage will live at the well, at the grotto.
Comes the death of *the victim*, the deer, a
sudden death and by maggots, by flies, in the time
of the end of the katuns, the fold of one katun.
Mandata.

Epilogue
TWENTY-SECOND YEAR / 8 MULUC

8 Muluc, on 1 Pop, *is the time of* the planted stone,
when we arrived—I, Ah Kauil Ch'el, with Napuc
Tun and Ah Xupan Nauat, the priests of the great
Halach Uinic, *the chief*, Hun Uitzil Chac Tutul
Xiu at the town of Uxmal in the land, the
province, the jurisdiction of Mayapan, *Banner
of the Maya*, Cuzamil, *Place of the Swallows*—at
the taking of the idol of Lord 3 Ahau. And so I
declare its command here at Nituntz'ala, here at
Pacat'aa, *Water View*, at Chulte.

I have composed the bird of the katun, which
truly originated within the charge of the katun

and out of the katun at the commencement of
the katun in 1 Ahau: he departed then from the
sky, he descended, he was buried underground.
He entered the reign of putrefaction, and then
came to pass the beginning of his birth, as we have
composed it, truly. Then he became man, the
ruler, the great Lord King. I composed it here at
the town of Bacalar, made it known from the
painted signs. The wise man may confirm it; he
will see it, if it does not run truly. I composed it
here in the land, in the town, of Salamanca, in
the division of the district, the great province,
here at the town of Chetumal in the land, the
province, of Tahuaimil. I completed putting it in
writing on 18 Zac, on 11 Chuen: we, Ah Kauil
Ch'el *and* Napuc Tun, residents of the town of
Uxmal on the fifteenth day of February in the
year 1544. Mandata.

A COMMENTARY ON THE CUCEB

The following remarks are offered as a detailed appendage to the Introduction (pp. 187–94) and with the assumption that the reader has some familiarity with Maya calendrical systems (described on pp. 269–72). Sources cited by author and date can be located in the Bibliography (pp. 274–77).

Cuceb

The title *Cuceb* appears in both the Tizimin and Mani versions. Translated "that which revolves," it brings to mind the so-called katun wheels pictured elsewhere in the Books of Chilam Balam (e.g., Roys 1933, figure 28), showing the look-alike faces of all thirteen Katuns in a revolving series. A connection between the Cuceb and the katun wheel, if indeed a connection exists, would suggest that the author had thought of the prophecy as measured not only against a Katun 5 Ahau but against the whole series of Katuns, or the entirety of time itself, a notion strengthened by the phrase "end of the katuns" in the closing passage of the text proper. (See Cuceb, entry for the twenty-first year.) The other two epic prophecies that have survived (Roys 1933, pp. 144–63, and Roys 1954) are both measured in terms of the whole series, lending an element of grandeur that is here missing, or suppressed.

The glyphs accompanying the title are evidently the sign for the day-name Cauac (Thompson 1950, figure 46), used as a quasi-phonetic for *ku* (see Thompson 1970, p. 278), coupled with what is apparently a symbolic bee, for which the Maya word is *cab*. Hence *ku-cab*, an approximate rebus for *Cuceb* (but see Thompson 1972, p. 28, item 3). The glyphs might also be read ideographically, in which case the *ku* yields "god," or "lord," while the bee's wings give "Bacab" (Thompson—1970, p. 278—is "reasonably confident" that bees' wings were a Bacab emblem). Hence the reading "Lord Bacab," entered here perhaps as a stamp of authority. Bacab, in fact, is a group of four deities—the four Bacabs—who, among other functions (e.g., they are patrons of beekeepers), serve as gods of change, ushering in new time periods. See commentary for the sixteenth year under *the katun of Mummer Opossum*. Possibly there is a specific allusion to the Bacab Ah Cantzicnal ("He of the Four Corners"), called by Landa "the greatest of the Bacabs" and associated in the Cuceb with the incoming, or new, Katun (see twelfth and sixteenth years); Ah Cantzicnal may, as such, be a stand-in for Amayte Ku ("Angular Lord"), who in turn is a manifestation of Itzam Na, the principal god of the Maya pantheon (see Thompson 1970, p. 229).

FIRST YEAR / 13 KAN

After a brief introduction, in which he imagines the inauguration of a Katun 5 Ahau, the prophet foretells a disastrous onslaught—a "descent"—of the Itzá and envisions a katun of sorrow, of warfare and drought (brought about by the sexual sins of the people). At the close of the katun a solar eclipse will blacken the sky and the guilty will "mourn."

13 Kan: The name and number of the sacred-almanac day coinciding with the first day of the calendar year in which our Katun 5 Ahau begins. Mention of 1 Pop, the first day of any calendar year, is added to clinch the identification. (For a description of the Maya calendar, see pp. 269–72.)

taken is the idol: To the composer of the Cuceb, the katun idol would have been no doubt a ceramic effigy with probably a compartment for a votive flame. But we know that the idol representing 5 Ahau has already been reposing in the temple for ten tuns (see commentary for the eleventh year, part I, under *A new cup is created* . . .), so that what is referred to here is perhaps a ceremony in which the idol is temporarily taken from the sanctuary and carried about in a procession celebrating the official commencement of his rule.

the year 1593: While it is true that a year 13 Kan began during 1593, there could have been no Katun 5 Ahau until 1599. As Roys observes, with characteristic caution, "This katun is, in a way, a fictitious one." But why 5 Ahau? The choice, of course, may have been dictated by pure chance. But the spectacular Santa Rita murals (Gann 1900) are also devoted to a Katun 5 Ahau—and none of the other katuns receives comparable treatment in surviving works of art or literature. Possibly, for reasons that have not come down to us, 5 Ahau was a chosen katun.

15 Tzec: Surely an error for 17 Tzec, the calendar date coinciding with 5 Ahau. The katun, of course, does not begin on 5 Ahau 17 Tzec. (A Katun 5 Ahau beginning in a year 13 Kan must commence with the calendar date 17 Ch'en. See pp. 269–72.) It is possible, nonetheless, that any calendar date on which 5 Ahau "speaks its name" would hold a measure of symbolic interest in the eyes of one about to embark upon a Katun 5 Ahau. Roys even suggests that it might have been the occasion for an anticipatory ceremony.

here I declare: The author identifies himself in the Epilogue as Ah Kauil Ch'el (see entry for the twenty-second year).

Mayapan: An important city of pre-Conquest Yucatan and for many years the capital of the Itzá confederation. In keeping with the mystical interrelationship between space and time, observed by the Maya in a number of interesting ways, each of the thirteen katuns was believed to have a place of origin—a geographical "navel"—and also a place of termination. In our text Katun 5 Ahau begins in Mayapan (Mayapan then becomes the "face" of the katun) and ends at Ichcaansihó, site of present-day Merida, capital of the state of Yucatan. This choice of Ichcaansihó as the "navel" and "face" of the new katun (see entry for the ninth year) suggests the importance of that city as the base of Spanish operations during the colonial period and hence, in the eyes of the Maya, the seat of Christianity. The advent of the new religion, or the "new teaching," as it is called in the entry for the thirteenth year, is closely identified with the coming of the new katun. Though our author is hardly a Christian, he obviously sees the similarities between the old and new doctrines. Moreover, as a member of the anti-Itzá, or Xiu, faction, he has politically aligned himself with the Spaniards in hopes of effectively routing the Itzá. Elsewhere in the Books of Chilam Balam, which are mainly Xiu writings, we find the Xiu exhorting the Itzá to accept Christianity and warning them of its terrible power.

child of the quetzal . . . descend: Quetzal is the Nahuatl word—whose Maya equivalent is *kuk* (or *yaxum,* meaning "green bird")—for the brilliant trogon (*Pharomacrus mocinno*) worshipped especially by the Mexicans. The entire phrase may mean "the foreigners, i.e., the Itzá, are coming."

devoured: Literally "bitten," or "eaten." The connotation is "wounded or slain in battle."

The dawning . . . the great tearing down: Suggests an attack.

ceiba be covered with seals: The kapok tree (*Ceiba pentandra*) is the Maya tree of life. Stamped with "seals," it becomes an omen of disaster, associated with warfare and hanging. (See entry for the eleventh year, part II.) The term *tz'alab* ("seal," or "mold," according to the Motul Dictionary) has often been translated "sign." In the present context the "seals," or "signs," suggest hieroglyphic symbols appearing in nature as an omen—similar to the biblical handwriting on the wall. See p. 93, note 96.

T'ul Caan Chac: An evil aspect of the rain god, Chac. T'ul Caan, literally "rabbit sky," is a sky producing nothing but useless, dripping rains.

Mourned . . . the plumeria: With its phalloid branchlets, milky sap, and deliciously scented blossoms, the plumeria (commonly known in English as frangipani) reminded the Maya of sexuality. The imagery here is of the guilty human community mourning the destruction of their world. (Indian societies harbored a deep-seated distrust of eroticism. If allowed to go unchecked, it might tear apart the social fabric.) The destruction of the world as a result of unbridled sexuality is also implied in Fragment D of Quetzalcoatl. See p. 87, note 74.

In its time, in its katun: Formulas comparable to the Isaianic "in that day."

Kinich Chaante: A name for the sun, possibly as a manifestation of the supreme god Itzam Na, whose power is to be eclipsed during this, the evil katun of foreign domination.

it shall be born in the sky: Here, perhaps, we have the first of several allusions to the flood monster Chac Uayeb Xoc, who appears to cause an eclipse by eating, or biting, the sun. See especially the pertinent phrases in the entries for the third and fifteenth years.

SECOND YEAR / I MULUC

In time of drought and alien rule, the Maya are obliged to yield up food, water, and clothing.

the mountains . . . speak: It would appear that the highlands are in some way symbolic of the seats of destiny, or divine power. Compare the phrase "In its time will the charge of the mountain descend" (eleventh year, part II).

Ah Uuc Chapat (*"Seven Centipede"*): This evil aspect of the earth (cf. Barrera and Rendón, p. 182), perhaps representing the underworld, is associated with drought in the entry for the fourth year—where it is coupled, moreover, with Ah Uucte Suy, an opprobrious name for the Itzá.

The charge will be seven, seven the surcharge: The personified katun is imagined as a traveler, bearing on his back the oppressive "charge," or burden, of fate. Together with the "charge," the traveler carries a kind of knapsack, in the manner of the ancient porters of Central America, known as the *pic,* or "surcharge." I take the passage to read: "The charge [i.e., fate's burden] will be seven [years of drought]." Likewise the surcharge. Cf. commentary for the thirteenth year, under *years of drought will be seven.*

Breechcloths . . . mantles: Taken by the conqueror as spoils of victory or to emphasize the humiliation of the defeated (Roys 1949).

childless generations: Evidently the Itzá are referred to here. But "childless" would appear to be more of a curse than an observation. Compare the prediction "Lost will be that which you knew, which was known of you," in the entry for the seventh year.

Mandata: "The abbreviations *ma* in the Tizimin and *mta* in the

Mani version probably mean *mandata* ('edict') from the Latin *mandatum*. Some of the katun prophecies are called *ordenansas*. This indicates the mandatory character of these predictions." (Roys's note.)

THIRD YEAR / 2 IX

Sudden violence (war) and drought fire are predicted. Screeching owls call for death. The people are plagued by insects. Neither town nor country escapes the devastation—though a time will come when the offending Itzá are indeed removed by the spirit of a new katun.

owl will cry at the crossing roads: The call of the owl is an omen of death; crossroads were associated with battle, presumably because warriors would lie in ambush at these points (cf. Roys 1949).

Ah Bolon Yocte: "He of Nine, or Many, Strides" is a god frequently associated with the katun, possibly representing the Katun as traveler, as the name suggests. Cf. Thompson 1970, p. 320.

Ah Bolon Kanan: Probably a reflection of Ah Bolon Yocte. Throughout this text, wherever names of gods, omens, monsters, etc., are paired, I take them to be synonymous or complementary. Often, as in *Ritual of the Bacabs*, paired elements are antithetical; but beyond the familiar earth-sky, red-white, and sun-moon couplings, there are no clear examples of antithetical pairing in the Cuceb.

the savannah land . . . the walled enclosure: I.e., country and town.

he that remains: I.e., the Itzá. Roys believed these references to a "remainder" implied that the prophecy was composed at a time when the main thrust of the Itzá per se had already been dissipated. We are dealing, then, with those who carried on in their name, perhaps their former cohorts or their descendants. (At the time of the Spanish Conquest, northern Yucatan was divided into a number of autonomous states, controlled by rival dynasties, including notably the Tutul Xiu and the Cocom. The Cuceb comes to us from the Xiu, who had reason enough to associate the Cocom with the hated Itzá.)

Buluc Ch'abtan: The tutelary spirit of Katun 3 Ahau (see Roys 1954, p. 39). In some passages Buluc Ch'abtan appears to be synonymous with 3 Ahau. (Remember that 3 Ahau is the *new* katun, the katun that will replace 5 Ahau. See p. 189.)

at the edge of the sea: I.e., where the katun will end—in the seaboard province of which Ichcaansihó was the capital city (see commentary for the first year, under *Mayapan*).

Chac Uayeb Xoc holds open his jaws: I.e., to eclipse the sun? See commentary for the first year, under *it shall be born in the sky*. See also commentary for the fifth year, under *Chac Uayeb Xoc* . . .

Three folds of the katun: The word "fold" implies the end of a tun or katun. The pages of the typical Maya hieroglyphic book were bound together like the panels of a folding screen and apparently contained prophecies for a series of tuns or katuns, one tun (or katun) to a page (e.g., the katun series in the Paris Codex). The reference here is to the third tun of Katun 5 Ahau.

FOURTH YEAR / 3 CAUAC

The drought-stricken Maya, driven from their towns, roam

through the forest in search of food and water. Some are caught (by the Itzá?) and sacrificed to the rain gods. The sufferings of the Maya come about as punishment for their own sins. In this time of hardship the weight of previous (oppressive) katuns can yet be felt, but with the close of Katun 5 Ahau will come the long-awaited removal of fate's harsh "burden."

3 Cauac: The accompanying glyph is the sign for Cauac.

well . . . grotto: As there are no rivers in northern Yucatan, communities were usually established near water-filled grottos or natural wells, called cenotes. But in time of drought, these, of course, could fail.

Ah Uucte Chapat: No doubt the same as Ah Uuc Chapat (see commentary for the second year), a personification here associated with drought. During dry spells human hearts might be sacrificed, especially those of slaves, captives, or subjugated peoples, who were thus "startled." The coupling with Ah Uucte Suy ("Seven Screech Owl") suggests that the Itzá are to blame. See commentary for the twentieth year, under *Ah Uucte Suy . . .*

trees . . . rocks: I.e., wilderness, as contrasted with the "well" and "grotto" of civilization.

of plumeria their bread: A play on the stereotyped phrase "of ramón is their bread." (The ramón, or breadnut, was a wild fruit eaten only in desperation.) While often a symbol of procreation pure and simple, the plumeria evidently means carnal sin in the present context (see commentary for the first year). The term "bread," moreover, while it usually denotes food, may here mean "destiny" (Roys 1954, p. 55, note 230). Freely rendered, the phrase might read "of sin is their destiny." Like the Aztecs, the Maya typically regarded drought—or any other natural disaster—

as a divine punishment for human sin. See commentary for the tenth year, under *punishment for guilt* . . . (The Itzá are often admonished in Maya scripture for their cult of the plumeria; but they are not specifically blamed in the Cuceb until the entry for the seventh year. See this entry and the accompanying commentary, under . . . *has loosened their breechcloths* . . .)

Then would he take up his burden: Probably refers to the turn of the katun, when Lord 3 Ahau will take the road.

The third tun would it be: The counting off of the katun here reaches the third tun.

and yet there would be Lord 13 Ahau Buluc Ch'abtan, Lord 11 Ahau, Lord 9 Ahau: Roys suggests that the writer, or some copyist, is remembering Katun 13 Ahau (during which the Spanish invasion occurred), Katun 11 Ahau (the katun of the actual Conquest), and Katun 9 Ahau (the time of Bishop Landa's inquisition), imagining that the evil influence of these three katuns is yet operative. Buluc Ch'abtan is coupled with 13 Ahau because he is the tutelary spirit of that katun—in addition to being the tutelary of Katun 3 Ahau. See Roys 1933, p. 134.

below and on high: Maya *cabal yokol,* implying that the Katun is lord of earth and sky, i.e., the universe. See commentary for the eleventh year, part I, under *cup . . . bowl.*

FIFTH YEAR / 4 KAN

The "waning" of Katun 5 Ahau is accompanied by bloodshed and war. The wrath of heaven will punish the guilty with floods and drought fires. Then will come Buluc Ch'abtan (spirit of the new katun); the Itzá will be dispatched; the old will be vanquished by the new; and the incoming Katun will mount his throne.

the time of the waning: The accompanying glyph shows five dots above the Cauac, or *ku* ("god"), sign together with the face-glyph denoting Ahau, all enclosed. I take it to read "the end (i.e., the enclosing) of Lord 5 Ahau." Note that the end, or waning, of 5 Ahau has nothing to do with the counting off of the katun by years, which here reaches 4 Kan.

flies: Swarming over corpses after a battle at the crossroads. (The microbe-like glyph with the triple enclosure may refer to the gathering of skulls, *ox kokol tzek*—literally, "much gathered skulls," or, etymologically, "three gathered skulls.")

upon his passing . . . dove will cry. Ulu!: These lines may allude to a lost myth in which the old Katun flees and is pursued through the forest by priests or by some figure representing the new time period. As he passes beneath them, the crying owls predict his death (see commentary for the third year, under *owl will cry . . .*). Likewise the dove with its mournful cry. The dove, moreover, betrays him to his pursuers, telling them which route the old lord has taken. The "Ulu!" is evidently a cry of anguish (cf. "Yulu Uayano!," Roys 1933, p. 116). The pursuit of the Katun is actually mentioned in the entry for the sixteenth year, q.v. For remnants of the supposed myth, see the folk tale entitled "De cómo en tierras de Yucatán fué perseguido Jesús" in Luis Rosado Vega, *El Alma Misteriosa del Mayab*, Mexico, 1957.

Chac Uayeb Xoc ("Great Demon Shark"). The trees will sink: A portent of flood? It seems not impossible that Chac Uayeb Xoc–Chac Mumul Ain represents an American species of the mythical water dragon, familiar in world folklore as a personification of ruinous floods and hence the antagonist of the drying sun.

In the latter role he effects an eclipse by "eating" the sun (cf. commentary for the third year, under *Chac Uayeb Xoc holds open his jaws*). For evidence that Xoc does indeed find his way to the heavens, see the opening lines of the entry for the fifteenth year, where he becomes what would appear to be a comet, causing the "face of the sun" to be "covered." See also commentary for the tenth year, under *over its face . . . will another descend*.

Ah Uuc Chuuah: Probably a personification of drought—a fitting role for the scorpion.

frogs will croak: I.e., hoping to coax the rain. The croaking of frogs was considered a rain charm. See Thompson 1966, pp. 239, 265.

The command will be loosened: A recurring figure of speech in which the force of destiny exerted by the Katun is apparently likened to the tightening of a rope. One is reminded of the personified tuns of the katun (shown by Gann, 1900, plate XXIX) linked at the wrists by a rope, as though captives of war. Interestingly, the word *katun* may also mean "war." Compare the phrases "Commander of Tuns" in the entry for the nineteenth year and "that which was loose will be tightened by Kukulcan" in the entry for the twentieth year.

in 4 Kan: The insertion of the year name is merely a formalism. See below, under *in the fifth tun*.

the white jaguar . . . the red jaguar: I.e., the Itzá. See below, under *the burrowing opossum and the red jaguar*. For whatever reason, names and epithets in Maya scripture are frequently separated into red and white components. In highly ritualized chants (e.g., the opening passage in the Book of Chilam Balam of Chumayel) an item may be separated into red, white, black, and yellow components, colors corresponding to the four world-directions.

Masuy: Sometimes spelled *Maycui.* Barrera and Rendón appear to read it as a variant of *Maycu,* a shortened form of Mayapan-Cuzamil, which may in turn stand for "the land of Yucatan." See commentary for the thirteenth year, under *Sacnicteil . . . Mayapan . . . Cuzamil.*

in the fifth tun: Once again we have the formalistic device of relating the count-off (here by tuns) to the subject matter of the prophecy. Buluc Ch'abtan, the tutelary spirit of Katun 3 Ahau, does not arrive, of course, until the end of Katun 5 Ahau. Here the katun is merely being "measured."

the painted signs: I.e., in the ancient hieroglyphic books, where prophecy was recorded.

Ah Itzá: The recurring *Ah* is simply a masculine prefix.

his command . . . his burden: I.e., that of Katun 3 Ahau. See commentary for the second year, under *. . . charge . . . surcharge.*

son of the day . . . of the night: The double epithet *u mehen kin, u mehen akab* ("son of day, son of night") seems to refer to the new Katun—or to Jesus Christ?—and hence, by extension, to those who would benefit by his coming (e.g., the Maya). But *u xotemalob kin, u xotemalob akab* ("the descendants of day, the descendants of night") in the entry for the twelfth year and elsewhere obviously refers to the Itzá.

the burrowing opossum and the red jaguar will bite one another: Roys believed these might be the names of Itzá military orders, which in the end would turn against another. The image itself suggests, however, that the underlying motif is that of a ritual combat, performed perhaps as part of the ceremony marking the close of the katun. The jaguar, a standard symbol of authority, would then represent the disfigured old lord—"like a jaguar is his head, disgusting is his body" (Roys 1933, p. 121)—

while the burrowing opossum could be identified with the Mummer Opossum, or Bacab, who ushers in the new katun (see entry for the twelfth year). In such a combat, evidently pictured on the mutilated east wall at Santa Rita (Gann 1900), the old would be vanquished by the new. The Itzá, then, are identified—or confused—with the defeated party. See "teeth shall be drawn from the jaguars of Ah Itzá" in the entry for the seventeenth year.

the sun and the earth come together: Reminiscent of the katun-ending ceremony fancifully re-created by J. E. S. Thompson (1966, pp. 224–32), in which the new katun is born precisely at sunset.

Then will he be seated: The idol of the katun receives offerings of food and drink as he presides, or "sits," in the sanctuary. Here we see the new lord, 3 Ahau, commencing his rule.

SIXTH YEAR / 5 MULUC

At the close of the katun the old lord will be disgraced and removed. But meanwhile the Maya must suffer his burden of drought in payment for their sins. Finally, when the katun has indeed ended, the hated Itzá will lose their water supplies and will themselves be forced into the wilderness.

5 Muluc: The glyph is "Muluc" (Thompson 1950, figure 46).

his eye will be pierced: Possibly the eye, or face, of the human surrogate was pierced. (The word for "eye" is also the word for "face.") The image is elsewhere used pictographically to indicate termination—for example, the stake driven through the four-angled face in the upper right-hand corner of the west wall at Santa Rita (Gann 1900), there marking the close of 7 Ahau. Here we have the close of 5 Ahau (and the birth of 3 Ahau). See p. 88, note 77.

vomits that which he swallowed: Perhaps the human surrogate, after a period of ritual feasting, is emetically purged—that is, purified—preparatory to his execution.

gives up his surcharge: I.e., to his successor, Lord 3 Ahau. See commentary for the second year, under . . . *charge* . . . *surcharge.*

Alone does he rule: The "guest" rule does not begin until the eleventh tun. See commentary for the eleventh year, part I, under *A new cup is created* . . .

Of sin is their drink: Literally, "Plumeria is their drink," which may mean "The Maya are stricken by drought because they have sinned." See commentary for the fourth year, under *of plumeria their bread.*

Then at that time: I.e., at the end of 5 Ahau.

a noise at the well: The clamor of certain bees who come in swarms to spoil or deplete the water supply. See similar allusions in the entries for the fifteenth and nineteenth years.

SEVENTH YEAR / 6 IX

In conjunction with ceremonies marking the close of 5 Ahau, the deliverer Lord Serpent triumphs over the spirit of the old katun and looks down from the sky as the human victim (representing the Katun) is purged and humiliated. Now the subject peoples rebel against the hated Itzá, who had introduced unwelcome sexual practices among them and had, moreover, sold them as slaves. As a result of ceremonial penances, the heavens open and the (fruitful) rains fall, while the Itzá are banished, dispersed, humiliated, forgotten.

6 Ix: The accompanying glyph is "Ix" (Thompson 1950, figure 46).

the bird . . . shall be composed: Roys takes the term "bird" to mean "augury." In the Epilogue (q.v.) the "bird of the katun" appears to mean the prophecy—that is, the Cuceb itself. In the present context, however, I believe it is the "bird" of 3 Ahau that is being composed (literally, "set in order") as the old katun turns, hence with the implied warning: "Beware, Itzá!" (The bird as prophet, or as a symbol of prophecy, is a folkloristic motif found in the Old World as well as the New.)

a time of penance: A period of fasting and penance would no doubt accompany or precede the ceremonies marking the turn of the katun, at which time the usual breechcloth and mantle would be exchanged for a ruder garment. See Barrera and Rendón, p. 182.

Ahau Can: Literally, "Lord Serpent"; freely rendered "Great Snake Father" by Thompson (1970, p. 186) and sometimes coupled with Hunab Ku (ibid., p. 186). There is a possibility that the Maya gods Hunab Ku ("One Lord" or "True God"), Itzam Na, and Oxlahunti Ku may represent, roughly, the concept of a supreme deity, with the figure of Itzam Na ("Iguana House") in the dominant role. Implicit in the name Iguana House is the idea of a four-cornered universe framed by the four-angled body of a cosmic dragon extending from the underworld to the heavens (Thompson 1970). In serpent form, in human form, or as a four-angled monster mask, he appears frequently on sculptured façades and in the hieroglyphic books. Although in the Cuceb there is no mention of Itzam Na by name, the epithets Ahau Can (seventh and tenth years), Ku Caan (twelfth year), and Amayte Ku (eleventh year, part I, and twentieth year) no doubt refer to him. Unlike Itzam Na, the shadowy Hunab Ku has no bodily form and no representation in Maya art. He is variously reported to be the father of Itzam Na or to be Itzam Na himself (cf. Thompson

1970, p. 204). Hunab Ku is twice mentioned in the Cuceb, once alone (thirteenth year) and once coupled with Oxlahunti Ku, or "Thirteen Lords," deities corresponding to the thirteen spaces of the Maya heavens (eighteenth year). The Oxlahunti Ku are sometimes treated as a single being, sometimes as an assembly of thirteen beings. Inasmuch as the Maya were fond of equating space with time and partly because the latter-day priests identified the Katun with the Christian concept of God in the person of Jesus Christ (see Epilogue to the Cuceb), I am led to suggest that the thirteen Katuns may have been a temporal reflection—that is, an extension in time—of the thirteen spaces of Oxlahunti Ku, and hence a parceling out, or a coming again—and again and again—of the supreme deity himself at regular intervals of 7200 days. For details, see commentary for the eleventh year, part I, under *Amayte Ku* and *when his eyes are unbound*.

Chac Bolay Ul ("*Great Predator Lord*"): Appears to be an epithet of the old Katun, 5 Ahau (who must yield the "jewel" of life to his successor, Lord 3 Ahau).

holder of the mat . . . vomits: See commentary for the sixth year, under *vomits that which he swallowed*.

Maax Cal: Literally, "monkey speaker"; freely, "he whose speech is false or lewd," i.e., the Itzá. Here, perhaps, we see the "children" rebelling.

Maax Kin, Maax Katun: Literally, "monkey of the time, monkey of the katun." Roys translates *Maax* as "rascal." The Itzá are meant.

. . . has loosened their breechcloths . . . sold were the children . . . of sin is his mouth: The supposed crimes of the Itzá bear witness against them. They have introduced unwanted sexual practices, possibly an erotic cult imported from Mexico, i.e., Nahua Mexico, or from the region between Yucatan and Mexico.

("They twist their mouths, they wink the eye, they slaver at the mouth, at men, women, chiefs . . ." reads a well-known passage from the Book of Chilam Balam of Chumayel.) Moreover, they have sold Maya captives as slaves. The term "children of Uuc Suhuy Sip" (Sip was—and still is—a Maya folk deity, a patron of hunters) probably refers to commoners only. Members of the ruling or priestly class were never made slaves, not even by an enemy. A similar, condescending regard for "the working people" is expressed in the Book of Chilam Balam of Chumayel (Roys 1933, p. 79) and in the well-known Aztec prayer to Tlaloc recorded by Sahagún ("Alas, the commoners are starving . . .").

north . . . west: Traditionally the directions from which one would expect disaster (Barrera and Rendón, p. 178).

drum . . . rattle: One of the murals at Santa Rita (Gann 1900) shows a god (Ah Bolon Yocte?), representing Katun 7 Ahau, beating a drum and shaking a rattle, evidently at the birth of 5 Ahau. The drum rests on the earth, the rattle is held in the air. Here, of course, the drum and rattle are being sounded at the birth of 3 Ahau.

a violent tearing, a ripping: I.e., thunder and/or lightning, presaging rain and fruitfulness as a sign that the god has been appeased. The idea is clearly set forth by the commentator of Codex Vaticanus 3738: ". . . they would placate him with these sacrifices, and especially with their own blood, which they would offer him. With these and other penances they placated the god in such a way that after they had performed these penances for a long time, there would appear above the earth a loud ripping [*una lacerta raspando*], giving them to understand that the punishment of heaven had ceased and that the earth would gladden and fructify . . . they depicted the sinner as a deer [i.e., in their ancient pictographic books] . . . to signify sterility they depicted a stone . . . to signify abundance of water they depicted a rent [*una lacerta*] . . . by means of a green cornstalk they signified fruitfulness."—Translated from the Italian in *Il Manoscritto Messicano Vaticano 3738, detto il Codice Rios*, ed. Duca di Loubat, 1900, p. 25.

motherless . . . fatherless: In other words, those who are disobedient to their elders or, by extension, those who are evil, i.e., the Itzá.

gone is your mask: In other words, "You, the Itzá, will have lost your authority to govern." See commentary for the thirteenth year, under *wooden mask shall laugh.* The imagery is perhaps derived from the figure of the dispossessed Katun, who must give up his mask. See commentary for the eleventh year, part I, under *Amayte Ku.*

your home: Roys has "your *temporary* home." For "temporary" read "usurped."

EIGHTH YEAR / 7 CAUAC

The knavish, monkey-like Itzá will be routed in battle. Desperate for water, they abandon their senses. The new Katun arrives; the old Katun departs. The power of the Itzá will be broken.

soot is removed: Implies a loss of power in the military sense. (Victorious warriors painted their faces black.)

kinkajou: A term of opprobrium, or perhaps a specific reference to an Itzá military order. See Roys 1933, appendix F.

he puts down his knee . . . : Crawling on the ground to lap up the last drops of water. Cf. the phrase "they shall be crouched" in the entry for the ninth year; also "They search, crouched on their shins" in the entry for the nineteenth year.

maddened: I.e., lewd. The Maya equated lewdness with insanity.

he departs: The old Katun yields to Buluc Ch'abtan, the tutelary spirit of 3 Ahau.

extinguished the fire: Implies a loss of power in the religious sense. (Regnant idols enjoyed a votive flame.)

Up to three folds of katuns: Katun 11 Ahau is the first katun in the Maya time-counting series, followed by 9 Ahau, then 7 Ahau. Thus, if we are now in 5 Ahau, we are "up to three folds of katuns." Note: "folds of katuns" is not to be confused with "folds of the katun"; see commentary for the third year.

NINTH YEAR / 8 KAN

The drought of 5 Ahau is harsh. But with the turn of the katun "comes the wind, the rain."

in Katun 5 Ahau: The accompanying glyph is the sign for Ahau.

they will be crouched: I take this to mean not the Itzá but the Maya, still suffering the "burden" of 5 Ahau.

sucte: Maya *zuuc* ("grass") + *te* ("tree")? An undetermined species.

Sicil, Kum: The squash, or calabash, and its seeds (a source of fat) were important food supplements.

At Ichcaansihó: See commentary for the first year, under *Mayapan.*

flame of the katun: See commentary for the first year, under *taken is the idol.*

rock will crack: An exaggerated description of drought.

tinamou: Maya *nom,* probably the rufescent tinamou (*Crypturellus cinnamomeus goldmani*), a Yucatec game bird somewhat resembling a partridge or a chicken. In the present context its cry symbolizes drought.

On the white savannah: I.e., the parched savannah. Compare the useless "white" rain predicted in the entry for the eighteenth year.

Ix Kan Itzam T'ul: Evidently an evil (and female) aspect of the great god Itzam Na, here identified with the useless, dripping rains.

Ah Nitob: The translation "wise ones" follows Barrera and Rendón. The allusion may be to those priests, or wise men, who devote themselves to the study of the katun (cf. Roys 1933, p. 151, note 4).

Ah Maycuc: Should perhaps read Ah Maycu ("He of Maycu")? See commentary for the fifth year, under *Masuy.*

will the breechcloths be white . . . : White garments are associated in the prophecies with the coming of strangers. (The ancient Toltec priests wore white.)

the lost ones: I.e., the Itzá (Roys 1949, p. 163).

comes the wind, the rain: Evidently the prophet here envisions the end of the katun and relief from its drought. See p. 345, notes 60 and 61.

comes the telling of destinies: At a time of ceremonial renewal, people are inclined to tell one another's fortunes, make "New Year's" resolutions, make wishes for the future (as they blow out birthday candles), or study their dreams for timely portents. Compare the final line of the Iroquois Ritual of Condolence, p. 168. Compare also the Old Testament Book of Joel (2:28): "And your sons and your daughters shall prophesy, your old men shall dream dreams, your young men shall see visions." (Although I do not like to stress Old World parallels, it should be pointed out that the reader who understands the Book of Joel will be greatly assisted in his understanding of the Cuceb. Especially useful in this connection is Theodore Gaster's treatment of Joel in his *Thespis*.)

TENTH YEAR / 9 MULUC

The spirit of "error," or religious infidelity, rules in the land. The world is corrupted by sin. Punishment for guilt—punishment by drought and solar eclipse—is the charge of Katun 5 Ahau.

9 Muluc: The banded tail and six dots appear misplaced if, as already suggested, they comprise the sign "Ix." (See entry for the seventh year and accompanying commentary, under *6 Ix.*) The "domino" glyph with two "strings" attached is the sign for "burden," or "destiny" (Thompson 1950, figure 46). The face-glyph, of course, is "Ahau."

Ah Uuc Yol Sip: This interesting name, literally "He Seven Heart of Error," appears to be associated with sin or with infidelity to the true religion. In the Chilam Balam of Chumayel (Roys 1933, p. 157) it is identified with "Caesar Augustus," while elsewhere in the same manuscript the figure of the Katun is identified with Christ. I do not think the name Ah Uuc Yol Sip should be considered a variant of Uuc Suhuy Sip ("Seven Virgin

Sip"), mentioned in the entry for the seventh year—at least not without qualification. Possibly the cult of the folk deity Sip had been discredited by the priestly hierarchy, so that in time his very name came to mean "sin," or "error" (cf. Roys 1949, p. 169, note 80). I believe that the Cuceb contains an implied contrast between the folk deity Sip and the priestly god Itzam Na, analogous to the contrast between Itzpapalotl and the great Spirit of Duality in the myth of Quetzalcoatl, Fragment C. See p. 76, note 28.

strength . . . vigor: Sexual vigor?

the aged engender: Even the old men and women are corrupted?

The eyes are uplifted: I.e., of those who adhere to the true religion, who yearn for the coming of Ahau Can. See commentary for the seventh year, under *Ahau Can.*

the stick . . . the stone: "To raise a stick, to raise a stone" means to be insolently disobedient (Roys 1954, p. 48). See commentary for the seventh year, under *motherless . . . fatherless.*

punishment for guilt is its face, is the face of Ix Chaante: The sins of the world are punished by drought. (Ix Chaante, "She the Beholder," appears to be an evil aspect of the drying sun.) Sexual sins in particular are emphasized by the Maya prophets. Drought, moreover, leads to famine, and from famine follow thefts, and—to quote Landa's testimony—"from the thefts slaves and selling those who stole. And from this would follow discords, and wars between themselves and other towns." Pestilence, though not necessarily related to drought, is also a product of sin; and all these ordeals are mentioned in one form or another in the Cuceb. Herrera y Tordesillas, a near contemporary of Landa, writes: "The afflictions and troubles which happened to this people, they were aware that they came upon them on account of their sins . . . They accused themselves of theft, homicide, the sin of the flesh, [and] false witness" (Landa, p. 219).

face of the youth: I.e., the sun. In certain Maya myths the sun is a youth (who courts the moon). See Thompson 1970, p. 237.

over its face . . . will another descend: A solar eclipse is indicated, recalling the prediction entered under the first year: "In its time, in its katun . . . would another power come over Ah Chaante."

ELEVENTH YEAR / 10 IX (PART I)

The new lord is installed. "Amayte Ku, *Angular Lord,* would he be."

fan . . . bouquet: Emblems of rulership, here pertaining to Lord 3 Ahau.

Amayte Ku: An aspect of the great god Itzam Na ("Iguana House"), who appears to be identified with any incoming, or new, Katun. In the Paris Codex the rulers of all thirteen katuns are shown seated on iguana thrones, where each is presented with a mask of the god Bolon Dz'acab ("Eternal One"), whom Thompson views as yet another manifestation of Itzam Na (Thompson 1970). See commentary for the seventh year, under *Ahau Can.*

cup . . . bowl: Follows Roys. Barrera and Rendón have "cup" and "plate," as did Roys formerly (e.g., 1933, p. 150). Although in one sense these receptacles appear to represent the offerings of food and water made to the katun idol, they appear in a second sense to symbolize the realm, or world, of the Katun. In a prophecy for Katun 9 Ahau we read, "Nine was its plate, nine was its cup" (Roys 1933, p. 150); and in the preamble to the Quiché-Maya *Popol Vuh,* the dual name of the supreme deity is given as "Lord of the Blue Bowl of Heaven, Lord of the Earth's Green Plate."

the setting in place of the stone: At the close of the 7200-day period an engraved stone would be set into the wall of the temple as a memorial to the Katun (Landa, footnotes 185 and 841). See commentary for the twenty-second year, under *the planted stone.*

And they will go out: The Itzá will be banished.

A new cup is created . . . : Although the preceding passage seems related to the changing of the rule at the close of the 7200-day katun, the several lines that begin here refer mainly to the installation of the new katun idol halfway through the term of his predecessor. (It is no coincidence that the prophet's count-off now reaches the eleventh year and the tenth tun.) From Landa's testimony we may reconstruct the worship of the katun idol as follows: for the first ten tuns, roughly ten years, he rules alone; then at the commencement of the eleventh tun the idol of his successor is set up beside him to share his rule as "guest" for the remaining ten tuns. During this second half of the katun the "guest" gradually absorbs the power of the "host" until at the close of the 7200-day period the old idol is discarded and the new lord rules alone. Although he cannot actually officiate as ruler until the start of his own katun, the new lord's reign has gathered such momentum during the guest years that at the hour of his formal birth he is virtually unstoppable. And so Destiny, whatever rash design she may have entertained, is presented with a *fait accompli.* The world—surely—will go on. (The recurring fear that the world might end at the close of a katun is vividly imagined by Thompson, 1966, p. 225.)

when his eyes are unbound: I.e., when he is no longer dead? (See commentary for the twenty-first year, under *Bound are his eyes.*) The idea that a new, or incoming, Katun is raised from the dead finds an echo in the Epilogue to the Cuceb (q.v.).

brackish the drink: During this, the drought-ridden rule of Katun 5 Ahau.

Yax Bolay Ul: I.e., Lord 3 Ahau, here installed as "guest," though not scheduled to rule for another ten tuns. Yax Bolay Ul, "Green Predator Lord," may also be translated "New Predator Lord," evidently a play on the name Chac Bolay Ul. See commentary for the seventh year, under *Chac Bolay Ul.*

P'iltec: In the Chilam Balam of Chumayel, P'iltec is a functionary who "conducts people to his lord" (Roys 1933, p. 101). Perhaps the allusion here is to a customary and onerous tribute of goods exacted in the name of the sun god by a militaristic ruling class at the close of each katun or half katun. (Has the name P'iltec been derived from the Nahuatl *Piltzinteuctli,* "the young sun," as suggested by Barrera and Rendón?) In the entry for the sixteenth year, relief is promised ("nor does he take tribute from those who would follow the proper road").

serpents are linked at the tail: An image associated with the end of one time period and the beginning of another. On the north wall at Santa Rita the figure marking the end of the first ten tuns of Katun 5 Ahau stands within a pair of linked serpents (Gann 1900; plate XXX, figure 8).

He takes the fire, does Ah Uuc Yol Sip: A reminder that we are still in the katun of sin. (See commentary for the tenth year, under *Ah Uuc Yol Sip.*) "To take the fire" is a figure of speech evidently derived from the custom of lighting a flame in the hollow compartment of an idol to whom one is paying cult. (The influence of Ah Uuc Yol Sip explains why the guest lord's water, mentioned above, is both brackish and insufficient.)

Comes the rule of the knee of the priest . . . : Suggests the sacrifice of the human surrogate at the close of the katun. From details spelled out in the Cuceb and from published descriptions of comparable Mexican rites, the following program emerges. On a prescribed date, perhaps forty or more days before the end of the katun, a young man is chosen to play the part of the outgoing god. For several or many days he presides in state, well attired and well fed. His term draws to a close. He is stripped of his clothing and emetically purged. As the text has it, there comes a time when "he vomits that which he begged." Moreover, he is publicly mocked, perhaps by one or more priestly functionaries, masked for the occasion. Then, perhaps, he is bound to a tree, a sapling of the sacred ceiba, and shot with arrows so that a little of his blood will drip into the earth. Possibly his eyes are also pierced at this time. Next he is dropped from a height, conceivably from a rooftop overlooking a court, onto an improvised altar, or "heap of stones." Four attendants seize the body as it lands. The priest steps forward, places his left knee on the victim's abdomen, and with a single stroke of the flint knife opens the breast and extracts the heart.

Ah Kin: Literally, "he of the sun," denoting a priest.

green-mantled knee: The priest wears a robe of green, symbolizing new life.

Ah Siyahtun Chac: The rain god, who is "comforted" at the coming of the new Katun. See commentary for the ninth year, under *comes the wind, the rain.*

Ahau Tun . . . Ah Niy Pop: Possibly the honorific titles of a superior chief. At the close of a katun, such chiefs were interrogated and deposed if found wanting. In some cases they may have been put to death, as hinted in the entry for the fifteenth year. See also Roys 1933, p. 89.

Ah Masuy: "He of Masuy." See commentary for the fifth year, under *Masuy.*

Ah Chac Chibal: Evidently an evil aspect of the sun, effecting punishment by drought. Cf. commentary for the tenth year, under *punishment for guilt . . .*

ELEVENTH YEAR/10 IX (PART II)

Here begins the second half, or what might be called "Book II," of the Cuceb. A number of fresh details are added, but the entries henceforth are little more than a set of variations on the material already presented in "Book I." And yet the momentum continues to build, year by year, until the prophecy reaches its logical conclusion in the entry for 7 Kan, the year in which the katun ends.

they run with their shields on their backs: Suggests a routed war party, fleeing with their shields held behind them—as the enemy pursues, still shooting.

ceiba: See commentary for the first year, under *ceiba be covered with seals.*

Mani: An important center in north-central Yucatan, home of the priest Chilam Balam.

May Ceh, Xau Cutz: I.e., Yucatan, formerly called "the land of deer and turkeys" (Landa, p. 41).

redbird . . . will dance: The dancing of the (blood-red) North American cardinal is a sign that the enemies of the Maya are to be slaughtered. See Luis Rosado Vega, *El Alma Misteriosa del Mayab,* p. 126.

Here shall it happen, for these are the birds . . . for his was the name given Ah Buluc Am, the diviner: An interpolation found only in the Mani version.

ix uixum: Evidently a bird. Roys does not translate. Barrera and Rendón read it as *yaxum,* i.e., quetzal.

Hapay Can: (*"Sucking Serpent"*): Probably another name for Ahau Can ("Lord Serpent"). See commentary for the seventh year, under *Ahau Can.* Roys, quoting Tozzer, notes that the Lacandon Maya believe in a certain evil spirit of this name who has "the form of a snake who draws people toward him with his breath . . . At the end of the world Nohochchacyum [the head of the Lacandon pantheon] will wear around his waist as a belt the body of Hapay Can." See Roys 1933, p. 67.

they prepare: Literally, "they prepare one another." The Itzá, in other words, are getting ready to die. The idea of *preparing* for death is common in Indian mythology. Recall that Quetzalcoatl "made his preparations" before fleeing Tollan (p. 57).

perching in swarms, the quail will cry out from the branch of the ceiba: An image rich with connotations. A full paraphrase might read, "Swarming like the numberless souls in the underworld, the evil birds of death come to weigh down the ceiba, i.e., the tree of life, warning (sexual?) sinners that death is at hand." For another instance in which the tree of life is compromised, see commentary for the first year, under *ceiba be covered with seals.* For the quail associated with the underworld, see Quetzalcoatl, Fragment A, p. 19; and as Barrera and Rendón (p. 183) have pointed out, the quail is linked with "sexual filth" in at least one of the ancient Aztec codices.

taken are your breechcloths: Throughout this prophecy the pronouns "you" and "your" refer to the Itzá.

they shall come forth: The Itzá shall come out into the wilderness.

TWELFTH YEAR / 11 CAUAC

He of the Two-Day Throne: A double entendre. The eleventh tun, whose name is 2 Ahau, could be called "He of the Two-Day (or Two-Time) Throne." But the same epithet also applies to the Itzá, probably because they were in some way connected with a Katun 2 Ahau (cf. Roys 1949, p. 172).

Ah Cantzicnal: Reported to be the "best and greatest of the Bacab gods" (Landa, p. 145). Inasmuch as the four Bacabs were believed to stand at the four corners of the world, and in view of Landa's remark, it would appear that Ah Cantzicnal ("He of the Four Corners") could stand for the group as a whole. See commentary under *Cuceb*, p. 224.

Ah Can Ek: The translation "He of Four Darkness" follows Barrera and Rendón. It and its companion epithet, "He the White Cowbird," possibly allude to the mythical parentage of the Bacab. Cf. *Ritual of the Bacabs* (Roys 1965, pp. 3–6).

Mummer Opossum: A role played by the Bacab in ceremonies marking the beginning of a new time period.

the wine of the katun: Roys believed the accompanying glyph might stand for "wine." Wine was used as a purge. (See commentary for the sixth year, under *vomits that which he swallowed.*) But if the wine was used to purge the victim, it was undoubtedly used also by the participants in general, both as an intoxicant and as a tonic. According to an early source quoted by Tozzer (in Landa, p. 92): "Some of the old men say that this was very good for them, that it was a medicine for them and cured them because it was like a good purge. With this they went about healthy and strong, and many grew to be very old."

11 Xul: The name Xul can mean "end." The number 11 (Maya *buluc*) is perhaps a play on the name Buluc Ch'abtan or on the name of the entry, 11 Cauac.

Ah Siyahtun Chac: An aspect of the water god. In other words, the Itzá will be thirsty.

The days of the katun are misery: The Itzá will be miserable during the new katun.

the numberless white ones: I.e., the Itzá. See commentary for the ninth year, under *will the breechcloths be white* . . .

THIRTEENTH YEAR / 12 KAN

12 Kan: The accompanying glyph is probably meant to be read "12 Kan." Each bar is "five," a dot is "one."

years of drought will be seven: One might suspect an allusion to Genesis 41:30. But the prediction accords with the quite convincingly Mayan idea expressed in the entry for the second year: "The charge [i.e., the burden of fate] will be seven [years of drought]." See p. 196.

a new teaching, according to . . . Chilam Balam: The famous priest Chilam Balam was supposed to have predicted the arrival of the Spaniards, and hence the coming of Christianity, a generation before the fact. (The so-called Books of Chilam Balam bear his name as a stamp of authority.) This mention of him may be intended as a warning to the Itzá or to their successors, whom the Maya (i.e., the Xiu) expected the Spaniards to chasten. See Roys 1933, p. 168. See also commentary for the first year, under *Mayapan,* and for the eighteenth year, under *Chilam Balam.*

Sacnicteil . . . Mayapan . . . Cuzamil: Collective name for all of northern Yucatan? See Roys 1954, p. 55, note 227.

hooded ones, lords of the hills: Translation uncertain. The reference is evidently to the Itzá, called elsewhere "strangers from the hills" (Barrera and Rendón, p. 40).

wooden mask shall laugh: As used in the Cuceb, the term "mask" or "wooden mask" is perhaps an emblem of authority, referring to either the Maya or the Itzá, depending upon context. Here the (Xiu) Maya would be meant. Cf. commentary for the seventh year, under *gone is your mask.*

FOURTEENTH YEAR / 13 MULUC

1 Oc: The almanac date immediately following 13 Muluc. The name Oc can mean "pace" or "footstep." See commentary for the twenty-first year, under *the pacing off of the katun.* The date here is evidently symbolic, not chronological.

the joint rule: I.e., the guest rule? See commentary for the eleventh year, part I, under *A new cup is created* . . .

Chac Mumul Ain: See commentary for the fifth year, under *Chac Uayeb Xoc* . . .

the katun of . . . *Five Sharpened Flint:* I.e., Katun 5 Ahau, whose miseries are sharp as the flint?

Place of the Great Piled Stone . . . *of the White Stone:* The Maya were deeply impressed by the cathedral built at the site of Ichcaansihó. See Roys 1933, pp. 125–6. See commentary for the first year, under *Mayapan.*

Ichcaansihó: Birthplace of the new katun. Barrera and Rendón (p. 157) translate *Ichcaansihó* as either "Face of the Birth of the Sky" or "Place of Many High Amoles." See commentary for the first year, under *Mayapan.*

Then will he seek out the son of the day: I.e., then will the Itzá accept Christ. See commentary for the fifth year, under *son of the day* . . ., and for the first year, under *Mayapan.*

FIFTEENTH YEAR / 1 IX

Ah Xixteel Ul: For *xixteel* Barrera and Rendón give the Spanish translation *rugoso*, suggesting the furrowed body of the shark. (The mysterious element *ul* is here rendered "lord," though it undoubtedly has a more specific meaning. Cf. Thompson 1970, p. 327.)

will appear: Or, following the lead of the Motul Dictionary, folio 460 recto, "will be gazed at purposefully from head to foot" (*ualic u xixtic uba*). The Mani variant is *yichtic uba* ("will be eyed").

Chac Uayeb Xoc: See commentary for the fifth year, under *Chac Uayeb Xoc* . . .

then will the fire be set . . .: "Suggests the appearance of a large fish at night in the phosphorescent sea off the coast of Yucatan" (Roys 1949, p. 160). But the context clearly indicates a celestial manifestation, perhaps a comet. (The dragon of Iroquois myth is identified as a meteor. See *Forty-third Annual Report of the Bureau of American Ethnology*, 1928, pp. 473 and 480. See also p. 190, above.)

Covered is the face of the sun . . . *the moon:* Solar and lunar eclipses—as well as comets, see preceding note—were conventional omens of doom. Cf. Fernando de Alva Ixtlilxochitl, *Obras históricas*, 1891–2, Vol. I, p. 57.

wooden mask: I.e., the Maya. See commentary for the thirteenth year, under *wooden mask* . . .

Xiuit: A Nahuatl word, probably a name for the Itzá. *Tziuit* is associated with the quetzal (Roys 1933, p. 121).

chiefs: Halach Uinic, literally "true man," was the usual title of a district chief. (*Uinicob* is the plural of *Uinic*.) See commentary for the eleventh year, part I, under *Ahau Tun . . . Ah Niy Pop*.

break into the grotto, the well: Cf. commentary for the sixth year, under *a noise at the well*.

Then did they see it in the surcharge . . . and by Ah Buluc Am: An interpolation found only in the Mani version. Of particular interest is the coupling of the fall of the katun with the "sinning of 1 Ahau." 1 Ahau is a name for the planet Venus, supposed to have emerged from the underworld on a day 1 Ahau (or 1 Acatl, i.e., Ce Acatl, according to the Aztec tradition). Venus, moreover, was identified with the god Quetzalcoatl, and there are hints in the Books of Chilam Balam that Quetzalcoatl was equated with the Lord of the Katun. See commentary for the twentieth year, under *that which was loose will be tightened by Kukulcan,* and for the twenty-second year, under *at the commencement of the katun . . .* For the sinning of Quetzalcoatl, see the Aztec myth, pp. 32–4.

Batabs ("*They of the Ax*"): Local chiefs, subordinate to the Halach Uinic.

SIXTEENTH YEAR / 2 CAUAC

the Katun paces itself to completion: The Katun as traveler completes his journey. See commentary for the twenty-first year, under *the pacing off of the katun*.

the knife descends, the penis descends: An image of retribution? The coupling of penis (*toon*) with knife (*taa*) is a common pun.

the cord will appear: Retribution in the form of drought. "Cord" could be freely translated as "sun's ray." See following note. Cf. Thompson 1970, p. 238.

and the arrow appears: "Arrow" may be a synonym for "cord" in this context, since solar rays are symbolic arrows. (See the preceding note, also note 57, p. 84.) Notice in the following lines of the translation that the "arrows come gathered in sheafs," suggesting an even more punishing form of drought.

precious stones: A figurative expression for "maize kernels," hence food.

Kinich Chaante: The sun as agent of drought. The emergence of the sun as a militant vindicator recalls the similar role of the planet Venus in Quetzalcoatl, Fragment C. See p. 83, note 53.

affliction shines down: The sun is oppressive.

sudden death: Pestilence?

binding of the burden: The burden of fate falls from the shoulders of the old Katun and is bound to the new. See commentary for the second year, under *The charge . . . surcharge.*

Co Kin . . . Co Katun: The evil old katun personified as a madman. (Madness is synonymous with lewdness.) With regard to the Katun's being "bound to the tree" and his heart "turned," see commentary for the eleventh year, part I, under *Comes the rule of the knee . . .*

nor would he go free . . . : Victims intended for sacrifice were ordinarily at liberty during the day. At night they were locked in cages.

his heart would be turned: I.e., sacrificed. See commentary for the eleventh year, part I, under *Comes the rule of the knee . . .*

headlong descent of the katun: An image linking the katun with the planet Venus—that is to say, the old Katun is dying, just as the dying planet (as evening star) falls "headlong" into the western horizon. Similarly Quetzalcoatl, in Fragment A, is called He-Who-Falls-Headlong.

the katun of Mummer Opossum: As already noted, the Mummer Opossum, or "Actor Opossum" as it has sometimes been translated, is a role played by the Bacab god in ceremonies ushering in new time periods. Here the Bacab is linked with the planet Venus (falling "headlong") and so included in the more or less synonymous company of Venus, Quetzalcoatl, Itzam Na, Ah Cantzicnal, and Jesus of Nazareth—all of whom are agents or avatars of the Katun. (Bartolomé de las Casas, *Los Indios de México y Nueva España*, ch. 123, quotes the testimony of a sixteenth-century Maya informant who equated Itzam Na with God the Father, and Bacab with God the Son.) The accompanying Cauac glyph stands for *ku* ("god"). See the discussion of this glyph in relation to the Bacab in the commentary for *Cuceb*, p. 224.

SEVENTEENTH YEAR / 3 KAN

Lord 3 Kan: The accompanying glyph reads "Kan" (Thompson 1950, figure 46).

Bound are the eyes of the lords of the world: May refer to the Katun, who represents not only himself but the entire series of thirteen Katuns. One is reminded of the blindfolding and mocking of Christ.

Great rains . . . revering his image: Fruitfulness and restitution shall be granted to the long-suffering Maya, adherents of the true religion. See commentary for the ninth year, under *comes the wind, the rain* and *comes the telling of destinies.*

takes the road: I.e., the road of the traveling Katun.

molbox: Written *mol box* (literally, "enclosing together") in the text. It appears to be a chronological term, associated with the end of the katun. See commentary for the fifth year, under *the time of the waning.*

EIGHTEENTH YEAR / 4 MULUC

Ah Ox Kokol Tzek: "He Three Heaper of Skulls" is a personification of death (by pestilence?).

bewailed are the flies: I.e., flies swarming over the corpses after a battle.

Bulucte-ti-Chuen: The phrase *ti chuen,* as it appears in *Ritual of the Bacabs,* has been translated "in the Chuen constellation" (Roys 1965, pp. 54, 55, 68).

. . . his face in its rule: I.e., the rule of Buluc Ch'abtan, tutelary spirit of Katun 3 Ahau.

The god will weep . . . : A parallel—but Christianized—passage in the Chilam Balam of Chumayel reads: "Tears shall come to the eyes of our Lord God. The justice of our Lord God shall descend upon every part of the world, straight from God upon . . . the avaricious hagglers of the world" (Roys 1933, p. 79).

They remember their mother . . . : Implies contrition on the part of the "motherless." See commentary for the seventh year, under *motherless . . . fatherless.*

Death will they suffer for three folds of katuns: Alternate translation: "Death will they, i.e., the Itzá, suffer for many folds of katuns."

Chilam Balam: Balam is the patronymic. The title is Chilan (*n* changes to *m* before *b*), signifying "interpreter"—one who interprets the will of the gods. Supposed to have been active in the town of Mani about the year 1500, Chilam Balam is generally regarded by Mayanists as the greatest of the pre-Conquest prophets. One may infer that he received his inspirations under the influence of narcotics (Thompson 1970, p. 186), that his prophecies were subsequently chanted or sung (Roys 1933, p. 167), and that he was a painter of hieroglyphic books (Roys 1954, p. 53, note 171). Drawing mainly upon the suggestions made in the present passage, one might be led to believe, furthermore, that he himself composed the prototype of the Cuceb, which would have been transcribed and adapted some fifty years later by the priest Ah Kauil Ch'el and his colleagues, later to be copied and recopied with additions and corruptions down through the seventeenth and eighteenth centuries. See commentary for the thirteenth year, under *a new teaching, according to . . . Chilam Balam*, and for the twenty-second year, under *I, Ah Kauil Ch'el*.

Napuc Tun . . . : See commentary for the twenty-second year, under *I, Ah Kauil Ch'el*.

Hunab Ku . . . Oxlahunti Ku: See commentary for the seventh year, under *Ahau Can*.

tree of the chapat: An image of drought? See commentary for the second year, under *Ah Uuc Chapat*.

anahte: Hieroglyphic book.

Ah Uuc Chapat: See commentary for the second year, under *Ah Uuc Chapat*.

Ah Uuc Yol Sip: See commentary for the tenth year, under *Ah Uuc Yol Sip*.

NINETEENTH YEAR / 5 IX

the Commander of Tuns: See commentary for the fifth year, under *The command will be loosened.*

the wooden drum: See commentary for the seventh year, under *drum . . . rattle.*

the Mummer Opossums: Should probably read "the burrowing opossums." See commentary for the fifth year, under *the burrowing opossum . . .*

Ah Uuc Tut: Literally, "He the Seven Bird," evidently a personification of the prophetic principle. Cf. commentary for the seventh year, under *the bird . . . shall be composed.*

In 11 Ahau they contend for the mat: The Spanish conquest of Yucatan occurred in a Katun 11 Ahau.

the masks of wood: The Maya (i.e., the Xiu) and the Itzá? See commentary for the thirteenth year, under *wooden mask . . .*

the mask of metal: The Spanish? See commentary for the thirteenth year, under *a new teaching . . .* (The text has "the wood mask of metal," here translated as though "wood mask" were a synonym for "mask.")

him who was two days sweet: I.e., the Itzá. See commentary for the twelfth year, under *He of the Two-Day Throne.*

three days powerful: Alternate translation; "many days powerful."

stepchildren: Literally, "adopted sons" (*mehentzilan*). The Itzá are meant. See Pérez 1898, p. 51.

evil: Maya *uenco.* Roys gives "shameless rascal."

Knifed in the Chest: The surrogate's heart is excised.

TWENTIETH YEAR / 6 CAUAC

Ah Uucte Suy . . . Ah Chac Mitan Ch'oc: Epithets linking the defeated enemy with the underworld, of which the owl (*Suy*) and the putrefaction of corpses are both conventional symbols. (A passage in the *Popol Vuh,* describing the underworld inhabitants and taken by Brasseur de Bourbourg and by Recinos to be a characterization of the Itzá, reads: "Their horrible faces frightened people. They were the enemies, the owls. They incited to evil, to sin and to discord."—Recinos, Goetz, Morley, p. 161.)

the shell drum, of the katun: Implies war. Drums and conch trumpets were sounded in battle—and the word *katun* can mean "war."

Ah Masuy: "He of Masuy." See commentary for the fifth year, under *Masuy.*

Tz'itz'omtun: A town on the northern coast of Yucatan.

Chac Hubil Ahau: A title suggesting warfare (evidently applied to the warlike Itzá). "The name Chac-Hubil-Ahau might be derived from either *hub,* a conch trumpet, or from its homonym meaning to overthrow and demolish walls" (Roys).

Sihomal: Possible name for Ichcaansihó. See commentary for the fourteenth year, under *Ichcaansihó.*

that which was loose will be tightened by Kukulcan: Apparently Kukulcan is here identified with the Lord of the Katun. (See commentary for the fifth year, under *The command will be loosened.*) *Kukulcan* is simply the Maya translation of *Quetzalcoatl*, the name of the Mexican deity whose cult was introduced into Yucatan by Toltec invaders ca. A.D. 1000. The Maya appear to have accepted the Toltecs—though not the Itzá, who arrived at the same time or shortly thereafter. See commentary for the fifteenth year, under *Then did they see it in the surcharge . . .*

the weeping ones: I.e., the Itzá. Similar enemies in the *Popol Vuh* are called "the sad ones, the unfortunate ones" (Recinos, Goetz, Morley, p. 161).

Yet . . . he shall not declare his command: Because in the year 6 Cauac he is still the "guest." See commentary for the eleventh year, part I, under *A new cup is created . . .*

the tree of the sacred clown: An image of new life, reminiscent of the vegetation rite described by R. Redfield (in *Maya Research*, Vol. 3): a sapling is felled in the forest and carried into the village, accompanied by a male clown dressed as a woman; dancing ensues. See p. 345, note 63.

Amayte Ku: See commentary for the seventh year, under *Ahau Can.*

yaxum spreads over the ceiba: Another image of new life. One is reminded of the "cypress of quetzal plumes" imagined in the famous Aztec hymn to the fertility god Xipe (Ángel M. Garibay, *Veinte himnos sacros*). The yaxum and the ceiba are Maya equivalents of the quetzal and the cypress.

the hunchback, the mask: I.e., the Itzá. "Hunchback" suggests one who is crippled by sin. "They sit crookedly on their thrones, crookedly in carnal sin" reads a typical description of the Itzá in the Chumayel book (Roys 1933, p. 169).

the thrice-greeted one: I.e., Lord 3 Ahau, but with no intended play on the number 3. The term *oxtescum* ("thrice-greeted one") is still a common invocation in Maya prayers (Roys).

seizure: Compare the phrase "seizing of the jewel from Chac Bolay Ul" in the entry for the seventh year and see the accompanying commentary, under *Chac Bolay Ul* . . .

TWENTY-FIRST YEAR / 7 KAN

7 Kan: The accompanying glyph carries the numeral 8, though 7 would be expected. But note that *Kan* means "maize," or "food" (see p. 271) and that the text contains an allusion to "Eight Heart of Food" (*Ah Uaxac Yol Kauil*). Possibly, then, the glyph is a pun.

Compelled by hunger, he sets up Ah Uaxac Yol Kauil: A better translation might read: "Compelled by hunger one sets up, etc." Ah Uaxac Yol Kauil is, of course, a patron of food, perhaps the maize god (Thompson 1970, p. 289). The entire passage down through "knife will be summoned . . . summoned the food" would appear to support the observation of the sixteenth-century Spaniard who found that, among the Maya, sacrifice was made "in order to buy food from the gods so that they might have much to eat" (Landa, p. 129, note 602).

Bound are his eyes: Alternate translation: "covered is his face." Compare the double phrase "covered is his face, dead is his face" (Roys 1954, p. 43).

13 Oc: The word *oc* means "footstep." Here again we have a date used symbolically.

the pacing off of the katun: I.e., the close of the 7200-day period, suggesting that time is measured in paces of the traveling Katun (Thompson 1950, p. 248).

4 Cauac: The almanac date immediately preceding 5 Ahau. 5 Ahau is the terminal date of the katun.

And he will rise up: The surrogate attains paradise. (According to a well-known theory, the sacrificial victim rises up to merge with the god whom he represents.) Landa describes the Maya paradise as "a delightful place, where nothing would give them pain and where they would have . . . a tree which they call there *yaxche*, very cool and giving great shade, which is the ceiba, under the branches and the shadow of which they would rest and forever cease from labor."

then again the true lineage will live: Literally, "established are their lineages." In other words, the Maya (i.e., the Xiu Maya) regain control.

death of the victim, the deer: The deer stands for the human surrogate, either as sacrificial victim pure and simple (see Barrera and Rendón, p. 179) or as the embodiment of sin. A pictograph on folio 7 verso of Codex Vaticanus 3738 shows the sinner symbolized by a deer. See the quotation from this codex given in the commentary for the seventh year, under *a violent tearing . . .* See also the vertical triptych on p. 60 of the Dresden Codex, depicting (1) the execution of the old lord, (2) the dying deer, and (3) the new lord's enthronement.

the time of the end of the katuns, the fold of one katun: See commentary under *Cuceb,* p. 223.

TWENTY-SECOND YEAR / 8 MULUC

8 Muluc: Here follows an epilogue, or what might be called the transcriber's afterword. The prophecy itself is complete at this point, as is the counting off of the katun by years (the katun would have ended during the twenty-first year, 7 Kan). And yet the year count moves on, demonstrating beyond a doubt that the chronological framework of the Cuceb has a life of its own.

the planted stone: The stone marker set in place as a memorial to the completed katun? See commentary for the eleventh year, part I, under *the setting in place of the stone.*

I, Ah Kauil Ch'el: It appears that the prophecy has been transcribed from a hieroglyphic source (or newly composed, using hieroglyphic manuals as guides) by the priest Ah Kauil Ch'el, assisted by fellow priests Napuc Tun and Ah Xupan Nauat, in the service of the superior chief (the Halach Uinic) Hun Uitzil Chac Tutul Xiu, who himself is a priest (as were such chiefs generally).

Tutul Xiu: Or simply Xiu, a putative Mexican (i.e., Nahua) lineage. The irony is that the Xiu, while scorning the "alien" Itzá, traced their own ancestry back to Mexico as a mark of princely distinction. Just as the Norman Conquest left its legacy of Francophilia among the privileged classes of England, so did the Toltec invasion (ca. A.D. 1000) leave a taste for things Mexican in Yucatan. See commentary for the third year, under *he that remains.*

town: The Mani copyist actually uses the Spanish word *villa.*

Uxmal: An ancient and hallowed ceremonial center (now a tourist attraction) controlled for many years by the Tutul Xiu.

Nituntz'ala . . . Pacat'aa . . . Chulte: Roys assigns these "places" to the region of Chetumal Bay on the east coast of Yucatan, far removed from the traditional Xiu centers of Mani and Uxmal. I would suggest that they are poetic names for the Chetumal area, just as *May Ceh, Xau Cutz* ("Deer Hoof, Turkey Claw") appear to be poetic names for Yucatan as a whole (see commentary for the eleventh year, part II, under *May Ceh, Xau Cutz*). Roys translates *Pacat'aa* as "Water View." *Nituntz'ala* and *Chulte* are untranslated. (Another of the surviving epic prophecies is said to have been "published" in the neighborhood of Chetumal Bay. See Roys 1933, p. 146.)

composed the bird: See commentary for the seventh year, under *the bird . . . shall be composed.*

at the commencement of the katun . . . the ruler, the great Lord King: An interpolation found only in the Mani version. Here again the Katun is identified with the planet Venus (see commentary for the fifteenth year, under *Then did they see it in the surcharge . . .*). Roys adds: "I suspect, however, that to the late eighteenth-century compiler of the Mani version, where we find the passage, it represented the descent of Christ into Limbo."

Bacalar . . . Salamanca: Bacalar, or Bakhalal, probably refers to the settlement near Chetumal Bay known in colonial times as Salamanca de Bacalar, or simply Salamanca.

Tahuaimil: Native district, or province, beside Chetumal Bay.

on 18 Zac, on 11 Chuen . . . on the fifteenth day of February in the year 1544: "I do not know how early Maya began to be written in European letters; the first example we know is dated 1557. Certainly it was not done as early as 1544, and a correlation of Christian and Maya dates at this time seems quite impossible" (Roys's note). Roys's refusal to accept 1544 as the date of the Cuceb's composition is probably based on the fact that Yucatan, though invaded by the Spanish in 1527, was not fully conquered until 1546. Yet it was the Itzá Maya who held out for so many years. The Xiu Maya (to whom the Cuceb belongs) were already cooperating with the conquistadors in 1531. Since it appears that the Aztec language was reduced to writing well within the first decade after the conquest of Mexico (1520–30), it seems not unreasonable to conjecture that the Xiu Maya were writing *their* language—and correlating their calendar—by 1544, whether or not this date can be validated by European records. But if we accept 1544 as the date of the basic text, we must allow for later interpolations, i.e., the presumed allusion to the cathedral at Merida (see commentary for the fourteenth year, under *Place of the Great Piled Stone* . . .) and the very doubtful but not impossible allusion to Bishop Landa's inquisition (see commentary for the fourth year, under *and yet there would be Lord 13 Ahau* . . .). The cathedral was started in 1561; the inquisition took place in 1562.

THE MAYA CALENDAR, THE ALMANAC, AND THE COUNTING OF TIME

Maya dates are determined by the intermeshing of two independent calendrical systems, the 365-day solar calendar and the 260-day sacred almanac, referred to in this book as simply the calendar and the almanac, respectively.

The calendar is easy to grasp. Its 365 days break down into eighteen "months" of exactly twenty days each, with an "unlucky" period of five days, called *uayeb*, falling at the end. (Though Maya astronomers had calculated the length of the solar year with exquisite precision, they declined to make leap year corrections for fear of interrupting the sacred sequence of days, thus permitting the calendar to slip gradually out of phase with the seasons.)

Unlike the calendar, the almanac is a purely religious device, bearing no apparent relationship to actual celestial phenomena. Each of its 260 days has a name and a number, determined by a rotating roster of twenty god names coupled with the numbers 1 through 13, which repeat in sequence until—after 260 days—all possible couplings have been exhausted.

The accompanying table (figure 3) gives both calendar and almanac dates for a 365-day year (the year with which the Cuceb begins) whose first day coincides with the almanac date 13 Kan. The god Kan in this case is called the "year bearer." Dates are written 13 Kan 1 Pop (the first day of the year), 1 Chicchan 2 Pop (the second day of the year), 13 Kan 1 Kankin (the 261st day, at which point the almanac, though of course not the calendar, begins to repeat itself), etc.

Note that the last day of the year, 13 Lamat (falling on 5 Uayeb), would be followed by 1 Muluc, the first day of the succeeding year. Hence Muluc is "bearer" for the second year of the Cuceb. Note also that the calendrical system is so constructed that only the gods Kan, Muluc, Ix, and Cauac can be year bearers.

In keeping with the notion that temporal concepts must have spatial equivalents, the Maya assigned each of their year bearers to one of the four world-directions, each of which in turn had its peculiar color. Thus Kan belongs to the east and to the color red, Muluc to north and white, Ix to west and black, Cauac to south and yellow. As we progress through the Cuceb, then, we move in a "circle," counterclockwise, passing from red to white to black to yellow to red, etc.

The following translations of the year-bearer names are given by Barrera and Rendón: *Kan* ("Precious Stone," a figurative name for maize, the jewel of life); *Muluc* ("Flood"); *Ix* ("Jaguar"); and *Cauac* ("Thunder"). But it must be remembered, as Thompson has pointed out, that these names do not stand for maize or flood, etc., as such, but rather for the gods who have dominion over them.

One might suppose that the passage of time would be reckoned in years or in repetitions of the sacred almanac. Yet such is not the case. The measuring of time is by 7200-day periods called katuns, of which there are precisely thirteen. When all thirteen have run their course—in other words, when 13 × 7200 days (roughly 256 years) have passed—the great "wheel" of the katuns is said to be complete, and, as it begins anew, history is believed to repeat itself.

By convention, the first of the thirteen katuns is inaugurated on the almanac day 1 Imix, which means that it will have to

Figure 3 / The Maya Year

#	Name	Pop	Uo	Zip	Zotz	Tzec	Xul	Yaxkin	Mol	Chen	Yax	Zac	Ceh	Mac	Kankin	Muan	Pax	Kayeb	Cumku	Uayeb
1	Kan	6	13	7	1	8	2	9	3	10	4	11	5	12	6	13	7	1	8	
2	Chicchan	5	12	6	13	7	1	8	2	9	3	10	4	11	5	12	6	13	7	
3	Cimi	4	11	5	12	6	13	7	1	8	2	9	3	10	4	11	5	12	6	
4	Manik	3	10	4	11	5	12	6	13	7	1	8	2	9	3	10	4	11	5	
5	Lamat	2	9	3	10	4	11	5	12	6	13	7	1	8	2	9	3	10	4	
6	Muluc	1	8	2	9	3	10	4	11	5	12	6	13	7	1	8	2	9	3	
7	Oc	13	7	1	8	2	9	3	10	4	11	5	12	6	13	7	1	8	2	
8	Chuen	12	6	13	7	1	8	2	9	3	10	4	11	5	12	6	13	7	1	
9	Eb	11	5	12	6	13	7	1	8	2	9	3	10	4	11	5	12	6	13	
10	Ben	10	4	11	5	12	6	13	7	1	8	2	9	3	10	4	11	5	12	
11	Ix	9	3	10	4	11	5	12	6	13	7	1	8	2	9	3	10	4	11	
12	Men	8	2	9	3	10	4	11	5	12	6	13	7	1	8	2	9	3	10	
13	Cib	7	1	8	2	9	3	10	4	11	5	12	6	13	7	1	8	2	9	
14	Caban	6	13	7	1	8	2	9	3	10	4	11	5	12	6	13	7	1	8	
15	Eznab	5	12	6	13	7	1	8	2	9	3	10	4	11	5	12	6	13	7	
16	Cauac	4	11	5	12	6	13	7	1	8	2	9	3	10	4	11	5	12	6	13
17	Ahau	3	10	4	11	5	12	6	13	7	1	8	2	9	3	10	4	11	5	12
18	Imix	2	9	3	10	4	11	5	12	6	13	7	1	8	2	9	3	10	4	11
19	Ik	1	8	2	9	3	10	4	11	5	12	6	13	7	1	8	2	9	3	10
20	Akbal	13	7	1	8	2	9	3	10	4	11	5	12	6	13	7	1	8	2	9

terminate (7200 days later) on the almanac day 11 Ahau. The second katun terminates on 9 Ahau, and by one of those striking coincidences typical of the Maya calendrical system, each of the katuns *must* end on a day Ahau. (The name Ahau means "lord" in the Maya language.) The Katuns themselves take their names from these terminal dates; in order, they are:

Lord 11 Ahau	Lord 1 Ahau	Lord 4 Ahau
Lord 9 Ahau	Lord 12 Ahau	Lord 2 Ahau
Lord 7 Ahau	Lord 10 Ahau	Lord 13 Ahau
Lord 5 Ahau	Lord 8 Ahau	
Lord 3 Ahau	Lord 6 Ahau	

Note that the sacred almanac conveniently clicks into the starting position, 1 Imix, as the katuns begin anew—because 1 Imix is the almanac date immediately following 13 Ahau, the terminal date of the last katun—confirming that the cycle has neatly exhausted all possible permutations. Time and history, at this point, have no choice but to repeat themselves.

As a minor elaboration, the katun is divided into twenty 360-day periods called tuns (the element *ka*, in *katun*, may in fact be a combining form of *kal*, meaning "twenty"). Interestingly, the tuns also terminate on a day Ahau and are named, like the katuns, accordingly. For Katun 5 Ahau, the katun of the Cuceb, the tun series reads as follows:

3 Ahau	•9 Ahau	2 Ahau	8 Ahau
12 Ahau	5 Ahau	11 Ahau	4 Ahau
8 Ahau	1 Ahau	7 Ahau	13 Ahau
4 Ahau	10 Ahau	3 Ahau	9 Ahau
13 Ahau	6 Ahau	12 Ahau	5 Ahau

Though none of the tuns is mentioned by name in the Cuceb, there is a possibility that the epithet "He of the Two-Day Throne" (see commentary for the twelfth year) is a play on the name of the eleventh tun, Lord 2 Ahau.

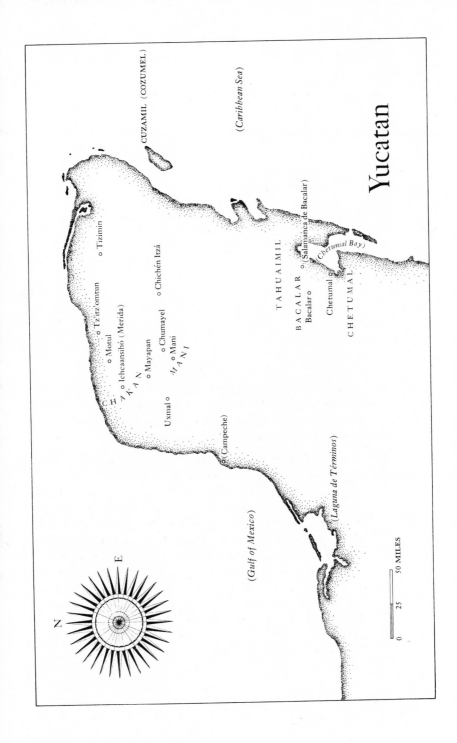

Yucatan

(Caribbean Sea)

CUZAMIL (COZUMEL)

o Tizimin

o Chichén Itzá

TAHUAIMIL

o (Salamanca de Bacalar)

(Chetumal Bay)

BACALAR

Bacalar o

Chetumal o

CHETUMAL

o Tz itz omtun

o Motul

o Ichcaansihó (Merida)

CHAKAN

o Mayapan

o Chumayel

Uxmal o

o Mani

MANI

Campeche)

o

(Gulf of Mexico)

(Laguna de Términos)

N

E

50 MILES

0   25

BIBLIOGRAPHY

1 / Primary sources

MS. Chilam Balam de Tizimin (Book of Chilam Balam of Tizimin), Museo Nacional de Antropología, Mexico, D.F. Photostatic copy at the Peabody Museum, Harvard University. The Cuceb occupies pp. 1–13 (folios 1–7).

MS. Book of Chilam Balam of Mani. Missing. Portions of the Mani book, however—or perhaps the Mani in its entirety—are preserved in a nineteenth-century manuscript known as Codex Pérez (the Cuceb falls on pp. 101–15), formerly owned by Josefa Escalante of Merida, Yucatan, now in the Museo Nacional de Antropología, Archivo Histórico del Instituto Nacional de Antropología e Historia, Mexico, D.F. A set of photographic negatives of the Codex Pérez, made by Ralph Roys for the Carnegie Institution, is now at the Peabody Museum, Harvard University. Note: the Codex Pérez is not to be confused with the "Perez Codex" described by Tozzer or with the hieroglyphic Codex Peresianus.

II / Translations of the Cuceb

Roys, Ralph L., "The Prophecies for the Maya Tuns or Years in the Books of Chilam Balam of Tizimin and Mani," *Carnegie Institution of Washington, Publication 585*, Contribution 51, 1949. Paleograph and English translation of the Cuceb, drawn from the Chilam Balam of Tizimin with variants supplied from the Mani text.

Barrera Vásquez, Alfredo, and Rendón, Silvia, *El Libro de los Libros de Chilam Balam*, 1948, second edition 1963. A treasury of Maya literature in Spanish translation. No paleographs. Page numbers cited in my commentary refer to the second edition.

Solís Alcalá, Ermilio, *Códice Pérez*, 1949. Paleograph and Spanish translation of the Codex Pérez. Must be used with caution.

Makemson, Maud W., *The Book of the Jaguar Priest*, 1951. An English version of the Book of Chilam Balam of Tizimin. Not in the mainstream of Maya research.

III / Art and literature of particular relevance to the Cuceb

Roys, Ralph L., *The Book of Chilam Balam of Chumayel*, Carnegie Institution of Washington, Publication 438, 1933, reprinted (by University of Oklahoma Press) 1967.

———— "The Maya Katun Prophecies of the Books of Chilam Balam, Series I," *Carnegie Institution of Washington, Publication 606*, Contribution 57, 1954.

Gann, Thomas, "Mounds in Northern Honduras," *Nineteenth Annual Report of the Bureau of American Ethnology, 1897–98*, Pt. 2, 1900, pp. 655–92. Includes color reproductions of murals discovered in a mound at Santa Rita—near Corozal,

British Honduras—evidently commemorating, at least in part, a Katun 5 Ahau.

Paris Codex. Hieroglyphic material pertinent to the cult of the katun. Largely undeciphered. A good edition is F. Anders's *Codex Peresianus*, 1968.

Dresden Codex. A fantasized katun-ending ceremony is illustrated on p. 60 of this famous hieroglyphic book. The newest and most useful edition is J. E. S. Thompson's *A Commentary on the Dresden Codex*, 1972.

Recinos, Adrián; Goetz, Delia; and Morley, Sylvanus, *Popol Vuh, The Sacred Book of the Ancient Quiché Maya*, 1950. Part II relates a series of adventures among underworld denizens who bear a resemblance to the Itzá. (Anyone interested in the *Popol Vuh* should also consult the new translation by Munro S. Edmonson, *The Book of Counsel: The Popol Vuh of the Quiché Maya of Guatemala*, 1971.)

Roys, Ralph L., *Ritual of the Bacabs*, 1965. A collection of medical incantations, peppered with cryptic allusions to the gods and monsters.

IV / History and ethnography

Landa, Diego de, *Relación de las cosas de Yucatan*, 1941, reprinted 1966. An English translation of Landa's sixteenth-century ethnography, edited, and with copious notes, by Alfred M. Tozzer. A storehouse of information.

Thompson, J. E. S., *Maya History and Religion*, 1970. Includes a useful summary of the gods and their attributes.

——— *Maya Hieroglyphic Writing: An Introduction*, Carnegie Institution of Washington, Publication 589, 1950, reprinted (by University of Oklahoma Press) 1960. A very thorough inquiry into the intellectual culture of the Maya, with emphasis on calendrics and the worship of time.

——— *The Rise and Fall of Maya Civilization*, 1954, second edition 1966. The most admired general account of the Maya. Also useful are S. G. Morley's *The Ancient Maya*, 1946, third edition 1956; and M. D. Coe's *The Maya*, 1966.

Anders, F., *Das Pantheon der Maya*, 1963. An encyclopedic treatment.

V / Language

Diccionario de Motul, edited by Juan Martínez Hernández, 1929. A sixteenth-century lexicon of surpassing importance.

Swadesh, M.; Alvarez, M. C.; and Bastarrachea, J. R., *Diccionario de elementos del maya yucateco colonial*, 1970. A useful introduction to the study of classic Maya.

Tozzer, Alfred M., *A Maya Grammar*, 1921, reprinted 1967. Includes an extensive bibliography.

Pérez, Juan Pío, *Coordinación alfabética de las voces del idioma maya que se hallan en el arte y obras del Padre Fr. Pedro Beltran . . .*, 1898.

——— *Diccionario de la lengua maya*, 1866–77.

The Night Chant

A NAVAJO CEREMONIAL

*"In old age wandering on a trail of
beauty, living again, may I walk."*

INTRODUCTION

An integrated system of component rituals, performed to the accompaniment of song cycles and reiterated prayers, the Night Chant epitomizes the mythos of Navajoism and gives expression to its ideals. In its narrowest use it serves as a form of therapy, conducted by a shaman (the *hatali*, or chanter) for the benefit of a principal communicant, customarily styled in anthropological writings as the "patient." But with the joining in of assistant singers, impersonators, new initiates, and assorted spectators, it becomes an occasion for general religious revival.

The ceremony opens at sunset and closes eight and a half days later at sunrise. During the first four days the patient purifies himself to the accompaniment of song and makes invocatory offerings to the gods. At midnight of the fourth day the sleeping gods awake. As the songs continue, the gods descend from their homes on high to appear in the sand paintings of the fifth through eighth days, wherein they "touch" their bodies to the patient's body so that he may absorb their power. The climax is reached at the beginning of the ninth day with the summoning of thunder. At this point the ceremony breaks free. In a figurative sense, it appears to burst under the tension created by an enormous containment of plus and minus "charges" (explained below). The songs that have "accumulated" over the previous eight days now "brim over," pouring out in an unbroken reprise that lasts the entire night—the night of nights—finally abating at sunrise as the patient, revitalized, faces east and inhales the breath of dawn.

The ceremonial method is twofold: on one hand the ritual repulses "evil," on the other it attracts "holiness." Accordingly, each of its separate rites may be categorized as either repulsive or attractive, as either purgative or additory. For the sake of balance, however, each ceremonial unit, though it may seem essentially "holy," will contain elements of "evil," and vice versa. In a typical prayer, for example, the words that imply healing:

> My mind restore for me.
> My voice restore for me . . .

are immediately followed by the words for exorcism:

> Today take out your spell for me.
> Today your spell for me is removed.

The tension created by the two opposing ideas operates at every level and may be looked upon as the ceremony's organizing principle.

As noted above, the individual rites tend to be predominantly repulsive in some cases, attractive in others. Taking a somewhat larger view, the entire first group of rites, comprising the first four days of the ceremony, can be classed as repulsive, the second four days as attractive. From a yet more distant vantage point, the nine-day ceremony as a whole proves to be an exercise mainly in attractivity—as recognized by native practitioners, who consider it a chant "according to holiness," distinguishing it from the so-called chants "according to evil," which place a heavier burden on the techniques of exorcism.

The nine-day program as a whole reveals a logical pattern; and even a casual glance will show how the various rites fit together in systematic groupings. (The plus sign is used in the table below to identify a unit considered primarily attractive, or healing; the minus indicates repulsion, or exorcism, including cleansing. The two units marked with an asterisk, although they are both attractive, have not been given a plus sign because they stand outside the general pattern of the ceremony. The second-day activity called "preparation of the many kethawns" has been marked with a plus enclosed in parentheses to indicate that it replaces the expected rite of attractivity, which here gives way to the exigencies of a too-busy day. The rites of Part III have not been marked at all, because as noted above, the plus-minus tension is here being neutralized.)

+ THE NIGHT CHANT

— *Part I / The Purification*

First Day / Day of the East
       Consecration of the lodge*
  —   First rite of exorcism (the breath of life)
  +   First morning prayer ritual
  —   First sweat bath
  +   The sacred mountains

Second Day / Day of the South
- — Second rite of exorcism (the evergreen dress)
- + Second morning prayer ritual
- — Second sweat bath
- (+) Preparation of the many kethawns

Third Day / Day of the West
- — Third rite of exorcism (the many kethawns)
- + Third morning prayer ritual
- — Third sweat bath
- + Amole bath

Fourth Day / Day of the North
- — Fourth rite of exorcism (the sapling and the mask)
  The vigil*
- + Fourth morning prayer ritual
- — Fourth sweat bath
- + The trembling place

+ *Part II / The Healing*

Fifth Day
- — Songs of exorcism, first session
- + First great sand painting

Sixth Day
- — Songs of exorcism, second session
- + Second great sand painting

Seventh Day
- — Songs of exorcism, third session
- + Third great sand painting

Eighth Day
- — Songs of exorcism, fourth session
- + Fourth great sand painting?

Part III / The Reprise

Ninth Day

        Dance of the Atsálei

        Dance of the Naakhaí

It should be borne in mind that each of the component rituals is accompanied by more or less continuous singing. Part III, then, is a reprise in the sense that it gives a final hearing to most (though not all) of the song cycles that have been used during Parts I and II, in effect drawing these two halves together. Note also that the first four days of the ceremony swing clockwise (the preferred term is "sunwise") through the four world-quarters—east, south, west, and north—completing the familiar circle that symbolizes nature in its entirety. Part II, in its fourfold structure, echoes the same sequence, giving repeated prominence to the number 4. Within this harmonious framework the participant seeks to identify his mind and body with the minds and bodies of gods; he strives to project himself into the realm of mythic time and to achieve the double goal of "old age" and "beauty."

Of particular significance to the ritualist are the deities Estsánatlehi ("Changing Woman") and Hastshéyalti ("Talking God"). Changing Woman personifies the earth as it progresses through maturity (summer), senescence (winter), and rejuvenation (spring). Talking God, a spirit power identified with the light of dawn, appears to represent, if indirectly, the sun. The "talking" attribute—evidently connected with the god's characteristic call, heard in the opening rite of the ceremony—has perhaps been adapted from Pueblo lore, where the sun is supposed to speak out as it breaks over the horizon. The identification of Hastshéyalti with the bluebird (*Sialia* sp.), especially as it sings in the morning, is a related concept. Numerous passages acknowledge the sun as the source of vegetable growth, the source of life itself, and therefore the ultimate antidote to disease and affliction of whatever kind. To identify with Hastshéyalti is to make one's own self invincible. In song the desire becomes explicit:

> Now Hastshéyalti I walk with.
> These are his feet I walk with.

But perhaps the greater achievement is to merge symbolically with the female earth, with Changing Woman, whose cult among the Navajo generally, if not in the lore of the Night Chant specifically, surpasses that of the sun. Though seldom mentioned by name, she lends her theme of growth and rejuvenation to various Night Chant songs and song cycles. And as the chanter prays, "Through the returning seasons may I walk," he asks that he may be made like her, always reviving, always becoming young.

The mythic deeds of a dozen or more deities are recollected in theurgic masques and dances and in the elaborate tableaux commonly known as sand paintings. (Though life may be transient, myth is eternal. And at least for a time one may live "forever" in the company of the gods and heroes.) Among the disparate myths epitomized in these procedures, the so-called Origin Legend deserves particular mention. Like the corresponding Aztec dogma, it postulates the existence of four previous ages, or worlds, each becoming successively more like the present, or fifth, world. Especially significant in both versions (i.e., the Aztec *Legend of the Suns* and the Navajo Origin Legend published by Matthews, 1897) is the penultimate Fourth World, in which human life as we now know it was formally created through the effort of the deity Quetzalcoatl, in the case of the Aztec story, or Hastshéyalti, in the case of the Navajo. As Matthews was the first to note, not a few of the Night Chant rituals pay tribute in one way or another to the events of the Fourth World. And the ceremony as a whole has sometimes been called the Dance of Hastshéyalti (i.e., the dance of the sun).

Ultimately the participant seeks the blessing asked for in the recurring formula *saa nagai bike hozhon* (*saa nagai:* "in old age traveling," *bike hozhon:* "the trail of ideality"), sometimes freely translated as "long life and happiness." But the phrase is a pun on the nearly homophonous *sa'aa nagai bigke hozhon*, approximately rendered as "may rejuvenation be achieved according to the ideal" (i.e., according to the example of Changing Woman). Hence the formula fully explored presents a paradox, a "mystery." The communicant expresses the desire for a happy old age and for the mystical rejuvenation that denies old age. Through the medium of the pun the realistic goal becomes mingled with the ideal; and while no translation can possibly convey the full meaning of the concept, Matthews's rendering, "In old age wandering on a trail of beauty," is as graceful and as evocative as any.

An army surgeon who pursued ethnography in his off-duty hours, and at his own expense, Washington Matthews (1843–1905) had already won acclaim for his *Grammar and Dictionary of the Hidatsa*—compiled during a tour of duty along the Upper Missouri—when in the autumn of 1880 he was transferred to Fort Wingate, New Mexico, near the southern boundary of Navajo country. Although his regular assignments left him little time, he nevertheless proceeded to familiarize himself with the Navajo language and was soon making forays into the surrounding countryside. On October 24, 1884, by then sufficiently competent to record texts, he was admitted to a medicine lodge during the performance of a major nine-day ceremonial. The resultant monograph, *The Mountain Chant* (1887), which was to become a model for future investigators, establishes Matthews as the father of Navajo studies and one of the pioneer figures in American anthropology.

Matthews might have continued his study of the Mountain Chant, but during that same autumn of 1884 he had witnessed the performance of another, more important ceremonial, evidently the most important of them all, the monumental Night Chant. To this he would devote his best energies during twenty remaining years of life, laboring toward the end under the strain of a debilitating illness. (Among its virtues the Night Chant is supposed to be specific for blindness, deafness, headache, paralysis, and insanity. But according to a fundamental principle of incantatory medicine, the chant can maim as well as cure. An improper attitude or simply a spiritual weakness on the part of the recipient may cause the remedy to backfire. In the opinion of many Navajos Matthews himself suffered the wrath of the chant—and in fact he did fall prey to both deafness and paralytic stroke.)

Since the turn of the century a number of other Navajo ceremonials have been described, but none with Matthews's completeness or consummate style. As for the Night Chant itself, it remains intimately connected with Matthews's name. Skimpy by comparison, and crude, is the version brought out by James Stevenson in 1891. Alfred Tozzer's description, published in 1909, consists of little more than a program. More recent students, including the late Berard Haile, have collected Night Chant materials, but these remain undigested. (Leland Wyman has promised a book on the Night Chant, and it is to be hoped that some of Haile's texts will be incorporated or at least discussed.)

The Night Chant as presented here is drawn primarily from Matthews's monograph of 1902, including without change all the song texts and prayers given in that work, as well as my own brief synopses of all obligatory rituals described therein. To these have been added various Night Chant materials brought out separately by Matthews, notably in his papers of 1894 and 1907, the result being as complete an assemblage as possible of those songs and prayers actually used in performance. The texts themselves were communicated to Matthews over a period of twenty years by the priests of the Night Chant, among whom the imposing but regrettably obscure figure of Hatali Natloi, "Laughing Chanter," undoubtedly deserves first mention.

It will be noticed that most cycles are represented by only one or two songs, while other cycles are missing entirely. This is partly because Matthews failed to obtain certain texts, but largely because he suppressed them if, as in so many cases, they were repetitious or lacking in verbal development.

An occasional term in italic indicates a gloss or interpolation suggested by Matthews himself. For native place names and

the names of deities, Matthews's orthography has been followed, with a number of simplifications to avoid phonetic
symbols. Vowels have the usual Continental sounds; a
doubled vowel means that the sound is prolonged. Consonants
and consonant combinations may be pronounced as in English. (Strictly speaking, the "accent" is not a stress but an
elevation in pitch. There is no accentuation in Navajo.)

THE NIGHT CHANT

With songs and prayers translated from the Navajo by
Washington Matthews, and with descriptions of ritual
procedure condensed from Matthews by John Bierhorst

PARTICIPANTS

The chanter
The patient
Assistants to the chanter
Singers
Impersonators
Relatives and friends of the patient

DRAMATIS PERSONAE

Hastshéyalti / "Talking God," the tutelary spirit of the Night
   Chant[1]
Hastshéhogan / "House God,"[2] companion to Hastshéyalti
Nayénezgani / "Slayer of the Alien Gods," the mythical deliverer
Tobadzhistshíni / "Child of the Water," companion to Nayénez-
   gani
Tónenili / "Water Sprinkler," the god of rain
Hastshéoltoi / "Shooting God," the god of hunting
Dsahadoldzhá / "Fringe Mouth," a god of succor

Hastshélpahi / "Gray God," a god of succor
Female Divinities
Male Divinities

THE SETTING

A conical lodge of timber and sod, roughly eight feet high at the center and twenty-five feet in diameter at the base. The curtained doorway faces east.

Part I / The Purification

FIRST DAY³ / DAY OF THE EAST

CONSECRATION OF THE LODGE. *Nightfall. The chanter enters and proceeds sunwise around the interior of the lodge, rubbing the four main timbers with meal. A crier stands at the door, calling* Biké hatáli hakú (*"Come on the trail of song"*).

FIRST RITE OF EXORCISM (THE BREATH OF LIFE). *Entering with relatives and friends, the patient takes his place at the seat of honor, directly west of the fire. Others sit to the north, south, and east. Twelve rings of bent sumac, each garnished with a breath-feather and trussed in yarn, lie waiting in a shallow basket. Hastshéyalti enters holding a collapsible square of peeled willow; he opens the square and slips it around the patient's waist, chest, shoulders, and head, uttering a cry* (Wu hu hu hú)⁴ *at each position. He withdraws. A Female Divinity enters, takes one of the rings, and touches it in turn to each of the patient's essential parts: soles, knees, palms, chest, back, shoulders, top of the head, cheeks, and mouth. Hesitating at the patient's mouth, she ravels*

out the yarn and exits dragging the attached ring. Her act is
repeated by Hastshélpahi, who removes a second ring, followed
by a second Female Divinity, who removes a third. Hastshéyalti
now reappears with the open square, and the entire sequence in
which three rings are unraveled is performed again—and again
and again, until all twelve rings have been removed:[5]

> From a place above, where he stands on high,
> Hastshéayuhi, where he stands on high,
> *says* "Your body is holy," where he stands on
>   high.

> From a house below, where he stands on high,
> Hastshéyalti, where he stands on high,
> *says* "Your body is holy," where he stands on
>   high.[6]

FIRST MORNING PRAYER RITUAL. *The chanter and his assistants pre-*
pare four kethawns (sacrificial offerings)[7] *as follows: four corn*
husks are filled with pollen, sparkling hematite, and "mixed
jewels" (bits of whiteshell, turquoise, jet, and abalone);[8] *four*
lengths of reed grass are cut and painted with representations of
the deities destined to receive them:

> A little one now is prepared. A little one now is
>   prepared.
> For Hastshéhogan, it now is prepared.
> A little message now is prepared,
> Toward the trail of the he-rain, now is prepared,
> As the rain will hang downward, now is prepared.

> A little one now is prepared. A little one now is
>   prepared.
> For Hastshéyalti, it now is prepared.

A little kethawn now is prepared,
Toward the trail of the she-rain, now is prepared,
As the rain will hang downward, now is prepared.[9]

The painted reeds are filled with native tobaccos:

Now the yellow tobacco am I.
Now the broad leaf am I.
Now the blue flower am I.
With a trail to walk on, that am I.

Now the narrow leaf am I.
Now the white mountain flower am I.
Now the blue flower am I.
With a trail to walk on, that am I.[10]

*The reeds, or cigarettes as they may now be called, are sealed
at each end with moistened pollen, figuratively lit with a piece of
rock crystal (held to the tip of the cigarette as if catching a ray
of sunlight from the smoke hole overhead), and placed inside the
husks with the jewels. The chanter applies pollen[11] to the patient's
essential parts, making a motion as if bringing it from the sun, then
takes the four completed kethawns (the first of which is sacred to
the Owl) and places them in the patient's hands. The patient
recites after him, line by line, the prayer:*

Owl!
I have made your sacrifice.
I have prepared a smoke for you.
My feet restore for me.
My legs restore for me.
My body restore for me.
My mind restore for me.
My voice restore for me.

Today take out your spell for me.[12]
Today your spell for me is removed.
Away from me you have taken it.
Far off from me it is taken.
Far off you have done it.
Today I shall recover.
Today for me it is taken off.
Today my interior shall become cool.
My interior feeling cold, I shall go forth.
My interior feeling cold, may I walk.
No longer sore, may I walk.
Impervious to pain, may I walk.
Feeling light within, may I walk.
With lively feelings, may I walk.
Happily may I walk.
Happily abundant dark clouds I desire.
Happily abundant showers I desire.
Happily abundant vegetation I desire.
Happily abundant pollen I desire.
Happily abundant dew I desire.
Happily *in earthly beauty* may I walk.
[*line untranslated*][13]
May it be happy before me.
May it be happy behind me.
May it be happy below me.
May it be happy above me.
With it happy all around me, may I walk.
It is finished in beauty.[14]
It is finished in beauty.

The prayer is repeated three times, essentially unchanged, in-
voking in turn (in place of Owl) the deities Hastshéayuhi,
Hastshéeltlihi, and Echoing Stone,[15] *each of whom is to receive*

*one of the four kethawns. Assistants now take the completed
kethawns outside the lodge and lay them down in prescribed
positions, thus yielding them (or "sacrificing" them) to the
intended holy ones. Singers within begin the Songs of the
Kethawns:*[16]

I

Across the Tshéyi Canyon from the other side he
    crosses,
On a slender horizontal string of blue he crosses,
For his kethawn of blue, upon the string he crosses.

Across the Tshéyi Canyon from the other side he
    crosses,
On a slender horizontal string of white he crosses,
For his kethawn of black, upon the string he
    crosses.[17]

II

In a beautiful manner now he bears,
For Hastshéhogan, now he bears,
A little message now he bears,
Toward the trail of the he-rain, now he bears.

In a beautiful manner now he bears,
For Hastshéyalti, now he bears,
A little mesage now he bears,
Toward the trail of the she-rain, now he bears.[9]

FIRST SWEAT BATH. *Midmorning. Assistants construct a small conical
sweathouse over a shallow pit approximately two hundred paces
east of the lodge. Carrying eight plumed wands (Stevenson
counted twelve) and led by the chanter, who strews pollen before*

them, the participants proceed in single file from the lodge to the
sweathouse, singing:

This I walk with, this I walk with.
Now Hastshéyalti I walk with.
These are his feet I walk with.
These are his limbs I walk with.
This is his body I walk with.
This is his mind I walk with.
This is his voice I walk with.
These are his twelve white plumes I walk with.
Beauty before me, I walk with.
Beauty behind me, I walk with.
Beauty above me, I walk with
Beauty below me, I walk with.
Beauty all around me, I walk with.
In old age, the beautiful trail, I walk with.
It is I, I walk with.[18]

Separating the wands into four males and four females (or six
and six per Stevenson),[19] the chanter plants them around the
sweathouse. The patient, entering through a curtained doorway,
sits beside the heated stones that provide the sweat bath, while
the chanter, outside, mixes two cold infusions, the ketlo (chant
lotion) and the klédzhe azhé (night medicine). The chanter sings:

In the House of the Red Rock,
There I enter;
Half way in, I am come.
The corn plants shake.

In the House of Blue Water,
There I enter;

Half way in, I am come.
The plants shake.[20]

Hastshéyalti and a Female Divinity appear, and as the patient emerges they massage his essential parts with the wands. The patient drinks the night medicine; he bathes himself in the lotion. The chanter sings:

At the Red Rock House it grows,
There the giant corn plant grows.
With ears on either side it grows.
With its ruddy silk it grows,
Ripening in one day it grows,
Greatly multiplying grows.

At Blue Water House it grows,
There the giant squash vine grows,
With fruit on either side it grows,
With its yellow blossom grows,
Ripening in one night it grows,
Greatly multiplying grows.

The sweathouse is dismantled; the party returns to the lodge. The chanter anoints the patient with pollen, inserting small portions of it into the patient's mouth—and into his own mouth—singing:[21]

Ína hwié! my grandchild, I have eaten.
Ína hwié! my grandchild, I have eaten.
Ína hwié! my grandchild, I have eaten.
  Hastshéhogan. His food I have eaten.
  The pollen of evening. His food I have eaten.
  Much soft goods. His food I have eaten.
  Abundant hard goods. His food I have eaten.

Beauty lying behind him. His food I have eaten.
Beauty lying before him. His food I have eaten.
Beauty lying above him. His food I have eaten.
Beauty lying below him. His food I have eaten.
Beauty lying all around him. His food I have eaten.
In old age wandering. I have eaten.
On the trail of beauty. I have eaten.
Ína hwié! my grandchild. I have eaten. Kolagane.[22]

The party withdraws.

THE SACRED MOUNTAINS. *Sprinkling dry pigments on the floor of
the lodge, the chanter prepares a small sand painting featuring the
four sacred mountains of the Navajo world; a trail leads into their
midst. At the doorway the crier issues his usual call:* Biké hatáli
hakú. *The patient enters, walking slowly along the "trail" to the
"mountains," followed by Hastshéyalti. The singers begin:*

In a holy place with a god I walk,
In a holy place with a god I walk,
On Tsisnadzhíni with a god I walk,
On a chief of mountains with a god I walk,
In old age wandering with a god I walk,
On a trail of beauty with a god I walk.

*The stanza is repeated three times, changing the name of the
mountain, in turn, to Tsótsil, Dokoslíd, and Depéntsa.*[23] *The
patient reaches the center of the picture; the chanter recites:*[24]

From the base of the east.
From the base of Tsisnadzhíni.
From the house made of mirage,[25]
From the story made of mirage,[26]

From the doorway of rainbow,
The path out of which is the rainbow,
The rainbow passed out with me.
The rainbow raised up with me
Through the middle of broad fields,
The rainbow returned with me.
To where my house is visible,
The rainbow returned with me.
To the roof of my house,
The rainbow returned with me.
To the entrance of my house,
The rainbow returned with me.
To just within my house,
The rainbow returned with me.
To my fireside,
The rainbow returned with me.
To the center of my house,
The rainbow returned with me.
At the fore part of my house with the dawn,[27]
The Talking God sits with me.
The House God sits with me.
Pollen Boy sits with me.
Grasshopper Girl sits with me.[28]
In beauty Estsánatlehi, my mother, for her
     I return.[29]
Beautifully my fire to me is restored.
Beautifully my possessions are to me restored.
Beautifully my soft goods to me are restored.
Beautifully my hard goods to me are restored.
Beautifully my horses to me are restored.
Beautifully my sheep to me are restored.
Beautifully my old men to me are restored.
Beautifully my old women to me are restored.

Beautifully my young men to me are restored.
Beautifully my young women to me are restored.
Beautifully my children to me are restored.
Beautifully my wife to me is restored.
Beautifully my chiefs to me are restored.
Beautifully my country to me is restored.
Beautifully my fields to me are restored.
Beautifully my house to me is restored.
Talking God sits with me.
House God sits with me.
Pollen Boy sits with me.
Grasshopper Girl sits with me.
Beautifully white corn to me is restored.
Beautifully yellow corn to me is restored.
Beautifully blue corn to me is restored.
Beautifully corn of all kinds to me is restored.
In beauty may I walk.
All day long may I walk.
Through the returning seasons may I walk.
[*line untranslated*][30]
Beautifully . . . will I possess again.
[*line untranslated*]
Beautifully birds . . .
Beautifully joyful birds . . .
On the trail marked with pollen may I walk.
With grasshoppers about my feet may I walk.
With dew about my feet may I walk.
With beauty may I walk.
With beauty before me, may I walk.
With beauty behind me, may I walk.
With beauty above me, may I walk.
With beauty below me, may I walk.
With beauty all around me, may I walk.

In old age wandering on a trail of beauty,
    lively, may I walk.
In old age wandering on a trail of beauty,
    living again, may I walk.
It is finished in beauty.
It is finished in beauty.[31]

The prayer is thrice repeated, substituting in turn the names of the other three directions (south, west, north) and their corresponding mountains (Tsótsil, Dokoslíd, Depéntsa). Kneeling, Hastshé-yalti takes sand from each of the "mountains" and applies it to the patient. The patient kneels: coals are removed from the fire and placed before him; over these the chanter sprinkles a powder of feathers and resin, giving rise to an incense inhaled by the patient. The coals are extinguished, the picture obliterated. The party withdraws.

SECOND DAY / DAY OF THE SOUTH

SECOND RITE OF EXORCISM (THE EVERGREEN DRESS). *The crier calls at sunset. The patient enters the lodge and is draped with the evergreen dress—garlands of knotted spruce symbolizing the bonds of disease. The twin war gods, Nayénezgani and Tobadzhistshíni,[32] appear. The singers begin:*

In a land divine he strides,
In a land divine he strides,
Now Nayénezgani strides,
Above on the summits high he strides,
In a land divine he strides.

In a land divine he strides,
In a land divine he strides,

Now Tobadzhistshíni strides,
Below on the lesser hills he strides,
In a land divine he strides.

Proceeding sunwise around the patient, the gods cut loose the
knotted garlands. The singers continue:

I

The Slayer of the Alien Gods,[32]
That now am I.
The Bearer of the Sun
Arises with me,
Journeys with me,
Goes down with me,
Abides with me,
But sees me not.

The Child of the Water,
That now am I.
The Bearer of the Moon
Arises with me,
Journeys with me,
Goes down with me,
Abides with me,
But sees me not.[33]

II

I am the Slayer of the Alien Gods.
Wherever I roam,
Before me
Forests white are strewn around.
The lightning scatters;
But it is I who cause it.[34]

I am the Child of the Water.
Wherever I roam,
Behind me
Waters white are strewn around.
The tempest scatters;
But it is I who cause it.

The gods withdraw. The chanter drops fragments of the ever-green dress over the patient's head. With a grass brush he makes motions as if brushing away an evil influence, at length brushing it out through the smoke hole in the roof. He sings:

The corn grows up, the rain descends.
I sweep it off, I sweep it off.

The rain descends, the corn grows up.
I sweep it off, I sweep it off.

Incense is administered in the manner previously described. The party retires.

SECOND MORNING PRAYER RITUAL. *The chanter and his assistants prepare two "long" kethawns sacred to the Hastshéyalti and Hastshéhogan*[35] *of a shrine known as Kininaékai ("House of Horizontal White"). Each of the kethawns is a tobacco-filled reed attached to a string, which, feathered at the end, passes through five perforated jewels: whiteshell, turquoise, abalone, jet, and, again, whiteshell.*[36] *The chanter places the kethawns in the patient's hands, leading him, line by line, in the prayer:*

In the House of Horizontal White,[37]
He who rises with the morning light,
He who moves with the morning light;

Oh Hastshéyalti,
I have prepared your sacrifice,
I have made a smoke for you.
His feet restore for him.
His limbs restore for him.
His body restore for him.
His mind restore for him.
His voice restore for him.
Today your spell take out for him.
This very day your spell is taken out.
Away from him you took it.
Far away from him it has been taken.
Far away from him you have done it.
Happily he will recover.
Happily he has recovered.
Happily his interior will become cool.
Happily, feeling cold may he walk around.
It is finished again in beauty.
It is finished again in beauty.
In beauty may you walk, my grandchild.
Thus will it be beautiful.

*For the benefit of the second "long" kethawn, the prayer is made
again, substituting "evening light" and "Hastshéhogan" in the
opening lines. Chanter and patient now repeat the procedure for
the four "short" kethawns (tobacco-filled reeds painted to represent the Naakhaí dancers of the ninth night of the ceremony).
Two are male, two are female. For the benefit of the first, the
chanter recites:*

With the blue face,
Oh Male Divinity!

I have prepared your sacrifice.
I have made a smoke for you.
[Etc.]

The remainder of the prayer reads the same as the seventh through final lines of the prayer pertaining to the first "long" kethawn, given above. For the second "short" kethawn, the prayer opens:

With the yellow streak,
Oh Female Divinity!
I have prepared your sacrifice.
I have made a smoke for you.
[Etc.]

Again the continuation is the same. For the benefit of the third and fourth "short" kethawns, the chanter and the patient simply repeat the two prayers just given. Thus inspirited, all six kethawns are taken outside to be sacrificed (i.e., deposited where the gods will find them). The patient receives the usual incense.

SECOND SWEAT BATH. *The rites of the previous morning are repeated, this time with the sweathouse built to the south of the lodge. The songs (unrecorded) are similar.*

PREPARATION OF THE MANY KETHAWNS. *Four tobacco-filled reeds and forty-eight wooden pegs (i.e., fifty-two kethawns) are prepared during the afternoon.*

THIRD DAY / DAY OF THE WEST

THIRD RITE OF EXORCISM (THE MANY KETHAWNS). *Nightfall. The crier calls, the party enters. The fifty-two kethawns are sacrificed in a rite similar in form to the first rite of exorcism (see above). Hastshéyalti enters with the willow square, applies it to the patient, and exits. Returning, he takes a kethawn, presses it to each of the patient's essential parts, then carries it outside the lodge. A Female Divinity enters and similarly disposes of a second kethawn, followed by Hastshéhogan, who disposes of a third, and a second Female Divinity, who disposes of a fourth. The basic sequence, in which four of the kethawns are removed, is repeated until all fifty-two are gone. Songs on High accompany the rite. The chanter administers the usual incense. The company retires.*

THIRD MORNING PRAYER RITUAL. *The pattern previously established for the morning prayer ritual is again followed, now with a set of eight kethawns sacred to gods of the shrine known as House Made of Dawn (in the distant canyon of Tsegíhi).*[38] *Four of the kethawns stand for the Atsálei dancers to be encountered during the ninth night of the ceremony; four nearly identical prayers accompany this group of kethawns. The first prayer:*

Tsegíhi!
House made of the dawn.
House made of evening light.
House made of the dark cloud.
House made of male rain.
House made of dark mist.
House made of female rain.
House made of pollen.
House made of grasshoppers.
Dark cloud is at the door.
The trail out of it is dark cloud.
The zigzag lightning stands high up on it.
Male deity!
Your offering I make.

I have prepared a smoke for you.
Restore my feet for me.
Restore my legs for me.
Restore my body for me.
Restore my mind for me.
Restore my voice for me.
This very day take out your spell for me.
Your spell remove for me.
You have taken it away for me.
Far off it has gone.
Happily I recover.
Happily my interior becomes cool.
Happily I go forth.
My interior feeling cold, may I walk.
No longer sore, may I walk.
Impervious to pain, may I walk.
With lively feelings, may I walk.
As it used to be long ago, may I walk.
Happily may I walk.
Happily with abundant dark clouds may I walk.
Happily with abundant showers may I walk.
Happily with abundant plants may I walk.
Happily on a trail of pollen may I walk.
Happily may I walk.
Being as it used to be long ago, may I walk.
May it be beautiful before me.
May it be beautiful behind me.
May it be beautiful below me.
May it be beautiful above me.
May it be beautiful all around me.
In beauty it is finished.
In beauty it is finished.[39]

THIRD SWEAT BATH. *Essentially the same as on the previous two days, but with the sweathouse built to the west of the lodge.*

AMOLE BATH. *Early afternoon. The chanter lays pieces of amole in a tightly woven basket, adds water, and hands the mixture to an assistant who beats it until the suds rise up in a froth. The chanter sprinkles pollen over the surface of the suds; the patient is lathered to the accompaniment of Darkness Songs:*

> The corn comes up, the rain descends.
> It foams, it foams.
>
> The rain descends, the corn comes up.
> It foams, it foams.[40]

The necklace and jewels of both the patient and the chanter are washed. The patient is rinsed and rubbed dry with corn meal.

> From his body, it is rubbed away.
> By Estsánatlehi, it is rubbed away.[41]
> With the white corn, it is rubbed away.
> Made of the corn root, it is rubbed away.
> Made of the corn leaf, it is rubbed away.
> Made of the corn dew, it is rubbed away.
> Made of the tassel, it is rubbed away.
> Made of the pollen, it is rubbed away.
> Made of the corn grain, it is rubbed away.
> In old age wandering, it is rubbed away.
> On the trail of beauty, it is rubbed away.

FOURTH DAY / DAY OF THE NORTH

FOURTH RITE OF EXORCISM (THE SAPLING AND THE MASK). *Hastshé-yalti, accompanied by Hastshéhogan, plants a sapling in the earthen floor of the lodge, bends it toward the patient, and ties it to a mask fitted against the patient's face. Sapling and mask fly back when released, drawing evil influences away from the patient's head.*

The Vigil[42]

Anointing the masks / The patient, followed by the chanter, his principal assistants, and others who so desire, scatters pollen on the masks of the gods (previously laid out on the lodge floor). Barely audible prayers accompany the rite. Afterward, pollen bags are passed through the audience, and anyone who wishes to partake—that is, ingest a portion of the pollen—may do so.

Sprinkling the masks / Women carrying dishes of ceremonial food enter and proceed sunwise around the fire. To the accompaniment of Wand Songs (unrecorded), the chanter prepares lotion (ketlo) in a watertight basket, scattering the surface with frost crystals.[43] Each of two assistants takes a plumed wand, dips it in the lotion, and sprinkles the masks and the spectators.

Feeding the masks / The masks are symbolically fed from a bowl of corn meal mixed with water, subsequently passed to the chanter, the patient, the principal assistants, and, sunwise, among the assembled guests—until it is empty.

Waking the masks / Midnight. Taking each mask in turn, the chanter shakes, or "wakens," it as he sings the Waking Song:

He stirs, he stirs, he stirs, he stirs.
Among the lands of dawning, he stirs, he stirs;
The pollen of the dawning, he stirs, he stirs;
Now in old age wandering, he stirs, he stirs;
Now on the trail of beauty, he stirs, he stirs;
He stirs, he stirs, he stirs, he stirs.

He stirs, he stirs, he stirs, he stirs.
Among the lands of evening, he stirs, he stirs;
The pollen of the evening, he stirs, he stirs;
Now in old age wandering, he stirs, he stirs;
Now on the trail of beauty, he stirs, he stirs.
He stirs, he stirs, he stirs, he stirs.

He stirs, he stirs, he stirs, he stirs.
Now Hastshéyalti, he stirs, he stirs;
Now his white robe of buckskin, he stirs, he stirs;
Now in old age wandering, he stirs, he stirs.
Now on the trail of beauty, he stirs, he stirs.
He stirs, he stirs, he stirs, he stirs.

The third stanza is repeated for each of the remaining gods,
substituting the name and attribute as follows until all the masks
have been "wakened":[44]

Hastshéhogan: his white kilt
Dsahadoldzhá: his bow of darkness
Gánaskidi: his white tobacco-pouch
Hatdastshíshi: his white leggings
Hastshébaka: his soft goods of all kinds
Hastshébaad: her jewels of all kinds
Nayénezgani: his stone necklace
Tobadzhistshíni: his ear pendants
Hastshéoltoi: her puma quiver

Hastshéltshi: his coral beads
Hastshézhini: his white beads
Tónenili: his jar of mixed waters
Tshohanoái: his abalone pendant
Klehanoái: his whiteshell pendant
Estsánatlehi: her plants of all kinds

The chanter prays alone:

In beauty may I dwell.
In beauty may I walk.
In beauty may my male kindred dwell.
In beauty may my female kindred dwell.
In beauty may it rain on my young men.
In beauty may it rain on my young women.
In beauty may it rain on my chiefs.
In beauty may it rain on us.
In beauty may our corn grow.
In the trail of pollen may it rain.
In beauty before us, may it rain.
In beauty behind us, may it rain.
In beauty below us, may it rain.
In beauty above us, may it rain.
In beauty all around us, may it rain.
In beauty may I walk.
Goods may I acquire.
Jewels may I acquire.[45]
Horses may I acquire.
Sheep may I acquire.
Beeves may I acquire.[46]
In old age,
The beautiful trail,
May I walk.

The remainder of the night is devoted to song cycles, selected at the discretion of the chanter.[47]

I

The sacred blue corn-seed I am planting,
In one night it will grow and flourish,
In one night the corn increases,
In the garden of the House God.

The sacred white corn-seed I am planting,
In one day it will grow and ripen,
In one day the corn increases,
In its beauty it increases.

II

With this it grows, with this it grows,
The dark cloud, with this it grows.
The dew thereof, with this it grows,
The blue corn, with this it grows.

With this it grows, with this it grows,
The dark mist, with this it grows.
The dew thereof, with this it grows,
The white corn, with this it grows.

III

This it eats, this it eats,
The dark cloud,
Its dew
The blue corn eats,
This it eats.

This it eats, this it eats,
The dark mist,
Its dew
The white corn eats,
This it eats.

IV

The great corn-plant is with the bean,
Its rootlets now are with the bean,
Its leaf-tips now are with the bean,
Its dewdrops now are with the bean,
Its tassel now is with the bean,
Its pollen now is with the bean,
And now its silk is with the bean,
And now its grain is with the bean.

V

Truly in the East
The white bean
And the great corn-plant
Are tied with the white lightning.
Listen! It approaches!
The voice of the bluebird is heard.

Truly in the East
The white bean
And the great squash
Are tied with the rainbow.
Listen! It approaches!
The voice of the bluebird is heard.[48]

VI

From the top of the great corn-plant the water
    gurgles, I hear it;
Around the roots the water foams, I hear it;
Around the roots of the plants it foams, I hear it;
From their tops the water foams, I hear it.

VII

On your farm the cloud is level with the corn,
On your farm the water is level with the corn,
On your farm the mist is level with the plants,
On your farm the mist is level with the pollen.[49]

VIII

The corn grows up. The waters of the dark clouds
    drop, drop.
The rain descends. The waters from the corn
    leaves drop, drop.
The rain descends. The waters from the plants
    drop, drop.
The corn grows up. The waters of the dark mists
    drop, drop.

IX

Since the ancient days, I have planted,
Since the time of the Emergence, I have planted,[50]
The great corn-plant, I have planted,
Its roots, I have planted,
The tips of its leaves, I have planted,
Its dew, I have planted,
Its tassel, I have planted,
Its pollen, I have planted,

Its silk, I have planted,
Its seed, I have planted.

Since the ancient days, I have planted,
Since the time of the Emergence, I have planted,
The great squash-vine, I have planted,
Its seed, I have planted,
Its silk, I have planted,
Its pollen, I have planted,
Its tassel, I have planted,[51]
Its dew, I have planted,
The tips of its leaves, I have planted,
Its roots, I have planted.

X

Shall I cull this fruit
Of the great corn-plant?
Shall you break it? Shall I break it?
Shall I break it? Shall you break it?
    Shall I? Shall you?

Shall I cull this fruit
Of the great squash-vine?
Shall you pick it up? Shall I pick it up?
Shall I pick it up? Shall you pick it up?
    Shall I? Shall you?

XI

I pulled it with my hand.
The great corn-plants are scattered around.
I pulled it with my hand.
The standing plants are scattered around.

Singing continues until a crier, shouting outside the door, announces the first streak of dawn. Singing concludes with the Daylight Songs:

> He has a voice, he has a voice.
> Just at daylight Sialia calls.[52]
> The bluebird has a voice.
> He has a voice, his voice melodious,
> His voice melodious, that flows in gladness.
> Sialia calls, Sialia calls.
>
> He has a voice, he has a voice.
> Just at twilight Sialia calls.
> The bird Tsholgáli has a voice.
> He has a voice, his voice melodious,
> His voice melodious, that flows in gladness.
> Sialia calls, Sialia calls.

The chanter prays, the patient withdraws.

FOURTH MORNING PRAYER RITUAL. *The chanter again follows the pattern established in the previous mornings' rituals, here using but a single kethawn (similar to the "long" kethawn of the third day). The accompanying prayers are directed to Hastshéyalti, Hastshéhogan, Dsahadoldzhá, Gánaskidi, Hastshébaka, and Hastshébaad. An assistant representing the mythical Tsenidzhenétyin ("He Who Carries toward a Rock Shelter") deposits, or "sacrifices," the kethawn.*

FOURTH SWEAT BATH. *This ritual receives its final performance, with the sweathouse built to the north of the lodge. Thunder Songs are used.*[53]

I

Thonah! Thonah![54]
There is a voice above,
The voice of the thunder.
Within the dark cloud,
Again and again it sounds,
Thonah! Thonah!

Thonah! Thonah!
There is a voice below,
The voice of the grasshopper.
Among the plants,
Again and again it sounds,
Thonah! Thonah!

II

The voice that beautifies the land!
The voice above,
The voice of the thunder
Within the dark cloud,
Again and again it sounds,
The voice that beautifies the land.

The voice that beautifies the land!
The voice below,
The voice of the grasshopper
Among the plants,
Again and again it sounds,
The voice that beautifies the land.

THE TREMBLING PLACE. *A small sand painting called Picture of the Trembling Place may be made during the fourth afternoon of the ceremony. (This rite is optional.)*

Part II / The Healing

FIFTH DAY

SONGS OF EXORCISM, FIRST SESSION (INCLUDING INITIATION). *Shortly after nightfall a basket is turned upside down on the floor of the lodge and beaten to the accompaniment of song.*[55] *Ushered in by Hastshéyalti and a Female Divinity, the initiates (mostly children) are sprinkled with corn meal and flagellated with a blade of yucca if male, or, if female, massaged with an ear of corn. The god and goddess unmask. In turn the initiates try on the mask of the Female Divinity; they sprinkle pollen on the masks; they inhale the incense.*[56] *The basket is turned up.*

FIRST GREAT SAND PAINTING. *Sprinkling powdered pigments on the floor of the lodge, the chanter and his assistants prepare the painting called Picture of the Whirling Logs—featuring Hastshéyalti, Hastshéhogan, and other gods of succor seated on the arms of a cross (which floats on the surface of a whirlpool), encircled by the ribbonlike figure of the rainbow goddess. When the work is complete, the chanter deposits meal on the sacred figures, plants the plumed wands around the outside of the picture, sets a cup of medicine between the "hands" of the rainbow, and sprinkles pollen. A Male Divinity enters, takes the cup, and after offering it symbolically to the pictured gods gives it to the patient to drink. Taking dust from the various bodily parts of the "gods," he applies it to the corresponding parts of the patient. Songs of the Whirling Logs accompany the rite:*

Grasshopper arrives,
From the east arrives,

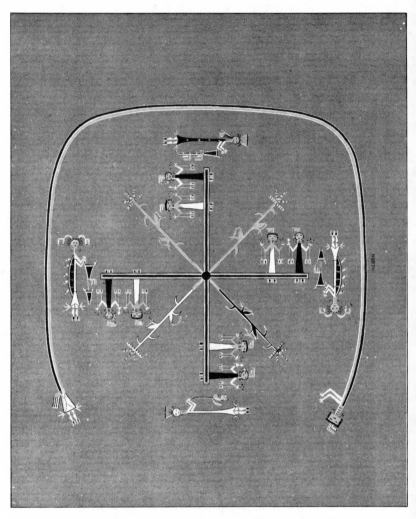

Figure 4 / The First Great Sand Painting: *Silnéole Yikál*
(Picture of the Whirling Logs). After Matthews 1902

The great corn arrives,
The child-rain arrives,[57]
In a way of beauty arrives.

Grasshopper arrives,[58]
From the west arrives,
Vegetation arrives,
Pollen arrives,
In a way of beauty arrives.

The Male Divinity withdraws. The chanter administers the customary incense. The picture is obliterated.

SIXTH DAY

SONGS OF EXORCISM, SECOND SESSION. *Again the basket is "turned down." As the singing draws to a close, the basket is "turned up" and hands are waved in the direction of the smoke hole to drive out evil influences (which the songs have captured and imprisoned beneath the basket). The patient inhales the usual incense.*

SECOND GREAT SAND PAINTING. *Again the ribbonlike rainbow surrounds the depicted gods (here representing the ninth-night Naakhaí dancers). The chanter and his assistants repeat the previous day's sand-painting ritual to the accompaniment of Songs on High.*

SEVENTH DAY

SONGS OF EXORCISM, THIRD SESSION. *Once again the basket is turned down. Songs on High continue. The basket is turned up.*

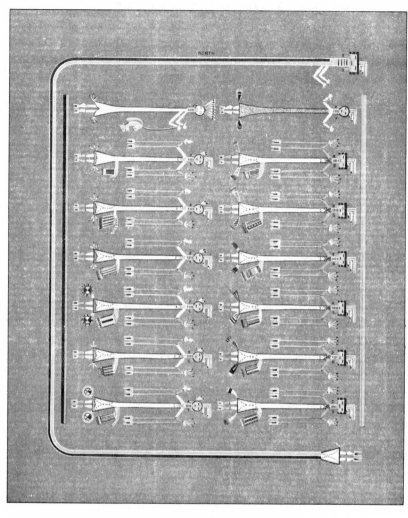

Figure 5 / The Second Great Sand Painting: *Naakhaí Yikál*
(Picture of the Naakhaí Dance). After Matthews 1902

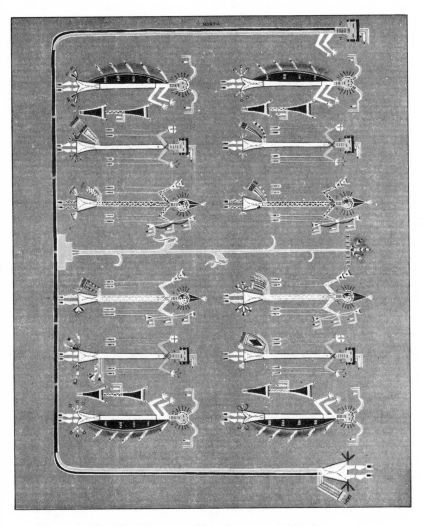

Figure 6 / The Third Great Sand Painting: *Dsahadoldzhábe Yikál* (Picture with the Fringe Mouths). After Matthews 1902

THIRD GREAT SAND PAINTING. *A modified rainbow encircles the representations of twelve deities, including those known as Fringe Mouths. While the work progresses, a second initiation takes place outdoors in front of the lodge (similar to the earlier, fifth-day initiation). Now, as a prelude to the sand-painting ritual, impersonators perform a rite of succor: the patient, approaching the lodge, meets Hastshéyalti, Dsahadoldzhá ("Fringe Mouth"), and a Male Divinity; the three gods, dancing, alternately approach and withdraw, holding a rattle to the patient's head and rubbing his body with meal. Turning sunwise, the patient enters the lodge, approaches the completed sand painting, and submits once again to the ritual described above for the fifth day. Singers begin the Songs of the Fringe Mouths (unrecorded).*

EIGHTH DAY

SONGS OF EXORCISM, FOURTH SESSION. *The basket is once again turned down. Songs of the Fringe Mouths continue. The basket is turned up.*

FOURTH GREAT SAND PAINTING. *In other nine-day chants of the Navajos a fourth great painting is customarily made on this, the eighth day of the ceremony. But in the case of the Night Chant, one of the sand paintings is said to have been withheld—or forbidden—by the gods.*[59] *In its place, Nayénezgani, Tobadzhistshíni, and Hastshéyalti perform a rite of succor similar to that of the preceding day. Afterward, inside the lodge, the patient (praying) presents a kethawn to each of the three impersonators.*

Part III / The Reprise

NINTH DAY

Four great fires are kindled on either side of the level space, or "dancing ground," in front of the lodge. Facing the lodge at a distance of some hundred paces stands the newly constructed "arbor," a circle of evergreen boughs to be used as the performers' changing room. Spectators, numbering in the hundreds, gather just beyond the fires along both sides of the dancing ground.

DANCE OF THE ATSÁLEI, OR THUNDERBIRDS. *The chanter's assistants paint with white earth the bodies of the dancers who will represent the four thunderbirds (of corn, of child-rain, of vegetation, and of pollen). The chanter sings:*

> Now the holy one paints his form,
> The Wind Boy, the holy one, paints his form,[60]
> All over his body, he paints his form,
> With the dark cloud he paints his form,
> With the misty rain he paints his form,
> With the rainy bubbles he paints his form,
> To the ends of his toes he paints his form,
> To fingers and rattle he paints his form,
> To the plume on his head he paints his form.

As the dancers repair to the arbor, the basket is turned down and singing begins anew. Fully costumed, the thunderbirds, led by Hastshéyalti, approach the dancing ground. A crier calls: Come on the trail of song. *The patient emerges from the lodge and sprinkles the dancers with meal. (Singing within the lodge continues unabated.) Addressing the thunderbird of pollen, the patient recites after the chanter, line by line:*[61]

In Tsegíhi,
In the house made of the dawn,
In the house made of the evening twilight,
In the house made of the dark cloud,
In the house made of the he-rain,
In the house made of the dark mist,
In the house made of the she-rain,
In the house made of pollen,
In the house made of grasshoppers,
Where the dark mist curtains the doorway,
The path to which is on the rainbow,
Where the zigzag lightning stands high on top,
Where the he-rain stands high on top,
Oh, male divinity!
With your moccasins of dark cloud, come to us.
With your leggings of dark cloud, come to us.
With your shirt of dark cloud, come to us.
With your headdress of dark cloud, come to us.
With your mind enveloped in dark cloud, come
     to us.
With the dark thunder above you, come to us
     soaring.
With the shapen cloud at your feet, come to us
     soaring.
With the far darkness made of the dark cloud
     over your head, come to us soaring.
With the far darkness made of the he-rain
     over your head, come to us soaring.
With the far darkness made of the dark mist
     over your head, come to us soaring.
With the far darkness made of the she-rain
     over your head, come to us soaring.
With the zigzag lightning flung out on high

over your head, come to us soaring.
With the rainbow hanging high over your head,
     come to us soaring.
With the far darkness made of the dark cloud on
     the ends of your wings, come to us soaring.
With the far darkness made of the he-rain on
     the ends of your wings, come to us soaring.
With the far darkness made of the dark mist on
     the ends of your wings, come to us soaring.
With the far darkness made of the she-rain on
     the ends of your wings, come to us soaring.
With the zigzag lightning flung out on high on
     the ends of your wings, come to us soaring.
With the rainbow hanging high on the ends of
     your wings, come to us soaring.
With the near darkness made of the dark cloud, of
     the he-rain, of the dark mist, and of the
     she-rain, come to us.
With the darkness on the earth, come to us.
With these I wish the foam floating on the
     flowing water over the roots of the great
     corn.
I have made your sacrifice.
I have prepared a smoke for you.
My feet restore for me.
My limbs restore for me.
My body restore for me.
My mind restore for me.
My voice restore for me.
Today, take out your spell for me.
Today, take away your spell for me.
Away from me you have taken it.
Far off from me it is taken.

Far off you have done it.
Happily I recover.
Happily my interior becomes cool.
Happily my eyes regain their power.
Happily my head becomes cool.
Happily my limbs regain their power.
Happily I hear again.
Happily for me *the spell* is taken off.
Happily may I walk.
Impervious to pain, may I walk.
Feeling light within, may I walk.
With lively feelings, may I walk.
Happily abundant dark clouds I desire.
Happily abundant dark mists I desire.
Happily abundant passing showers I desire.
Happily an abundance of vegetation I desire.
Happily an abundance of pollen I desire.
Happily abundant dew I desire.
Happily may fair white corn, to the ends of the
     earth, come with you.
Happily may fair yellow corn, to the ends of the
     earth, come with you.
Happily may fair blue corn, to the ends of the
     earth, come with you.
Happily may fair corn of all kinds, to the ends
     of the earth, come with you.
Happily may fair plants of all kinds, to the ends
     of the earth, come with you.
Happily may fair goods of all kinds, to the ends
     of the earth, come with you.
Happily may fair jewels of all kinds, to the ends
     of the earth, come with you.

With these before you, happily may they come
    with you.
With these behind you, happily may they come
    with you.
With these below you, happily may they come
    with you.
With these above you, happily may they come
    with you.
With these all around you, happily may they
    come with you.
Thus happily you accomplish your tasks.
Happily the old men will regard you.
Happily the old women will regard you.
Happily the young men will regard you.
Happily the young women will regard you.
Happily the boys will regard you.
Happily the girls will regard you.
Happily the children will regard you.
Happily the chiefs will regard you.
Happily, as they scatter in different directions,
    they will regard you.
Happily, as they approach their homes, they will
    regard you.
Happily may their roads home be on the trail of
    pollen.
Happily may they all get back.
In beauty I walk.
With beauty before me, I walk.
With beauty behind me, I walk.
With beauty below me, I walk.
With beauty above me, I walk.
With beauty all around me, I walk.

It is finished in beauty,
It is finished in beauty,
It is finished in beauty,
It is finished in beauty.

With minor variations the prayer is thrice repeated, once for each of the other three dancers. The dance begins. Singers within the lodge now yield to a second company of singers outdoors:

The corn comes up, the rain descends,
The corn plant comes therewith.
The rain descends, the corn comes up.
The child-rain comes therewith.

The corn comes up, the rain descends.
Vegetation comes therewith.
The rain descends, the corn comes up,
The pollen comes therewith.

When the outside singers have finished, the inside singers resume:

Above it thunders,
His thoughts are directed to you,
He rises toward you,
Now to your house
Approaches for you.
He arrives for you,
He comes to the door,
He enters for you.
Behind the fireplace[62]
He eats his special dish.
"Your body is strong,
"Your body is holy now," he says.

The dancers proceed to the arbor, unmask, then retire to the
lodge for silent prayer. (The singing in the lodge continues with-
out interruption.)

DANCE OF THE NAAKHAÍ. *Twelve gods (the Naakhaí dancers)*
emerge from the arbor, accompanied by Hastshéyalti and the
chanter. Tónenili tags along.[63] *Just as the lodge singing ceases,*
the outside singers begin the familiar prelude:

> Óhohohó héhehe héya héya
> Óhohohó héhehe héya héya

The prelude is followed by either traditional or improvised verses.
The dance begins. Stopping and starting at regular intervals, the
outdoor singing (and dancing) alternates with the lodge singing,
so that the night—the entire night—is filled with song.[64] *The*
indoor program becomes a reprise of song cycles heard during
the previous eight days, with some new items added.[65] *Dawn*
arrives. The singing ends with the Finishing Hymn:

> From the pond in the white valley—
> The young man doubts it[66]—
> He takes up his sacrifice,[67]
> With that he now heals.
> With that your kindred thank you now.

> From the pools in the green meadow—
> The young woman doubts it—
> He takes up his sacrifice,
> With that he now heals.
> With that your kindred thank you now.

The basket is turned up and the drumstick (of twisted yucca leaves) taken outside by an assistant, who pulls it apart, sprinkling pollen on the shreds, repeating in a low voice the benediction:

Thus will it be beautiful,
Thus walk in beauty, my grandchild.[68]

The patient, facing east, inhales the breath of dawn.[69]

1 / The Navajo name as given by Matthews is *Klédzhe Hatál* (*Klédzhe:* "according to the night," *Hatál:* "a chant"—hence "Night Chant"). Most modern students, however, refer to the ceremony simply as "Nightway," noting that the single term *Klédzhe* is sufficient to specify it. See Berard Haile, "Navaho Chantways and Ceremonials," *American Anthropologist*, Vol. 40, 1938, pp. 639–52.

2 / The deity Hastshéhogan ("House God"), with his unmistakable farm and home associations, would appear to be a Navajo *kulturgeist*. As are culture spirits elsewhere, Hastshéhogan is identified with the light of the western sun, the traditional source of fecundity and food crops. By the same token he represents but one half (the "feminine" half) of a split personality, whose "masculine" counterpart is Hastshéyalti ("Talking God"), the personified light of the eastern sun and the advocate of dawn and birth. (Hastshéyalti stands for the white light of morning, Hastshéhogan for the yellow light of evening.) By phonetic manipulation the element *hogan* can be made to sound somewhat unlike the familiar word for house, or hogan, and more akin to a subverbal cry—analogous to the *Wu hu hu hú* (see p. 292 and note 4) of Hastshéyalti. For this reason the name has lately been

translated "Calling God" (see Wyman 1970, p. 175), neatly emphasizing the deity's companionship with Talking God (see note 4) and bringing the interpretation more in line with the view of mid-twentieth-century Navajos who consider the etymology "House God" to be of secondary importance or even irrelevant.

3 / The Navajo day begins at sunset.

4 / Talking God's utterance resembles the call of the personified sun (*Hu hu!*) heard at daybreak in Pueblo rituals (see E. C. Parsons, *A Pueblo Indian Journal, 1920–21*, p. 45). There would appear to be a connection between the voice of the sun, the breath of the sun, the breath of dawn, and the breath of life. See notes 2 and 69.

5 / Though principally exorcistic, the ritual makes use of both the additory and purgative aspects of wind. Hastshéyalti's willow square, circumscribing a "concentration" of winds, imparts or invigorates the breath of life. (See Stevenson, p. 238; and compare the Fourth World episode—Matthews 1897, pp. 68 ff.—in which a group of four gods, led by Hastshéyalti and abetted by Wind, create First Man and First Woman; cf. p. 68, note 4, above.) The whirlwind-like rings, on the other hand, suggest the swiftness of the wind (Matthews 1902) and hence its peculiar ability to carry off infection. The knots in the yarn symbolize the pent-up evil of disease (Kluckhohn and Wyman, p. 79); unraveling draws it out and the escaping wind-rings bear it away. (Compare the Iroquois prayer: "We return thanks to the wind, which, moving the air, has banished diseases"— Lewis Morgan, *League of the Ho-dé-no-sau-nee*, 1851, p. 202.)

6 / In the present context Hastshéayuhi ("Superior God") is perhaps best considered as a reflection of Hastshéyalti, emphasizing his celestial aspect. (The song is one of twenty-six Songs on High.)

7 / *Kethawn* is a Navajo word (commonly translated "prayer-stick") denoting a wide range of invocatory, coercive, or sacrificial offerings. In the case at hand, "precious" food (an ear of jewels) and tobacco (a ritual cigarette) are inspirited with a coercive prayer and delivered to the gods as sacrifices in exchange for healing. The kethawn is a "message" in the sense that it conveys the substance of the accompanying prayer.

8 / The colors of the jewels—white, blue, black, and yellow—are the colors of the four cardinal points, east, south, north, and west.

9 / The song is a poetic generalization. The intended deities are generalized as Hastshéhogan and Hastshéyalti; the blessing to be obtained through the medium of the kethawn is generalized as rain (see note 61). (He-rain, or male rain, is rain accompanied by thunder. She-rain, or female rain, is rain without thunder.)

10 / The first stanza refers to *Nicotiana Palmeri*, the second to *N. attenuata* (Matthews 1902).

11 / Matthews recognizes pollen, the most important of all the medicines used in Navajo ritual, as an "emblem of peace, of happiness, of prosperity." According to Reichard, the word for pollen means, literally, "it-spreads-light-in-all-directions."

12 / All disease is attributed to supernatural spells. And most, if not all, deities work evil as well as good.

13 / Matthews was unable to translate *Hozhógo dáshe elkídzhe ah hwenído*.

14 / This line is analogous to the Christian amen (Matthews 1897, p. 275).

15 / It is difficult to determine the significance of these four rather obscure supernaturals. Owl is the proverbial sorcerer in certain

mythologies, but in Navajo lore he is often benign. Hastshéayuhi, typically paired with Hastshéyalti (see note 6), occasionally surfaces in myth with a full-fledged personality of his own—mostly mischievous. Hastshéeltlihi is said to inhabit ruined Pueblo dwellings (considered shrines by the Navajo). Echoing, or "Talking," Stone personifies an echoing cliff wall. (Matthews 1902, Reichard 1950.)

16 / The first of these two songs pertains to gods in quest of kethawns, the second to kethawn bearers in quest of gods.

17 / In former times, writes Matthews, there was something like a spider's web, a kind of suspension bridge, across the Chelly Canyon (Tshéyi Canyon) on which the holy ones crossed. Hastshéayuhi crossed on a blue string, Hastshéyalti on a white.

18 / In these last two lines the singer would appear to be saying, "I *am* old age, I *am* the beautiful trail." As Wyman has shown, the twin concepts "old age" and "beautiful trail" (or "long life" and "happiness," as he prefers to render them) may sometimes be thought of as persons. Occasionally "they" may even be characterized as boy and girl ("long-life-boy, happiness-girl"), emphasizing "their" perennial youthfulness. (Wyman 1970, pp. 28–30, 135.)

19 / This commemorates the separation of the sexes in the Fourth World (Matthews 1902).

20 / Both this song and the one that follows belong to a group known as Songs in the Rock. The mythology of the cycle is unrecorded, but it probably tells of a hero who travels to the Red Rock House (an unidentified Pueblo ruin, regarded as sacred) in quest of fertility, or abundance. One is reminded of the culture hero's journey to the house of the reddening sun (in Algonkian myth) and the fabulous vegetables of Tollan (see p. 39). The terms "Blue" and "Water'" are antithetical to "Red" and "Rock";

for an explanation, see the second part of note 33.

21 / This "food song" is the only item from the song-myth of Dawn Boy that Matthews could definitely place in the Night Chant ceremony. (A distinction must be made between the lore of the Night Chant and the ceremony itself. In the former category are several great myths accounting for the origin of ritual procedure, an untold number of song-stories, like the myth of Dawn Boy, and various lesser myths that serve as mnemonic keys to the lengthier song cycles. Together these comprise a vast "library" of the Night Chant, from which the chanter draws certain prayers and songs for ceremonial use. Much of the material is deliberately held in reserve. Some of it may be tabooed.) For Dawn Boy, see Matthews 1907.

22 / According to Matthews the phrase *Ína hwié* is "meaningless." *Kolagane* is a familiar nonsense word included for the sake of euphony. (The term "my grandchild," a form of address often heard from the lips of supernaturals, imparts a special tone of blessedness. In myth, the song is sung by Dawn Boy himself. See note 21.) For a detailed interpretation of the song as a whole, see pp. xiv–xv.

23 / The four sacred mountains—Tsisnadzhíni (Pelado Peak, New Mexico?), Tsótsil (Mount Taylor, New Mexico), Dokoslíd (Humphreys Peak, Arizona), and Depéntsa (Hesperus Peak, Colorado?)—stand at the four corners of the Navajo world: east, south, west, and north, respectively. In this context, however, they are regarded as the four mountains of the Fourth World, subsequently transported to the present, or Fifth, world (Matthews 1902).

24 / The prayer that follows continues the theme announced in the preceding song and developed in the accompanying ritual. Like the heroes of myth, the patient has followed a holy trail to each of the four sacred mountains (seats of the gods). Acquiring

their power, he returns to his home by means of a rainbow (the swift, easy road traditionally used by supernaturals) and finds his familiar surroundings beautified.

25 / A clearer translation of this line would be "From the hogan made of mirage," emphasizing that a conical, Navajo-style dwelling is envisioned, not a Pueblo-style adobe or rock house. While the preceding song stresses the mountain's loftiness, here in the prayer the focus is on its form, regarded as an apotheosized hogan, the ideal home of a god (see Reichard, p. 452). "Mirage" refers to the typical mirrorlike glint associated with desert heat; in Navajo lore it appears to represent a precious, or exalted, form of sunlight, viewed as male generative power (cf. Reichard, pp. 66, 495). The mountain, in a sense, has become a house of the sun; and in fact the four sacred mountains are supposed to have been sun substitutes during the sunless Fourth World. See Reichard, pp. 17, 250. (Note how this line and the two that follow progressively narrow the devotee's attention from house to "story" to doorway. Progressionism is a conventional feature of Navajo ritual poetry—used again below, in a somewhat different manner, to get the patient-hero back into his own house.)

26 / Matthews's poetic "story" is misleading. "Base," or "lower part," would be more correct.

27 / The "fore part" of any house would be to the east, in front of the occupant, whom we must imagine to be seated at the yuni (the place of honor behind the fire, facing the doorway).

28 / Grasshopper Girl (or Cornbeetle Girl, as modern students prefer) symbolizes "female generative power," just as Pollen Boy, with whom she is often coupled, symbolizes "male generative power" (Reichard, pp. 422, 457). Note that this line together with the three preceding lines expresses in figurative terms the formula:

With beauty before me,
With beauty behind me,
With beauty above me,
With beauty below me.

29 / The return to the mother (or grandmother) is a characteristic motif of the Navajo hero myth. (For examples see Spencer, passim.) Bear in mind that in Navajo myth the hero is often literally a child. Jungian mythologists (emphasizing ontogenetic parallels) tend to regard *any* hero's adventure as a symbolic separation from the mother. Note that the departing Quetzalcoatl, p. 34, sings of leaving his "mother." (And note that the youthful heroes of the *Popol Vuh* are reluctantly given up by the "grandmother" who anxiously awaits their return.)

30 / Matthews was unable to translate all or part of this and the following four lines. (For the Navajo text, see Matthews 1907, p. 52.)

31 / Source for this prayer: Matthews 1907.

32 / Nayénezgani ("Slayer of the Alien Gods," or "Monster Slayer") is the principal hero of Navajo mythology; he is the war god, the child of Father Sun and Mother Earth (and the approximate analogue of Quetzalcoatl in his warrior aspect). His presence in ritual suggests exorcism, or "evil chasing." Like other major gods, Nayénezgani has an alter ego, Tobadzhistshíni, a more passive, or "feminine," counterpart who generally accompanies him.

33 / It is to be expected that the war god would be identified with the planet Venus. A moment's reflection will confirm that Venus does indeed arise, journey, and go down with the sun (imagined by the Navajo as an anthropomorphic figure carrying a disc, hence the epithet "Bearer of the Sun"), though the sun of course does not "see" it. In a Wichita myth given by Edward Curtis

(*The North American Indian*, Vol. XIX, 1930, p. 88), the morning star says, "You people may not see me during the day, but I journey on." The second stanza, pertaining to Tobadzhis-tshíni ("Child of the Water"), turns out to be pure nonsense—at least from an experiential point of view—though structurally it is quite valid. Notice that it simply reiterates the first stanza, substituting an antithesis for each key element, "sun" becoming "moon," "Slayer of the Alien Gods" becoming "Child of the Water." (Child of the Water, said to have been conceived by the earth through the agency of dripping water, provides a satisfying antithesis to Slayer of the Alien Gods, who was also conceived by the earth, but through the agency of sunlight.) All the Night Chant song texts are composed in antithetical pairs. If, as in a few cases, the twin stanza is missing, it has merely been suppressed, either by Matthews or by the chanter himself. The twin stanza is always artificial and, in some cases, egregiously "nonsensical."

34 / Lightning in the present context is evidently imagined as the war god's weapon against evil, acquired from his sun father (who provides sunbeam arrows for clear days, lightning arrows for dark days). See Matthews 1897, p. 113; Reichard, p. 18.

35 / Many a Navajo shrine has its own Hastshéyalti and Hastshéhogan.

36 / Matthews writes: "At the White House the patient is supposed to stand in the center of the world; for this reason the string is attached to the middle of the kethawn. The white cotton string represents the biké hozhóni, the beautiful or happy trail of life so often mentioned in the songs and prayers, which the devotee hopes, with the aid of the gods, to travel. 'With all around me beautiful, may I walk,' say the prayers, and for this reason the string passes through beautiful beads, which by their colors symbolize the four cardinal points of the compass. 'With beauty above me, may I walk,' 'With beauty below me, may I walk,'

are again the words of the prayers; so the string includes feather and hair of the turkey, a bird of the earth, and of the eagle, a bird of the sky. 'My voice restore for me,' 'Make beautiful my voice,' are expressions of the prayers and to typify these sentiments the string includes feathers of warbling birds whose voices 'flow in gladness' as the Navaho song says." (Note that the "beautiful trail" passes through the four colors—white for east, blue for south, yellow for west, black for north—and back again to the first one, white, the color of dawn. For an interpretation, see p. 92, note 93.)

37 / Describing the well-known White House, Matthews writes: "In the Chelly Canyon, Arizona, there still stands in an excellent state of preservation a remarkable ruined cliff-house built of yellow sandstone, two stories high . . . Its upper portion is painted white, horizontally; its lower unpainted portion is yellow . . . The Navahoes do not think this the result of a mere whim, but that it is intentional and symbolic. White is the color of the east in Navaho symbolism, and they suppose the upper story was sacred to Hastshéyalti, or Talking God, who was a god of dawn and of the east. Yellow is the symbolic color of the west, and they suppose the lower story belonged to Hastshéhogan, or House God, who was a god of the west and of the evening twilight." —Matthews 1902, p. 89; 1907, p. 29.

38 / If the proper materials are available, the chanter may prepare an additional kethawn, sacred to the sun itself. (This would tend to confirm that the presumed Pueblo ruin called House Made of Dawn, as well as the White House of the previous morning's ritual, is in some way analogous to the dwelling place of the sun. Possibly, like the jeweled palace of Quetzalcoatl, they replicate— on earth—the sun's home in the heavens.)

39 / Source: Matthews 1907, p. 54.

40 / This is but one of ten Darkness Songs. Another, not used

during the bath (but heard during the ninth-night reprise), is as follows:

> For my sake bluebird approaches, for my sake bluebird
>   approaches.
> The rain sprinkles, the corn comes up.
> The rain sprinkles, the rain descends.
>
> For my sake bluebird approaches, for my sake bluebird
>   approaches.
> The rain sprinkles, the rain descends.
> The rain sprinkles, the corn comes up.

41 / The bath is intimately connected with the mythology of the earth mother, Estsánatlehi. See Wyman 1970.

42 / Here begins a series of ritual acts to "waken" the sleeping gods; the episode marks a turning point. During the first half of the Night Chant the patient is cleansed so that he will be acceptable to the gods. Now the gods are made ready to "appear" in the curative sand paintings to which the second half of the ceremony (the Healing) is largely devoted.

43 / Like many other Indian ceremonies, especially those belonging to tribes that practice horticulture (as do the Navajo), the Night Chant "must be performed only during the frosty weather, in the late autumn and the winter months—at the season when the snakes are hibernating" (Matthews 1902, p. 4). Here again the serpent is associated with cultural activities. See p. 190. A sick person requiring a Night Chant in summer may be treated with excerpts, never the full ceremony (Reichard, p. 102).

44 / Herewith the Night Chant pantheon. Of the sixteen gods included, several are too obscure to be easily characterized (for details, see Reichard and, especially, Matthews 1902). Hastshéyalti and Hastshéhogan have been discussed elsewhere (e.g., in note 2), as have Nayénezgani and Tobadzhistshíni (see notes 32 and 33).

Hastshébaka ("He Divinity") and Hastshébaad ("She Divinity")
are generalized male and female gods; Hastshéoltoi, the god of
hunting, is imagined as a berdache, according to Matthews, and
referred to as "she" (possibly Hastshéoltoi is a berdache—i.e., an
American Indian male transvestite homosexual—because the
ancient Navajo hunting economy has in recent centuries given
place to the more sedentary livelihood of farming); Tónenili is
the god of rain. For Tshohanoái ("Bearer of the Sun") and
Klehanoái ("Bearer of the Moon"), see note 33. Estsánatlehi, the
earth mother, is considered too sacred to be represented by a mask
(nor does she figure in any of the Night Chant sand paintings);
as he reaches her verse in the song, the chanter shakes a Hastshébaad mask (Matthews 1902, p. 32).

45 / "Goods" and "jewels" (elsewhere translated by Matthews as
"soft goods" and "hard goods") refer to hides, furs, robes, and
man-made articles, in the case of the former category, and shells,
turquoise, and colored stones, in the case of the latter—in other
words, precious possessions.

46 / The occasional mention of domesticated animals (horses,
sheep, beeves) represents what is apparently the only non-
aboriginal intrusion in all this lore.

47 / The eleven songs that follow belong to a Night Chant cycle
celebrating the growth of corn and other crops in a miraculous
garden of the sun. Actually the group comprises thirty songs, but
most of these are essentially repetitions and have therefore been
omitted. The cycle is known as Songs in the Garden of Hastshéhogan ("House God," the western, or "feminine," aspect of the
sun). The source is Matthews's paper of 1894.

48 / In the second-to-last line of both stanzas, "It" refers to rain,
presaged by thunder. The bluebird symbolizes joy, happiness.

49 / In the accompanying myth a goddess says to Hastshéhogan,

". . . the dark cloud has descended to the ground; the water is at the feet of your corn" (Matthews 1894).

50 / Our present "earth surface" world was preceded by four earlier, nether, worlds, layered one on top of the other within the earth womb. When the people of the Fourth World crawled up into the sunlight, they were said to have "emerged" into the Fifth World. Thus the phrase "since the time of the Emergence" is roughly equivalent to saying "since the world began."

51 / The squash, of course, has neither "silk" nor "tassel." See note 33.

52 / Sialia: the Latin name for the bluebird genus. (Tsholgáli, named in the second stanza, is an unidentified bird that sings in the evening.)

53 / Matthews did not record the Thunder Songs of the Night Chant. I have taken the liberty of including in their place the two Thunder Songs from Matthews's *Mountain Chant*, following the suggestion of Kluckhohn and Wyman (pp. 64-5).

54 / An onomatope for the sound of thunder.

55 / Exorcism is suggested not by the songs themselves but by the manner of performance. As Matthews observed during the exorcistic singing of the sixth day, the inverted basket imprisons a residue of evil (see the synopsis of "Songs of exorcism, second session," p. 320). According to an informant quoted by Kluckhohn and Wyman, the amole drumstick cleans things—"like pounding dirt out of the patient's body."

56 / Note that a second initiation is performed during the afternoon of the seventh day. Among the numerous ceremonials of the Navajo, only the Night Chant includes such rites—and this alone would be sufficient to distinguish it as the sine qua non of

Navajo ceremonialism. (To attain the highest privileges, according to Matthews, one must go through the initiation four times, twice at night and twice during the day. After the fourth time, one is permitted to wear the masks and impersonate the gods.)

57 / Child-rain is rebounding rain, as from a puddle (Matthews).

58 / Grasshopper: a symbol of "female generative power" (Reichard). See note 28.

59 / Matthews 1902, p. 212.

60 / Wind is the precursor of rain. Before he becomes rain, the dancer must be wind (or "Wind Boy," emphasizing his youthfulness). The connection between wind, rain, and salvation is also implicit in the Cuceb. See p. 243. See also note 61. (The white paint used by the dancers is a symbol of life. See p. 92, note 92.)

61 / In the great prayer that follows, the Night Chant reaches its climax; the prayer for rain is the prayer for salvation. Envisioning deliverance, the Maya prophet writes: "And in the wind-swollen sky *there shall be* the house of storms" (Ralph L. Roys, *The Book of Chilam Balam of Chumayel*, p. 159). From the Book of Joel (2:28): "And it shall come to pass afterward, that I will pour out my spirit upon all flesh." See note 60.

62 / I.e., at the yuni. See note 27.

63 / Tónenili, the rain god, here plays the role of clown, dancing out of step, mimicking the other dancers, and getting in their way. To the list given in note 60—wind, rain, salvation—must be added a fourth term: comedy. Compare the Cuceb, entry for the twentieth year: ". . . the tree of the sacred clown will arise: comes compassion . . ."

64 / Hence the name *Night Chant*.

65 / A song cycle whose use is unspecified (other than that it should be reprised during this final night) is the group known as Songs of the Long Pot, two of which are given by Matthews:

I

The corn comes up, the rain descends, O long pot!
The rain descends, the corn comes up, O long pot!
The water trickles *on the leaves*. The water trickles.

The rain descends, the corn comes up, O long pot!
The corn comes up, the rain descends, O long pot!
The water trickles *on the leaves*. The water trickles.

I I

My great corn plants,
Among them I walk.
I speak to them;
They hold out their hands, *i.e.*, *leaves*, to me.

My great squash vines,
Among them I walk.
I speak to them;
They hold out their hands to me.

Probably the "long pot" refers to a cooking utensil belonging to the prototypal hogan of mythic days—a sacred relic viewed solely in the mind's eye. See Wyman 1970, p. 15.

66 / "The young man doubts it"—an ironical aside, glancing at the irreverence of youth.

67 / I.e., "the god takes up his sacrifice."

68 / Source: Matthews 1898.

69 / Nowadays, according to Sapir (1942, p. 257), the patient

inhales the breath of dawn as his last act in the ceremony. But Matthews, who makes no mention of the gesture, may never have witnessed it. It must be understood that the Night Chant as presented here, with the possible exception of this final detail, is the Night Chant learned by Matthews from Hatali Natloi in the late nineteenth century. A Night Chant performed today, while similar in broad outline, would vary considerably in its finer details.

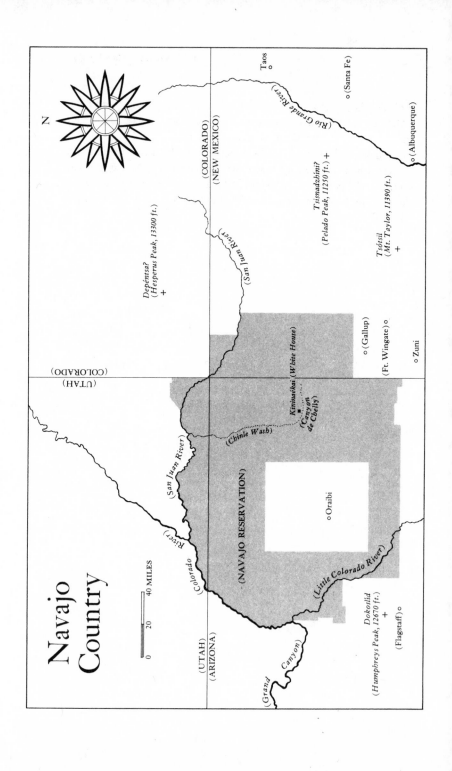

Navajo
Country

Scale: 0 20 40 MILES

(UTAH)
(ARIZONA)

(Grand Canyon)

(Colorado River)

(San Juan River)

(UTAH)
(COLORADO)

Depéntsa?
(Hesperus Peak, 1300 ft.)
+

(San Juan River)

(COLORADO)
(NEW MEXICO)

(NAVAJO RESERVATION)

(Chinle Wash)

Kininaekai (White House)
■ (Canyon
de Chelly)

o Oraibi

(Little Colorado River)

Dokoslid
(Humphreys Peak, 12670 ft.)
+
o (Flagstaff)

o (Gallup)

(Ft. Wingate) o

o Zuni

Tsisnadzdini?
(Pelado Peak, 1250 ft.) +

Tsótsil
(Mt. Taylor, 11390 ft.)
+

Taos o

o (Santa Fe)

(Rio Grande River)

o (Albuquerque)

N

BIBLIOGRAPHY

I / Selected works of Washington Matthews

The Night Chant: A Navaho Ceremony, Memoirs of the American Museum of Natural History, Vol. VI, 1902. Still in print as of 1973 (available from Walter J. Johnson, 111 Fifth Avenue, New York).

"Navaho Myths, Prayers, and Songs," *University of California Publications in American Archaeology and Ethnology*, Vol. V, 1907. A posthumous work, edited by Pliny Earle Goddard.

"Songs of Sequence of the Navajos," *Journal of American Folklore*, Vol. 7, pp. 185–94, 1894.

"The Mountain Chant: A Navajo Ceremony," *Fifth Annual Report of the Bureau of American Ethnology*, pp. 385–467, 1887.

Navaho Legends, Memoirs of the American Folk-lore Society, Vol. V, 1897, reprinted 1969. Includes the Navajo Origin Legend.

"Some Sacred Objects of the Navajo Rites," *Archives of the International Folk-Lore Association*, Vol. I, pp. 227–47, 1898.

MSS. Washington Matthews Collection, Museum of Navaho Ceremonial Art, Santa Fe, New Mexico. The collection is described in an unpublished catalogue by Elsbeth E. Freudenthal on file at the museum. I have not seen the collection, but judging from an abstract of the catalogue, prepared for me by Constance Darkey, the museum's librarian, the following items would appear to be of interest: no. 155 (twenty-five pages of notes on the Night Chant), no. 361 ("Yebitcai Dance —Sergeant Barthelmess's Description—Jan. 1884"), no. 383 ("Night Chant Songs of Long Chanter"), no. 508 (eight small pages of notes labeled "Parts of the Yebitcai I didn't see"), no. 589 (a small notebook labeled "Yebitcai November 1890").

II / *Other descriptions of the Night Chant*

Stevenson, James, "Ceremonial of Hasjelti Dailjis," *Eighth Annual Report of the Bureau of American Ethnology, 1886–87,* pp. 229–85, 1891.

MS. Nightway. Father Berard Haile Collection, University Library, University of Arizona, Tucson. A miscellany of Night Chant items collected by Berard Haile, including a holograph notebook of Night Chant prayers and songs.

Tozzer, Alfred M., "Notes on Religious Ceremonials of the Navaho," *Putnam Anniversary Volume*, pp. 299–343, 1909.

Curtis, Edward S., *The North American Indian*, Vol. I, 1907, reprinted 1970. Includes a description of the Night Chant and striking photographs of Night Chant god-impersonators.

III / *Religious lore and general ethnography*

Reichard, Gladys A., *Navaho Religion: A Study of Symbolism,*

1950, second edition 1963. An indispensable guide to Navajo religious concepts.

Kluckhohn, Clyde, and Wyman, Leland C., *An Introduction to Navaho Chant Practice, With an Account of the Behaviors Observed in Four Chants*, Memoirs of the American Anthropological Association, no. 53, 1940, reprinted 1969.

Wyman, Leland C., *Blessingway*, 1970. The Navajo blessing-rite lore. An extensive repertory of myth, song, and prayer, fundamental to the study of Navajo ceremonialism.

Spencer, Katherine, *Mythology and Values: An Analysis of Navaho Chantway Myths*, Memoirs of the American Folklore Society, Vol. 48, 1957, reprinted 1971. Useful for its scrupulous abstracts of the chant myths.

Sapir, Edward, *Navaho Texts*, 1942.

Kluckhohn, Clyde, and Leighton, Dorothea, *The Navaho*, 1946, paperback edition 1962. The best general account of the Navajo.

Kluckhohn, C., and Spencer, K., *A Bibliography of the Navaho Indians*, 1940.

INDEX

9; principal village of, 122

Ce Acatl ("1 Reed"), 9, 12, 21–4 passim, 73, 75; meaning of name, 71

ceiba (kapok tree): shot with arrow, 62, 93; and green bird, 219, 263; groves of, 221; identified, 93, 227; in paradise, 265; and quail, 207, 251; as sapling, 249; covered with seals, 195, 206, 227; as tree of life, 92, 227

centipede, see Ah Uuc[te] Chapat

Chac (Maya rain god): of the Dripping Sky, 196; evil aspect of, 227; as Ah Siyahtun Chac, 205, 208, 249, 252

Chac Bolay Ul, 200–1, 208, 239, 248

Chac Mumul Ain ("Great Slime Crocodile"), 197, 210

Chac Uayeb Xoc ("Great Demon Shark"), 219; takes chiefs, 212; as culture "serpent," 191; as flood monster, 227, 233–4; holds opens his jaws, 197, 230; set in the sky, 211; "trees will sink," 199

chalchiuitl, defined, 74; see also emerald

Changing Woman, see Estsánatlehi

chanter (in Navajo ritual), role of, 281

Chapultepec, 16, 56, 89, 96

"charge" of fate, defined, 228

Chelly Canyon, see Tshéyi (Chelly) Canyon

Chetumal, 222, 266–7

Chichén Itzá, 74

Chilam Balam (the priest): and Christianity, 253; home of, 250; life of, 259–60; word of, 209, 216

Chilam Balam, Books of, 191–2, 223, 226, 253, 256; Chumayel Book, 90, 193, 234, 240, 244, 248, 259, 263, 345; Mani Book, 192; Tizimin Book, 192

child-rain, xxii, 321, 325, 330; defined, 345

chili, 23, 44, 45, 46; sexually "hot," 80. See also peppers

Chimalma, 24, 74

Chimalpahin Cuauhtlehuanitzin, Domingo, 5–6, 82

Cholula, 94, 95

Christ, see Jesus Christ

Christianity, xvii, 70, 76, 80, 192, 226, 253, 259; Christian amen, 335

cigarette, 294; see also tobacco

Cihuacoatl, 19

Cinteotl ("Spirit of Maize"), 11, 65

Cipactonal, 20

Citlallatonac ("Light-of-Day"), 17, 26, 67; identified with Milky Way, 72; as father of Quetzalcoatl, 74